The
LONG
JOURNEY

Reindeer and Humans
from Palaeolithic to Anthropocene

REIDAR ANDERSEN & OLAV STRAND

First published in 2026 by Whittles Publishing, an imprint of Porto Press.

The editors have made every effort to ensure the accuracy of information contained in this publication, but assume no responsibility for any errors, inaccuracies, inconsistencies and omissions. Likewise, every effort has been made to contact copyright holders. If any copyright material has been reproduced unwittingly and without permission the Publisher will gladly receive information enabling them to rectify any error or omission in subsequent editions.

British Library Cataloguing in Publication Data
A CIP record for this book is available from the British Library

ISBN: 978-1-84995-707-6

Cover and text design by Raspberry Creative Type, Edinburgh

Printed and bound in Great Britain by CPI

To order please go to our website www.portopress.com or contact our distributor, BookSource, 50 Cambuslang Road, Clydesmill Industrial Estate, Glasgow G32 8NB. Telephone 0141 642 9192

Porto Press Ltd
3 Connaught Road
St Albans
AL3 5RX

www.portopress.com

Paper from responsible sources

CONTENTS

Meetings in the mountains   1

PART I   5
The reindeer and humans   7
The pionéer   10
Contribution to the history of our globe   14
Reindeer hunters by the Mediterranean   21
What the next 500,000 years are all about   31

PART II   35
The second hunter and the reindeer   37
The art of survival   47
The Neanderthal kitchen   52

PART III   57
The spectacular interlude   59
Neanderthals die – long live the Neanderthal!   68

PART IV   71
Reindeer hunter found in a rabbit hole   73
Rulers of the mammoth steppe   78
A 30,000-year hunt for reindeer   88
The girl from Altamira   99
Hunters at the edge of the ice   104

PART V   109
Into the land beyond   111
Sol rising from the sea   117
The day when only the mountain people survived   119
The settlers   122
The country becomes multicultural   125
Iron creates 'Klondike atmosphere'   128
The reindeer people who became Sami   131
The beer-brewing Sami take to the mountains   133
Wild reindeer hunting in Várjjat   136
Wide distribution of Sami products   138

PART VI   141
Welcome to the Middle Ages!   143
Kings and clergy dominate the reindeer hunting on Dovre   150
My ship is loaded with...   157
From hunting culture to nomadic reindeer husbandry   160
The battle for the outfield   163
A popular theory that caused great harm   167
The new reindeer populations   169
The last outpost of the wild reindeer   172
A new era   176

PART VII   177
Hunters enter America   179
Behind nature and culture – the hunters' communion with the spirits   182
Missionary idea has major consequences   187
Now warning lights are flashing in the circumpolar northern regions   194

PART VIII   199
Circumpolar cultural and ecological sorrow   201
The situation in Eurasia   202
The situation in North America   208
Norway – the recognisable history   216

PART IX   219
The rulers of the globe   221
Reindeer don't bathe with hippos!   226
'Green shift' threatens untouched nature   232
Could the unthinkable happen?   234

Epilogue   236
References   238

'We cannot win this battle to save species and
environments without forging an emotional bond
between ourselves and nature as well – for we will not
fight to save what we do not love.'

STEPHEN JAY GOULD

MEETINGS IN THE MOUNTAINS

The Northern Hemisphere

Three people sat by a large rock in a steep mountain pass. From here, they overlooked their world and found shelter from the wind coming from the south. It wasn't a strong wind, just a gentle breeze, but it was icy cold and forewarned a new and more brutal season.

The people by the rock were freezing. They knew all too well that this land would soon demand more from them. They gazed northward, their eyes tired from searching. Always seeking north, first during the long journey, later for many days from the same rock. They no longer wanted to go further north; it was too far. The journey home could be dangerous.

So, they sat there, waiting and watching, watching and waiting. It was a quiet day. Barely a sound could be heard. The mountain was endlessly empty, not a single sign of life from what they had hoped to find here. But then, suddenly, just before all hope was replaced by the feeling of *no, it's not going to happen, they're not coming, we're in the wrong place* – hope returned.

At first, only a small dot appeared on the horizon – a shade of colour barely different from the background. Then it had gone again. A deceitful little dot that ignited futile hope. But then it was back. It became larger, clearer, and in motion. Hope rose by the rock. Hope turned into realisation. And then they were there – grown out of the mountain that had nurtured the herd. At first, just like a narrow stripe – later a stream, then a river. Several rivers. The reindeer flowed forward in rows. Mountains and plains filled with life. Calves and females, nervous under watchful eyes. Heavy bucks with wide antlers and long fur glowing in the sun. The three by the rock came to life; waiting had turned into the predator's intense concentration. Now there was only one thing that mattered – the herd and the hunt.

This description could fit an autumn day anywhere in the northern regions. The three by the rock could have been Native Americans, Innuits in Canada or Greenland. They could have been reindeer herders or hunters in Siberia. They could have been involved in reindeer husbandry in Sápmi, Sábme, or Saemie, the Sami areas in Norway, Sweden, Finland and Russia, or wild reindeer hunters in Norway.

The description could be from our time, or it could be from the Viking Age, Iron Age, or earlier Stone Age. The three by the rock could be like us, or they could be people from a completely different time. The common denominator across time and space is the reindeer.

Our shared history with the reindeer is a long journey both in time and space, stretching back to the first humans who lived in Europe. It's a history full of big questions and stories that are not just about nature and reindeer; it's also a story about where we come from, how we have evolved, the relationship we have had and have with nature, and how humans managed to survive in Europe through several major ice ages.

It's also a story of people who built animal pit fall traps, of how iron and reindeer laid an economic foundation for what would become Norway, and how churches were erected by people who gained wealth and power from the animal in the high mountains. Today, above all, it's a story of an impending climate catastrophe and how we will manage to preserve the last remnants of wild nature, our own cultures and our identity.

The story of humans and reindeer begins as most stories do, with a beginning, and once upon a time. And once upon a time, there were people in Europe who lived a simple life, on the verge of what was possible. At times they lived well in a warm world, at other times they experienced biting cold and conditions they had very little chance of mastering. Perhaps humans disappeared from Europe during these cold periods, but when the climate became milder, new hunters from our genus entered this part of the world.

Although we do not know all the details of these people's lives, new research results, and findings at these people's settlements, have made it possible to imagine what life was like back then. But it's not easy. In our technological world, where a stream of innovations makes it difficult to follow the development from one generation to another, it can be hard to imagine that the standard tools of our earliest ancestors, the stone hand axes, did not change significantly over 40,000 generations. Nevertheless, we know enough to recreate the lives of some selected individuals, and we know for certain that people similar to those we have described have lived and that they were entirely dependent on reindeer for many thousands of years of their existence.

Closer to our own time, it is easier to see these people and the relationship they have had and have with the reindeer, although we have lost much along the way to today. Among many indigenous peoples in Europe, North America and Asia, both language and cultural identity have been weakened through many years of colonisation and assimilation policies. Additionally, in today's human-dominated overheated world, there are fewer and fewer areas of untouched nature. We can ask the question – have we reached the end of our long common journey with the reindeer?

Our hope is that knowledge of the long history we have with the reindeer or caribou can motivate us to find solutions that preserve not only the reindeer but also the identity and cultures still based on the animal, which is Europe's and North-Americas most important living cultural heritage.

PART I

They arrived in Europe almost simultaneously, the two of them. The reindeer through a winding path from South America, via North America and Beringia furthest east in Russia, before crossing the Ural Mountains and starting its journey south-west into Europe. Man, on the other hand, started in Africa and entered Europe furthest south. One adapted to a life surrounded by snow and ice, the other entirely depended on warmth from a scorching sun. Claiming that two such different species would form strong bonds and become mutually dependent on each other would have given high odds. But that's how it turned out!

THE REINDEER AND HUMANS

Even though they are not entirely certain, some researchers believe that a distant relative of the reindeer lived in South America more than 10 million years ago. Over time, a mountain-adapted animal evolved, eventually ending up in Beringia – the vast steppe tundra area that formed a land bridge between present-day Russia and North America about 2 million years ago. And it is in this area that the reindeer evolved into the animal we know today.

On the other side of the Atlantic Ocean, the first traces of our own genus are found on the banks of the Awash River, in eastern Ethiopia. A 2.8-million-year-old lower jawbone of our relative shows that the teeth have acquired a shape and size different from those of older so-called bipedal – two-footed – inhabitants of Africa. Many believe that climatic changes at that time led to the development of our own lineage. If so, it wouldn't be the last time climate played a crucial role in this story.

Then there's the matter of naming, a previously rather unclear process. It was the very little, modest Swede Carl Nilsson Linnaeus who, in the mid-1700s, came up with the ingenious principle that all species should have a Latin name consisting of a genus name first, followed by a species name. He was so pleased with his own idea that, at the age of 33, he believed he was on a par with Newton and Galileo, and when he was later ennobled, he quickly changed his name to Carl von Linné.

How successful his naming of the reindeer and humans is up for debate. That our lineage was named *Homo*, which means 'person' or human in Latin, we can understand. But many argue that calling us, the latest in the *Homo* genus, *sapiens* – the wise – is something we haven't quite lived up to. Linnaeus didn't quite hit the mark with the naming of the reindeer either. The species name, *tarandus*, he had picked up from Greek, Roman and German writings. How Aristotle and, somewhat later, Julius Caesar had meet the reindeer is not known, but they provided good descriptions of the animal. It is more explicable that some German theologians and naturalists in the 1500s described an animal they called tarandus, especially since the Swedish king Gustav I had given ten reindeer as a gift to his friend Albert, the Duke of Prussia. But Linnaeus missed the mark with the genus name. The reindeer was inscribed in his work *Systema Naturae* as *Cervus tarandus*, suggesting that the reindeer belonged to the same genus as the deer. That was completely wrong. This is why the English spy, and later naturalist, Charles Hamilton Smith is now credited with the name *Rangifer*. He had read *De animalibus*, written by Albert the Great in the 1200s, where in chapter 268, 'Dicitur Rangyfer quasi ramifer', a detailed description of 'Rangyfer' with a branched antler (ramifer) is given.

So, it is *Rangifer tarandus* that, over 1 million years ago, begins its migration southward in Europe. Those who do not join the migration but continue their lives in North America will later be called caribou. The Mi'kmaq people in Canada observed that the animal used its antlers as a snow shovel – qalipu in their language, a word most interpreted as caribou, and one they found to be a fitting description. Therefore, caribou became the name of the reindeer for all eternity in North America. But much would happen before the reindeer encountered the Mi'kmaq people. In Europe, the reindeer would eventually encounter various types of hunters. It didn't remain entirely unchanged itself, as significant climatic shifts would affect both Rangifer and *Homo* over the next hundreds of thousands of years. In Europe, we find the first traces of the *Homo* genus in the Spanish mountain areas north-west in the country. Is it here that the first encounters between the two occur?

FIG 1. Ever since the first humans entered Europe about 1.2 million years ago, climate has been a major factor in the history of human presence and their relationship with reindeer. During this period, the climate has changed dramatically some twenty times, with alternating warm and cold periods. The line in the figure shows changes in temperature, the map shows some of the most important archaeological sites discussed in the first parts of the story of humans and reindeer.

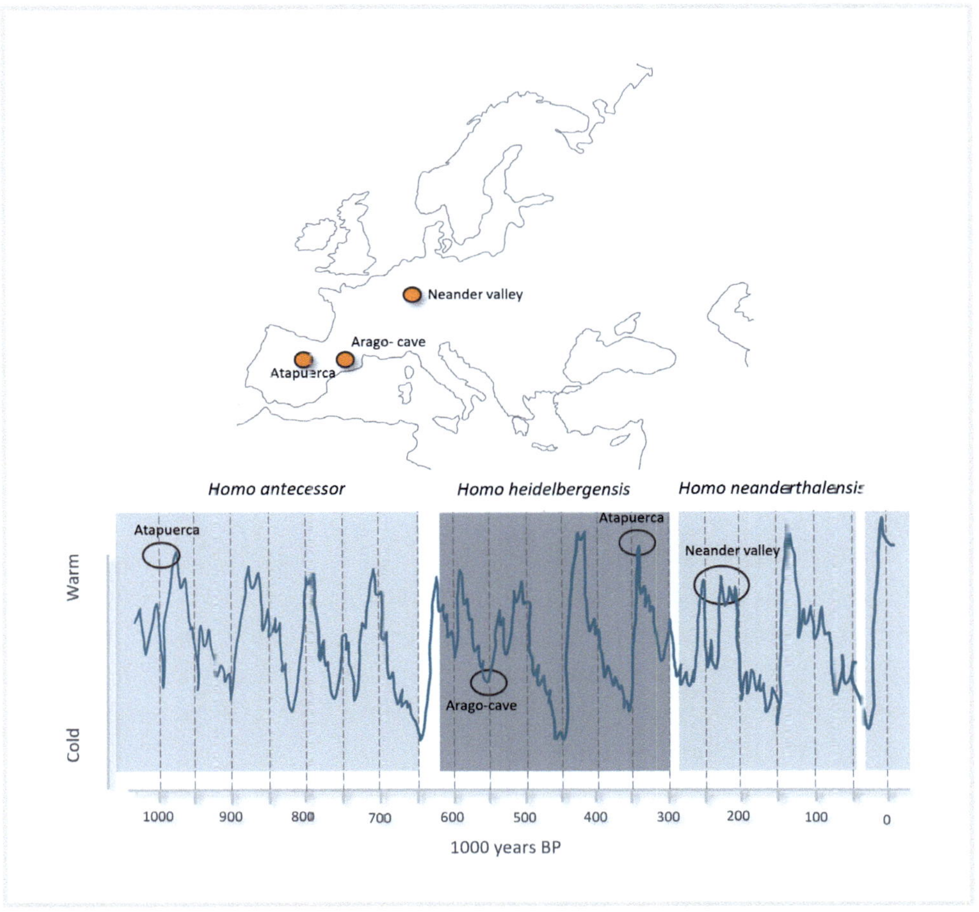

THE PIONÉER

Atapuerca, Spain 1.2 million years ago

If you had been present up here in the Spanish mountainous region near the source of the Ebro River 1.2 million years ago and seen the man approaching his dwelling, you would probably have assumed he belonged to your own group. You might have noticed that he walked in a slightly peculiar manner, but that's about it, for his facial features remarkably resemble those of us modern humans. If you sat next to him on the bus on your way to work one morning, you might not have reacted. That is, of course, if he were dressed in a somewhat more civilised manner.

Although his nose is somewhat broader than yours, his jaw is delicate in a way you wouldn't expect from a caveman. His smile reveals that the front teeth in his upper jaw closely resemble your own, although they are slightly larger. The size of his head indicates room for a relatively large brain, and he carries himself upright and sturdy, very unlike the slightly stooped fellow you had imagined. The man is tall, probably up to about 5 feet 11 inches.

But then there's his gait. His knees are small and thin, providing little room for the attachment of powerful tendons like your own. However, his ankle bone is exceptionally large; the same can be said for the big toe of the man. Taken together, this results in a gait you don't see every day, and which has now taken him to the edge of what looks like a large sinkhole. He disappears into the hole and is gone.

It's not recommended that you visit him at home. There are several reasons for this. Down there still lie the bone remains of his son, who died at only 5 or 6 years old. Had you taken a look at the teeth of this son, you would have seen that the first permanent molars in both the upper and lower jaw were unused. He obviously died before he could use them. This suggests a developmental time comparable to that of children in modern humans, indicating that the boy had plenty of time for intellectual development.

You would have found the rest of the cave floor covered with stone tools and bone remains. There is a great variety of both. Fine-grained chert is apparently the most commonly used material for making the roughly hewn stone axes, but remnants of quartz and limestone are also scattered around. Some of the stone material he must have collected far from the dwelling, indicating that the man's hunting grounds were vast. But it's the bone remains that make the cave a less appealing living space. There are enormous quantities of them, many from deer, and on the freshest ones the stinking rotten meat still hangs. There are no remains of fires, so hot meals haven't been served.

In the pile of bone remains, you would have found the best reason to decline any dinner invitation from the man. He is a cannibal. Most of the human bones are smashed with the powerful stone axes, apparently to access the fat-rich marrow. But it's the treatment of the skulls that would have made the greatest impression. They all bear marks of countless cuts – far more cuts than the skulls of the deer and horses, which are also found in the bone heap. Access to the brain has evidently been important. Whether these were ritual actions reserved for the tribe's enemies or if they consumed their own is still unclear, but knowledge of Europe's first inhabitants comes precisely from this area.

It was during the construction of a railway line to some mining areas in the Sierra de la Demanda, just outside Burgos, that in the 1850s they cut through limestone areas in the Atapuerca mountains and exposed the caves Gran Dolina (large sinkhole), Galería Elefante, and Sima de los Huesos (pit of bones). It was the results of archaeological excavations in these caves that, 140 years later, would give Atapuerca UNESCO World Heritage status. Today, international teams of archaeologists have reached the bottom of the cultural layers inside the caves and can document continuous human use over 1.2 million years!

Although the construction of the railway was what really accelerated the exploration of the caves, they had been known to the locals for a long time. Descriptions of what was then called the Atapuerca cave date back as far as 1576, and stories of people going down into the caves and looting treasures have existed for just as long.

In earlier times, there were many theories about why the caves contained so many bones. While some believed it was floods that had washed dead people into the caves, others thought it must have been a cemetery for poor workers who had their livelihood in the area. The greatest confidence was placed in the theory that the bone remains were dead soldiers who had fallen on September 1, 1054, in what is described as the Battle of Atapuerca.

The battle had been fought between two brothers: King García Sánchez III of Navarre and King Ferdinand I of Castile. The youngest, Ferdinand, already had some experience in warfare. Twenty years earlier, he had killed his childless brother-in-law, King Bermudo III of León, in the Battle of Tamarón and given the kingdom as a gift to his wife, Bermudo's sister. Ferdinand also won the Battle of Atapuerca, leaving behind a multitude of dead soldiers on the battlefield. That these had been thrown into the caves and given rise to the bone heaps was thus considered the most likely explanation.

The archaeological excavations would uncover a much more exciting story. In Galería Elefante, a tooth and parts of a jaw dated to be over 1 million years old were uncovered. Simple worked stone tools were also found. In Gran Dolina, many different cultural layers have been uncovered, and in one of these, in 1994, eighty bone fragments from a total of five or six humans were found. These were dated to be between 850,000 and 780,000 years old. Subsequent excavations uncovered new human bones. In total, anthropologists have now brought out 170 fossil bones from the cave and into their laboratories.

The number of bones from the prey animals found inside the caves is also formidable. Just in the sinkhole where our friend the pioneer lived, remains of over a hundred deer have been found. Is this where we will find the bone remains of Europe's oldest reindeer? Detailed examinations of the bone material reveal that the animals have been butchered. Stone knives have left cut marks on most of the bones. Based on the types of bones found in the cave, it appears that the smaller species were carried whole down to the cave, while for larger animals, heavy meat parts like thighs and forelegs seem to have been transported individually to the dwelling. It has now been revealed that the pioneers brought home 16 different species of mammals to the cave, but there are no bone remains of reindeer. With the exception of wild boar, the other species have now disappeared from the earth's surface. However, many of these have left behind close relatives, such as fallow deer and deer.

Based on the archaeological and biological findings, professionals are now drawing two interesting conclusions. First, there are good indications that the hunters were able to cooperate in small groups and share the work. It is unlikely that they were solely dependent on animals killed by larger predators. Only a fraction of the bones examined have tooth marks from predators, despite the fact that in the three caves in Atapuerca, 166 different cave bears have been found, as well as several specimens of the now extinct European lion, wildcats, wolves, red foxes and lynxes.

Secondly, pollen studies from plants have shown that, at this time, olive trees and beech trees grew together with hazelnut and chestnut trees here. Nuts from these trees surely contributed to providing the pionéer with a welcome change from the raw meat diet, but there's no food for reindeer. Both the pollen studies and the prey animal remains indicate that these people lived in a warm climate, or as anthropologist Clive Finlayson put it, a piece of Africa in Europe.

During their time on earth, the pioneers also ventured as far north and west as England, which says something about the climate. It was evidently liveable for a hunter with simple clothing and without the ability to kindle a warming, life-giving fire. The continuous calcareous area between England and France has been easy to cross for Europe's first inhabitants on both two and four feet, and those on two feet first settled in Happisburgh, a day or two walk north-east of present-day London. Here we find the earliest evidence of human activity in England. Not only have stone tools been found here, but, incredibly, also the footprints of the hunter!

On this day over 800,000 years ago, the hunters must have been looking for seafood. On mud flats at what was then the mouth of the Thames, a group of five children and adults left fifty footprints, some of them detailed enough to see the shape of the toes. Based on the length of the footprints, it is assumed that the group consisted of individuals between 0.9 to 1.7 metres tall. Around them, on the grassy plains at the river's mouth, horses, mammoths and bison grazed, and the climate is assumed to have been like that of southern parts of Sweden and Denmark today. At a dwelling further south, examinations of insect fauna and flora show that the climate at times has been even warmer and drier, not unlike what we find around the Mediterranean today.

A freezing cold wind from the north must then gradually have pushed the pioneer southward. Olive groves and oak trees will now give way to grassy steppes and eventually tundra. A new ice age was on its way, a term as unknown to the pioneer as it was to us modern humans until recently. In the next 800,000 years, it will be the 20 or so shifts between warm and cold climates that will define which plants, animals and humans will inhabit the European continent. And without the presence of reindeer during the most climatically challenging periods, the prehistory of our own genus would look completely different.

CONTRIBUTION TO THE HISTORY OF OUR GLOBE

The end of the 19th century and the beginning of the 20th century was a time of expeditions and great discoveries, and the results of these fundamentally changed people's worldview in just under a century. The Bible's texts stating that the Earth was 6,000 years old, that the first humans were named Adam and Eve, and that the Great Flood was the direct cause of the state of nature gradually lost their supporters. The belief that fossils of extinct animals were concrete evidence of the havoc caused by the Great Flood also waned. Gradually, a large puzzle of observations and theories was pieced together into a whole, and we came to understand that there had not only been one, but many ice ages.

A small piece of this puzzle is found just north of South Kensington Station in London, where Peter Alexander runs the sale of antique furniture in his highly esteemed Reindeer Antiques. The choice of name is not coincidental. During the construction of this railway station, fossilised bones from an animal adapted to Arctic conditions, namely reindeer, were found. At the same time, construction work at Trafalgar Square uncovered remains of hippos and elephants, while a woolly rhinoceros was found under Battersea Power Station. This happened in Victorian Britain, when the British Empire was in its most magnificent period. The nobility simply found it unfitting to believe that reindeer had roamed around Hyde Park and that hippos had inhabited Trafalgar Square, in the heart of London itself. It just wouldn't do! Moreover, the discovery of an animal adapted to life in snow and cold alongside an almost hairless animal adapted to Africa's scorching sun was an impossibility. The island's climate is not compatible with the habitat requirements of any of these species. Therefore, the findings were flatly rejected.

Around the same time, Tsar Nicholas I received a message that an elephant had been found in Siberia. This piqued the tsar's interest, and he sent word to the botanist Michael Adams. Although Adams was originally on a diplomatic journey to China, he was promptly instructed to proceed to the remote discovery site near the mouth of the Lena River and ensure that the elephant was brought to St. Petersburg. When a Russian tsar gives an order, it is followed, but in his report to the tsar, Adams clearly expressed his 'discomfort at riding on a reindeer for days on end'.

Adams managed to salvage the elephant, pack it up and send the carcass to St. Petersburg. He also collected large quantities of wool and hair from the unwieldy beast, and, according to his own account, it took ten men to lift half of the skin with wool and hair into a boat for further transport.

Now, the discussions began. How had an African animal made its way all the way to Siberia? It is the year 1806, and the theory proposed by the German zoologist Johann Philipp Breyn about the elephant being transported northward by the Great Flood still held strong. Therefore, the elephant discovery was interpreted as yet another proof of the havoc caused by the Great Flood. However, parts of the elephant's hair and skin were sent to several foreign universities and museums, including to the Frenchman Charles Cuvier, who was the foremost expert of his time on fossils and taxonomy. Due to the unique and intact condition of the find, Cuvier concluded that this was not an elephant, but a mammoth – an extinct Arctic animal – that had lived in these areas under different climatic conditions. At this time, some researchers had thus understood that there had once been animals adapted to a much colder climate.

At the same time, lively discussions were taking place in geological circles regarding large boulders found in the most peculiar locations. One of these boulders was in Switzerland and was so large that it had its own small chapel on top and its own name, Pierre des Marmettes. This formidable granite boulder had somehow moved a whole 40 kilometres from Val Ferret near Mont Blanc, which is the nearest source of granite. Such stones high up in the landscape and in inexplicable positions raised questions about whether floods and water (of the Great Flood type) could really have moved them. It also seemed strange that these stones had sharp edges. They were not worn and shaped as they would have been if they had been moved in a flood, and doubts began to arise about the correctness of the Great Flood as an explanation for large stones and elephants that were clearly in the wrong place. Of all things, it was a Norwegian geology professor who was on a trip to the West Coast of Norway who would come up with the best solution to these strange observations.

When the Danish-born Norwegian professor Jens Esmark was baptised in Houlbjerg Church in North Jutland by his father, the parish priest, in the spring of 1763, the baptismal font was actually carved from a glacial erratic of Norwegian red granite. It is not known if anyone in the congregation had pondered how a large boulder had been transported to Denmark, but it would be the modest Professor Esmark who, after a three-month journey on the West Coast with two students, made one of the greatest discoveries ever made in Norway. The result was an article with the somewhat cautious title 'Contribution to the History of our Globe', published in the *Magazine of Natural Sciences* in April 1824. Here, Esmark asserts that 'in short, we will find, in all countries, whether they are mountainous or lowland, the same traces of the work of ice masses. It is particularly in Norway that I have found many evidences of the effects of enormous ice masses that have now disappeared.'

Esmark and his two students had, during their journey on the West Coast, managed to navigate by sea up to the Sognefjord. They realised that to make it home to Christiania (now the capital Oslo) before the autumn lectures began, they had to take the route from Oppstryn via Sunndalen and Rauddalen to Bråtan in Skjåk. On the trip, they had to cross the pass of Kamperhamrane at 1,200 metres, where the northern tip of the Jostedalsbreen glacier had to be traversed. It was when they descended on the east side of the glacier that the realisation struck. And, to be fair, it was probably the student Otto Tank who initiated it all.

The glacier, which had retreated slightly after the 'last ice age' around 1750, had left behind a long and high ridge of gravel. Tank immediately pointed out that the ridge was strikingly similar to the ridge they had seen earlier in their journey at sea level in Stavanger. Suddenly, they understood what they had seen there at Lyngenfjorden: what the locals called Vassrygg was an enormous moraine, carved up by a glacier. Esmark later wrote: 'The similarity is so striking that anyone who has the opportunity to make this comparison must grasp the same ideas.' The conclusion was therefore clear: at some point in the past, enormous glaciers must have reached all the way down to the coastline.

Geir Hestmark writes in his book about Jens Esmark that he did not only settle for establishing that an ice age had occurred: 'He also sought its cause.' To explain how such a massive climate change could occur, he launched a theory inspired by observations of recurring comets – a theory about changes in the Earth's orbit around the sun. If the orbit had once been more elliptical like that of comets, rather than nearly circular as it is now, this could lead to cooling when the Earth was farthest from the sun.

This would turn out to be a central element in modern scientific explanations of why there have periodically been long periods of cold and ice ages. But much work and several discoveries still remained before our understanding of the ice age truly became solid. The last and very important piece was found at the bottom of the Pacific Ocean.

The puzzle falls into place

Independent of Esmark's work, two Swiss researchers were mapping glaciers to assess flood hazards after a glacier fall that caused significant damage in the areas around Martigny in the Swiss Alps. Their work showed that glaciers could explain the presence of erratic boulders and many moraines. They assumed, however, that glaciers had once been much larger and introduced the concept of 'monster glaciers'. But the results from both Esmark and the Swiss researchers received little attention, and the topic became rather quiet.

It would take almost 100 years from Esmark's first article for the idea of an extensive period of cold climate and glaciation of large areas to be widely accepted. During this time, overwhelming geological evidence was gathered to support this. In Germany, England and Switzerland, geologists found moraine deposits that must have originated from several different glacial periods, and they named the different periods after the respective river valleys they had worked in. But it is the Swiss scientist Louis Agassiz who undeservedly received much of the credit for the concept of ice ages and monster glaciers.

The venerable Agassiz was originally an expert on fossil fish and a student of the famous Carles Cuvier (the one who realised that the elephant in Siberia was a mammoth), which gave him great weight in the scientific community. He was initially skeptical of the idea of monster glaciers but changed his mind, to the extent that he later devoted almost all his time to mapping the former extent of glaciers. At a gathering at the prestigious Swiss Academy of Sciences, he went all out. The politely conservative members of the Academy had great expectations of a neat lecture on fossil fish – but that's not what they got. Instead, they were treated to a loud presentation on monster glaciers. Not only that, Agassiz concluded in his fervor that ice had covered the whole of Eurasia and well into the Mediterranean. The term 'ice age' or 'Die Eiszeit' stuck after this meeting.

With the growing understanding that there had been periods in Earth's history where ice had covered large parts of the land, there came a need to know the reasons why this had happened. Could it happen again? Would reindeer once again find grazing areas around Kensington Station? It was a near-genius, and very hard-working Serbian engineer named Milutin Milankovitch, and a rather original Scot who would find the causes of the ice ages.

Between 1860 and 1880, the Scot, James Croll, after a varied career as the owner of a tea shop, insurance agent, hotel manager and caretaker, had already developed his own theory for the formation of ice ages based on the amount of heat the Earth receives from the sun. Today we refer to this as albedo effects. In short, the amount of heat absorbed depends on the surface's ability to reflect sunlight (like snow and ice) or the ability of dark surfaces (like open sea) to absorb heat. These are highly relevant conditions today. The melting of sea ice in the Arctic (which reflects a lot of sunlight) causes more open sea (which absorbs heat more easily). The melting of ice in the polar regions, therefore, has a self-reinforcing effect on temperature rise as the oceans absorb more heat as more and more sea ice melts.

Milutin Milankovitch built on these ideas and calculated how much energy and heat the Earth receives from the sun through different parts of its orbit around the sun. There are three aspects of the Earth's orbit that determine how much heat we receive through sunlight. The shape of the orbit itself varies from nearly circular to elliptical over periods of 100,000 to 400,000 years. The tilt of the Earth's axis varies with a period of 41,000 years and, finally, movements in the Earth's rotational axis vary with a periodicity of 19–23,000 years. The reason for these variations is gravitational effects from other planets (especially Jupiter) on Earth.

Milankovitch calculated how these forces affected the Earth's orbit and then what effects the variations in orbits had on how much heat the Earth received at any given time. This was a near-monstrous calculation job performed solely with a slide rule, a lot of complicated equations, paper and pencil. He spent about 20 years on this job, which was published in German in 1941. His work was not in vain. We would soon gain knowledge of ice ages, and especially interglacials, confirming his calculations.

If knowledge of the ice ages was difficult for many to comprehend, knowledge of the dramatic climatic changes was no less challenging to understand. Constantly new discoveries of so-called geological layers with fossils of warm-adapted species sandwiched between layers of fossils of typically cold-tolerant species helped increase this knowledge, and documented what we now refer to as interglacials; warm periods between two cold climate periods.

The fact that reindeer and hippos had both inhabited the centre of London could now be explained; they had not been there at the same time. Even in Norway, where during the last ice age maximum there was a 3,000-metre-high cap of ice over large parts of the country, traces of wildlife have been found. In the cave systems in Ofoten, cave explorers found remains of 100,000-year-old wolves, seals and various bird species. Ofoten teemed with life during the warm period of that time, and from earlier times we know of finds of 30,000-year-old bone remains from birds and animals in Skjonghelleren in Møre and Romsdal, and 40–50,000-year-old mammoth molars in Gudbrandsdalen. This means that even during the long periods referred to as ice ages, there have been shorter periods of much more favourable and warmer climates.

It is the geologists Cesare Emiliani and Nicholas Shackleton who must share the credit for our ability today to measure the timing of cold and warm periods accurately and far back in time. Cesare knew that calcite, which is one of the most common minerals in the Earth's crust and the main component in the shells of molluscs, contained varying amounts of the oxygen-16 and oxygen-18 isotopes. He believed that the variations were due to varying ocean temperatures. By drilling cores from the ocean floor and measuring the ratio between the two isotopes, he could see which periods had warm and cold seawater.

Nicholas, the great-grandson of the famous polar explorer Ernest Shackleton, was not surprisingly more concerned with glaciers. He found that as glaciers grew, they absorbed more of the light oxygen-16 isotope at the expense of the heavier oxygen-18 isotope. The variations in the ratio between these two isotopes thus revealed not only the ice ages themselves but also the shorter periods, which we today call marine isotope stages, with warm and cold periods within each ice age. In the cold periods, therefore, there was more oxygen-18 in calcite because the lighter variant was bound in the glaciers.

From the entry of humans into Europe there have been at least 21 major changes in temperature (in scientific communities called marine isotope stages). Thus, the climate has changed 20 times, to some extent dramatically. Time and again, steppe and tundra areas have turned into lush, forested areas, only to become barren tundra again. In its journey from Beringia in the east and into Europe, the reindeer has therefore experienced many different climatic conditions. In warm periods, reindeer have had to migrate north-eastward to colder climates again.

The first physical evidence of the reindeer's entry into the central parts of Europe was discovered by the Finnish paleontologist and author Björn Kurtén. In some gravel deposits outside Süssenborn in Germany, he found an antler that a reindeer buck had shed between 680,000 and 620,000 years ago. Those who have analysed samples of the Greenland ice and ocean sediments see that this was a cold period. It was followed by a shorter warm period before the Earth again entered a cold period that the scientific communities call marine isotope stage 14. We are now 563–524,000 years back in time, and the reindeer has followed the steppe tundra all the way down to the Mediterranean.

REINDEER HUNTERS BY THE MEDITERRANEAN

Caune de l'Arago, France 550,000 years ago.

Up at the limestone cave Caune de l'Arago, about 30 kilometres from the Mediterranean, one can now overlook the rolling vineyards of Côtes du Roussillon. Incredibly, it's not difficult to imagine that this must have been a fantastic starting point for successful reindeer hunts. Just west of the cave, the Verdouble River has cut through the rocks, creating a steep canyon that cannot be crossed by either prey or humans. On the elongated flats south of the cave, where the Mediterranean can be seen in the distance, hunters would have a good overview of grazing animals and ample time to position themselves strategically where the game would have to cross the river winding through the area. Despite the landscape now being dominated by vineyards and heat-loving tree species, it's possible to envision a different, mostly treeless landscape and the reindeer hunters who once inhabited it. These people resembled, but were different from, the Pioneer we encountered in the Spanish mountains and are often referred to as Heidelberg men. One of the truly significant changes that has occurred is that humans now master fire, and for the first time we encounter people who we know lived in a truly cold climate.

By using our imagination, we can envision two of these individuals. For several days, they had been sitting at the cave entrance, overlooking the river and the hunters waiting for the reindeer herds. During these days, they had observed a pattern to what had been happening down by the river. Several times in the last few days, the herds had arrived, and each time the hunters met the animals in the river, but had not reached the herd before it had crossed back onto dry land and disappeared into the hills on the north side. The two are siblings, he a boy, she a girl soon to become a woman. He is younger, she a year older. Together, they are stubborn individuals. When others went one way, they easily went another. They found their own solutions and saw things differently from everyone else, an ability that would come to mean a lot for their people.

From the cave entrance, they saw a herd of about a hundred animals on migration that would likely cross the river on their journey north. Before the hunters had taken their usual positions down by the river, the two were on their way up a steep slope on the other side of the valley. From here, they could see that the rest of the group had started to gather down by the river, where they would once again try to meet the reindeer. The valley was quite wide and flat here. The river winding through the valley was not very large or particularly deep. The deepest pools were a couple of metres deep; otherwise, it was shallow, and the gravel bottom was clearly visible in the clear water. The problem was that the hunters didn't know where the reindeer would cross so they spread out along the river, with a long distance between each hunter.

As the two began the steepest climb, the herd had come all the way down to the river. Now the same thing happened as had happened several times before. The herd stood for a while, as if taking a thinking break. No reindeer wanted to be the first to cross the river, and the herd began to mill slowly around without any of the animals taking the initiative. For a while, it seemed like some were being pushed into the river, but then they retreated onto land again, and some of the animals lay down. Then, the whole herd lay down. All this was a great strain on the hunters waiting. Those closest to the herd couldn't move, and those lying further away couldn't get closer. So, all they could do was wait – wait for the reindeer to decide to move on. Thus, the game between hunters and reindeer continued.

The reindeer were not in a hurry. The girl and the boy became tired, listening to the occasional hum of insects, but otherwise nothing. Time crawled by, and their eyes began to close; they were almost asleep. They were brought back to reality by a shout down by the river. The reindeer were coming. Half the herd had already entered the river, but they had also spotted the hunter waiting. The first animals threw themselves to the side and rushed up the river, spraying water. The closest hunter threw the spear, but it didn't hit anything. The herd formed a wedge, stretched out and sped towards the shore. They crossed the river, and in between two waiting hunters they burst through. It was almost a perfect repetition of what had happened in the past few days.

Countless times from the cave entrance, the brother and sister had seen the herds flee after escaping the hunters down by the river. Positioned 80 metres above the river, the cave was the perfect vantage point. Although the reindeer probably smelled the hunters hidden behind small built-up stone walls and natural hiding places, they didn't seem very frightened. But when the hunters attacked the animals crossing the shallow river, there was always panic. Although the hunters by the river sometimes succeeded, it usually went as it did today. And they had observed a clear pattern. Scared animals always tried to get higher up in the terrain, and as a rule the herd would pass through the small pass where the two were now waiting. The two had done something unique, something new, and had used what they had seen to anticipate where the reindeer would come. The simple but ingenious plan was simply to let the reindeer come to them at a place where they often came and where it was easy to be a hunter.

So, they got ready and grabbed their spears, she with her right hand, he with his left. They smiled knowingly at each other. Some from the group had made the spears from some evergreen trees that grew further down by the big water. Although the spears were considerably longer than them, they were easy to handle. They could no longer see the herd, but they heard the panting and the distinctive rattling sound of a moving reindeer herd. Then it was there, the huge buck. She was ready when she saw the large antlered head emerge.

She thrust the spear toward the animal, and she hit it just behind the front leg. Her brother, standing to her left, waited. The moment after, the buck was out of sight. In her peripheral vision, she saw another animal – it was behind the rock and out of her brother's sight as he was hidden behind the stone. He sensed that she had seen something, leant forward, and gave a push with his right hand just before the animal was about to turn around. New animals passed by, some in the tracks of the first, others on the upper side of the mountain pass. There were many of them, but the hunters hardly noticed them. They ran as fast as they could up to the top of the ridge to get an overview; once up they saw the two animals.

One lay still on the downside of the ridge, the other lay a few metres further ahead. The two spears were still in both animals. It didn't take long for the hunters to get down to them. The reindeers' feet were already stiff and immobile; their eyes were open, but a gray film blocked all visual impressions. While the brother stood petrified as he looked at the one dead animal, she took out two stone meat cutters from a leather pouch. She had reckoned that her brother hadn't brought his.

They were reindeer hunters by the Mediterranean. For as long as they could remember, reindeer had been their most important prey. The animal had provided them with what they needed – meat, fat-rich marrow, and fur that protects against the cold. In this regard, they were not different from the hunting group located further east. Occasionally, they ventured eastward into the neighbouring hunting areas. The occurrences of the fine stone draws them there – stone that could be fashioned into blades and scrapers of a much higher quality than what they got from using stone from their own area.

Occasionally, they encountered hunters from other clans, and we can assume that these encounters were characterised by friendliness and the sharing of knowledge and ideas. The conversations may not have been long and detailed, but the topic was familiar – the weather and hunting. They have certainly noticed that it has not become easier to survive the coldest periods, and the exchange of experiences that make both dwelling places, hunting techniques, and clothing more suitable in the increasingly colder climate is not only useful but vital for a people living a life right on the edge of what is possible.

Reindeer land at Côtes du Roussillon

In the Arago cave, archaeologists have painstakingly dug through the cultural layers of this 10-metre-wide and 30-metre-deep cave, reaching progressively older cultural layers. Seven metres down in the cave, the activity of the hunters who lived here during a cold period more than half a million years ago is now documented. And what they find is fantastic. The people who lived here hunted reindeer! And not only did they occasionally catch a reindeer, three out of four prey animals brought into the cave are reindeer.

The French like systematic and orderly presentation, and at the nearby museum the findings archaeologists have made are presented in a clear manner. Bone material from prey animals that the hunters brought into the cave over hundreds of thousands of years is linked to the prevailing climatic conditions at any given time, leaving no doubt: a series of cold and dry periods have been replaced by shorter periods of warm and humid climate, and the composition of prey animals reflects the varying climatic conditions. The earth was in a cold climatic period 550,000 years ago. At this time, today's Côtes du Roussillon was a steppe-like and more or less treeless landscape. Almost exclusively, reindeer bone remains are left on the cave floor, and the preservation conditions inside the dark cave must have been good because it is difficult to understand that the large quantities of jaws with intact teeth presented in the museum's showcases are more than half a million years old.

On the days the hunters did not hunt reindeer, it is mouflon, ancestor to today's sheep breeds, deer, horse, rhinoceros, and thar, a now-extinct relative of the ibex in the Alps, that are brought into the cave. Further up in the cave's cultural layers, the activity is shown 50,000 years ahead in time. The earth is now in an interglacial period. It is a forested landscape the hunters oversee from the cave. Then it is red deer and roe deer they hunt, and these two species constitute the majority of the bone material left by the hunters. Only occasionally is a reindeer brought home to the cave.

Fifty thousand years ahead in time, the horse is the dominant prey, followed by deer, mouflon, thar, and bison. Reindeer and musk oxen are also found, but in very modest numbers. So, 10,000 years later, 440,000 years BCE, something interesting happens. We are now in the midst of what people in the Alpine regions call the Mindel glaciation, and the climatic conditions worsen. But evidently, the reindeer have left the hunting area. They have moved further north in Europe, while the far less migratory musk ox has remained, now constituting nearly three-quarters of the hunters' diet. An occasional woolly rhinoceros is also brought home to the cave.

Hunting woolly rhinoceros and other large prey animals is not a solitary endeavour! Therefore, everything indicates that coordinated hunting strategies were already established in the settlements down by the Mediterranean more than half a million years ago. This, of course, requires some form of communication, and it requires access to weapons with greater range than handheld stone axes could provide.

In 1911, amateur historian Samuel Warren from Sussex found what he initially thought was part of an antler, but which he subsequently presented to the venerable Geological Society in London as the tip of a spear. The approximately 40 cm long, 420,000-year-old piece of yew was pointed at the end, but the majority of academics at the time estimated that the planning required to fashion the spear and then use it for hunting far exceeded the cognitive abilities of early humans.

It was not until 1995 when archaeological excavations at Schöningen in Germany at a huge open-pit coal mine revealed ten well-preserved wooden spears that the spearhead from Sussex had its renaissance. The Schöningen spears were found in what used to be the shoreline of a large lake. For just under 400,000 years ago, there has been significant activity from both humans and prey animals in a warm interglacial period. Sediments from the shoreline have covered both the spears and bone remains from the prey animals, providing excellent preservation conditions. So much bone from horses was uncovered alongside the spears that archaeologists initially thought there had been a single episode of mass animal slaughter, and that this had taken place in the autumn since a large number of bones from foals were uncovered. However, subsequent investigations have confirmed that horses have been hunted in many different seasons, meaning that the area has been visited many times.

Nine out of the ten spears are made from the trunks of slowly growing spruce trees; the last one is made from pine. The spears vary in length from 1.84 m to 2.53 m, and it is evident that the weapon makers have a good understanding of the properties of the wood. The spearheads are all formed from the hard wood outside the centre of the tree, to avoid the softer wood core, and resemble in design the spears used in today's competitions. The largest diameter, and thus the centre of gravity of the spear, is found in the front third of the spear. Additionally, the spears are sharpened both at the front and back, which improves aerodynamics.

The finding of 12,000 animal bones bears witness to the effectiveness of the spears as hunting weapons. Many of the bones bear cut marks from various types of stone tools used to separate the meat from the bone, indicating collaboration in the butchering process. Both the construction of the spears themselves and other findings attest to a cultural and social structure that until recently was not believed to be possessed by these early hunters. These are hunters with good technical skills; they could plan a hunt and collaborate in killing large and fast animals.

The extensive archaeological excavations in the Arago cave have so far revealed that various hunter groups have used the cave over a period of 600,000 years and, thus far, nearly 150 bones of the hunters have been found. Most of them are teeth. The oldest belonged to a reindeer hunter 555,000 years ago. In total, it is estimated that the bone remnants come from about thirty different individuals, almost half of them children. Based on the development of the teeth, one can estimate how old they were at the time of death. Based on this, the expected lifespan is calculated to be between 20-25 years, a quarter of what a modern hunter can expect today. Life cannot have been easy. That they could survive in warm periods in forested areas and grasslands where grazing roe deer resided is one thing, but that reindeer and woolly rhinoceros kept these people alive during climatically tougher conditions is another, and testifies to a great ability to adapt to varying climatic conditions.

The interpretations of the extensive material obtained show two fundamental aspects: while there is a broad consensus that the species composition of the hunters' prey in the different cultural layers reflects varying climatic conditions, and that the reindeer is the most important species when conditions are at their toughest, there is correspondingly significant disagreement about who these people were and what kinship they have to us.

The family history of Europe's first reindeer hunter

The first discovery of what would later be called *Heidelbergensis* was made on October 21, 1907. In a gravel pit in Mauer, about ten kilometres south-east of Heidelberg, the 'labourer' Daniel Hartmann made a discovery that later led to him being named an honorary citizen of Mauer at the age of 94, and even having a street named after him. He found a robust lower jawbone 24 metres down in the gravel pit and spontaneously exclaimed, 'I have found Adam.' The jawbone had small teeth but was unlike modern human jaws in having extremely large and heavy bones. The unique characteristics of this Mauer jawbone led to it being considered as belonging to a new species and being named after the nearby town, hence the name *Homo heidelbergensis*.

A little over a decade later, a skull was found in Kabwe, Zambia, which is also believed to have belonged to the Heidelberg people. This was the first time fossilised remains of our ancestors had been found in Africa. The skull indicated that the owner had both primitive features, including a broad face and thick, curved brow ridges, but at the same time provided space for a brain of 1280 cm^3. Thus, the first, and potentially intelligent, reindeer hunter had habitat in both Africa and Europe.

Was it a European heidelbergensis that was found inside the Arago cave? The bone remains of what would later be named Tautavel Man were found in 1964 in a cultural layer that was 455,000 years old. Discussions in the academic community about who this hunter truly was began immediately. Both the 'upright man' *Homo erectus* and the Neanderthals were mentioned. Others pointed out similarities with both and believed Tautavel Man must be a transitional form, a kind of pre-Neanderthal. An attempt to call the man *Homo erectus tautavelensis* was quickly dismissed, and the majority of experts agreed that the skull belonged to one, or perhaps two, individuals of Heidelberg descent. The skull is actually a reconstruction based on two half-skulls; some anthropologists believe these come from two different individuals.

It wasn't until 1993 that English anthropologists made their first discoveries of this hunter. In Boxgrove, West Sussex, a shinbone (tibia) and two teeth were found, dated to be 480,000 years old. Although the shinbone had gnaw marks from a predator, it could be seen that the owner of the bone was more robustly built than modern humans. The muscle attachments on the back of the bone indicated that this person had very large and powerful leg muscles.

The limestone cliffs where the hunter resided were evidently an attractive place and, in addition to human remains, a large number of bones from the prey they left behind have been found. Reindeer would not have been on the menu, but the discovery of bones from horses and rhinoceroses show that meat meals would have been served. The dwelling place has gradually been flooded so that remains of flint workings have been buried without being disturbed. Almost miraculously, it is therefore possible to see slaughter sites and places where the Heidelberg people made their tools. The sites with tool production are so well-preserved that it has been possible to reconstruct how these people made their hand axes.

Fossilised bone remnants and traces of these hunters have now been found in many European countries, and as far east as India. However, most anthropologists admit that *Homo heidelbergensis* is poorly defined and seemingly comes in many different versions. Some describe this hunter as short-legged and robust, while others as long-limbed and slender. If the family history of the first reindeer hunters had been unclear previously, the discussions reached a new level just a few years ago when analyses of bone material from Gran Dolina, the sinkhole in Atapuerca where our friend the pioneer lived, were made.

Until recently, the immigration history of our genus to Europe was simple and easy to understand for us non-experts. The upright man – *Homo erectus* – was the first to step out of Africa and spread out across Asia and possibly Europe. These died out and were replaced by a new immigrant from Africa – the Heidelberg people. These Heidelbergers underwent a development that, both in Europe and Africa, ended with a so-called speciation. In Europe, they gave rise to the Neanderthals, in Africa to us modern humans. After we modern humans migrated out of Africa, we lived in Europe alongside the Neanderthals for a few thousand years before we eventually became the only human species on the planet.

However, there has been a veil of obscurity over the earliest history of our lineage. Since genes undergo chemical degradation when temperatures are above freezing, the scientific communities working on examining human genetic material – genomics – have not found genetic material older than 400,000 years. Older parts of history have therefore been based on how skulls and mandibles have changed in shape and size over time. Now, new analysis methods have shed new light on the oldest family history of *Homo*, and we can even learn a new term right away – proteomics.

Proteomics is the analysis of proteins in the enamel and dentin of teeth attached to old mandibles that has given researchers new insights. Enamel and dentin are the two hardest tissues in the human body, and, because of their hardness, durability and strength, teeth represent the skeletal elements most likely to be preserved in geological deposits after death, and are capable of surviving a wide range of destructive effects caused by mechanical, chemical, physical or thermal changes. Once teeth are formed, they are therefore not subject to the same type of decay as other bones. This means that the proteins present while the individual lived can be analysed in fossils up to 2 million years old.

This opens up entirely new and groundbreaking investigations. The way the proteins in our bodies are assembled is determined by our genes. The composition of the proteins found in enamel and dentin can therefore provide us with information about an individual's genetic code. In a way, geneticists here are 'reading the book backwards'. By analysing the proteins in tooth enamel, they can reconstruct the genetic code, and using that genetic code, they can then estimate the relationship between living and extinct human types.

The Spanish researchers already believed 20 years ago that morphological features in the oldest finds in Atapuerca differed so drastically from previous finds of what was termed *Homo heidelbergensis* that they gave the earliest 'Atapuerca people' a new species name – *Homo antecessor*. Not a random choice of name. *Antecessor* means pioneer or explorer in Latin. And that's what these people were.

Now, the new analysis methods have provided opportunities to analyse the tooth enamel of pioneers that are over 800,000 years old, and the results have not only provided new insights into the evolution of the human lineage but also sparked discussions in the scientific communities. They showed that *H. antecessor* may be the last common ancestor of Neanderthals and modern humans, and that the branching points in the human family tree reach much further back in time than was previously possible to demonstrate. These results thus shed a critical light on the significance of *Homo heidelbergensis* for the development of our own species. But so far, no traces of *antecessor* have been found in Africa. An African *antecessor* must exist if they are to be our ancestors, for all fossil material shows that our own species *Homo sapiens* originated in Africa.

Regardless of what name we put on the first reindeer hunters down by the Mediterranean, the story of these people is exciting. For how can a species developed under tropical conditions in Africa survive for several hundred thousand years in a much cooler Europe? And how can a species sharing the same genetic material evolve so differently on the two continents that it results in two new species, Neanderthals in Europe, and us modern humans in Africa?

WHAT THE NEXT 500,000 YEARS ARE ALL ABOUT

Humans and reindeer are like most organisms. They can react to changes in environmental conditions in only three different ways: they can move to new areas, adapt to the new environmental conditions, or die. The story of the *Homo* genus and the reindeer will contain examples of all three. The reindeer is the quintessential wanderer of the animal kingdom, always seeking out areas with the most favourable environmental conditions. The first reindeer hunter, in his eagerness to adapt to the environment, will wipe himself out but give rise to two new species of reindeer hunters. One – the Neanderthal – will fail to adapt to the environmental conditions and die The other – us modern humans – will not only adapt to the environmental conditions but will also largely change the environmental conditions. And that's what the next half a million years will be about.

Europe has generally been a rather cold place over the past hundreds of thousands of years. The occasional warm periods, during which a life-giving sun melted glaciers and laid the foundation for new life, were short compared to the truly cold periods. There's no doubt that the European climate suited *Rangifer* (reindeer) better than the *Homo* genus, as Beringia provided a better evolutionary setting for adaptation to the cold than the eastern parts of Africa.

For a species that can survive in a landscape dominated by ice and snow for eight months of the year, cold is not a problem. Reindeer can maintain their body temperature even when the mercury drops to around -40°C, and newborn calves can maintain a constant body temperature at -25°C. Each hair in their fur has hundreds of air bubbles that provide excellent insulation, and the air breathed in is warmed up in the muzzle before reaching the lungs. When traversing snowy terrain, their broad hooves provide excellent flotation while also functioning as digging tools when snow covers grazing plants. Even though their legs are not covered in the same type of fur as their bodies, reindeer can maintain their body temperature by having veins carrying cold blood from the feet positioned right next to arteries carrying warm blood from the heart, allowing for heat exchange. However, they are less tolerant to heat. If the temperature rises above 10°C, even young reindeer try to shed body heat, and at temperatures nearing 25°C, both body temperature and heart rate increase, making life difficult.

While the term 'climate refugees' is relatively new, organisms have always attempted to sustain life by seeking out environments they are best suited for. Reindeer, being the great wanderers of the animal kingdom, have always responded to changes in climate by migrating to new areas with favourable conditions. Thus, changes in climate and environmental conditions led the mountain-adapted South American animal, which later became reindeer, to end up in Beringia about two million years ago. Environmental changes also made it possible for our earliest relatives, such as the erect *Homo erectus*, to move from Africa into Asia about two million years ago, and for the European pioneer *Homo antecessor* to venture into the Spanish highlands 1.2 million years ago. Many anthropologists believe that conditions related to crossing the Sahara were crucial for our ancestors to migrate from Africa to other continents. During cold and dry periods, poorly equipped migrants would have found it impossible to cross this vast desert area.

Not only is Europe generally colder than Africa, but climate conditions have also been highly variable. Therefore, in addition to the physiological challenges posed by cold, immigrants had to cope with the environmental changes associated with a varying climate. Menus had to be adapted quickly. New and previously unknown prey animals and plants had to be incorporated into the diet, necessitating changes in traditional hunting and gathering methods. The threat landscape also changed as new predators entered the hunting grounds. Only those who could adapt to the new conditions survived.

Many are familiar with the simplified version of Darwin's pioneering work, 'survival of the fittest', and expect that an organism's development is solely governed by genetic material, genes. This view has now been abandoned by scientific communities. Genetic information is important, but most species can influence their own development by continuously responding to environmental conditions. Biologists have now found many examples of non-genetic inheritance, and terms such as plasticity, epigenetics, niche construction, and cultural inheritance frequently appear in scientific literature. The reindeer hunters in the Arago cave can be associated with all these concepts.

Even though fossil bone material from our earliest relatives is limited, it can still be asserted that, like our reindeer-hunting friends in the Arago cave, they came in many different variations, some slim and long-limbed, and others broad and short. The reasons for this are that most organisms are capable of responding to different environmental conditions. For the reindeer hunters in the Arago cave and their relatives in Africa, responses to environmental conditions would be so significant that they would disappear as a species themselves, leaving behind two new species, one on each continent.

Regardless of whether the scientific communities in Atapuerca ultimately prove that the pioneer *antecessor* is the ancestor of both Neanderthals and modern humans or whether it was *Heidelbergensis* who came to Europe from Africa 6–700,000 years ago, we can assume that the first reindeer hunters in the Arago cave were relatively long-legged, upright and slender hunters with body proportions not unlike those of modern humans. This adaptation to more tropical conditions is a trait that is well known among most mammals and many other organisms, leading to the association of two different 'ecological rules' with the phenomenon.

German Carl Bergmann was the first to establish in 1847 that most mammals inhabiting cold climates have larger body mass than species under warmer conditions. The reason for this is that reducing the ratio of surface area to volume minimises heat loss. With the same explanation, American Joel Allen determined that animals in cold environments have shorter extremities than species in warmer climates.

Warmth was not characteristic of the environment the reindeer hunters in the Arago cave would experience over the next three to four hundred thousand years. Therefore, it would not be advantageous to carry traits adapted to a tropical climate. Changes were necessary. Gradually, the broad nose, with its large nostrils that had previously cooled and dried the air before reaching the lungs, was replaced with narrower and longer noses capable of warming and moistening the cold and dry air the reindeer hunters breathed in. The body gradually became wider, and the feet shorter, eventually resulting in a body shape that reduced heat loss.

Our distant relatives thus exhibit a significant degree of what we can call malleability. For even though the main pattern is that our neural pathways are genetically determined and formed similarly in all individuals, further development after birth is significantly influenced by the individual's interaction with the environmental conditions it grows up in. Our genes also do not behave in the same way all the time. Chemical components can mark different genes and turn them on and off, depending on environmental conditions; this is what biologists call epigenetics. When we consider that all cells in the body contain exactly the same genetic material but that some 'receive instructions' to become blood cells, others liver cells, we understand that the effects of this adaptability are tremendous. In fact, the effects of adaptations to different environments can be so significant and rapid that they lead to the formation of new species.

In addition to the gradual changes in the first reindeer hunters themselves, who became increasingly better adapted to the climate, they also began to influence their own surroundings. They made the environment more habitable – they mastered fire, and they built small huts using hides from their prey. Therefore, 400,000 years ago, a fire burned at Terra Amata – 'the beloved land' – near the old town of present-day Nice. Just 20 metres above the Mediterranean Sea, on what was then a beach, hunter groups established themselves for long periods. The huts were simple, but it must have been a relief from life inside the dark, damp caves and shelters they had previously used. Soon, fires burned outside small huts from Beeches Pit in England to Vértesszöllös in Hungary. The changes in quality of life must have been significant.

For the first reindeer hunters in the Arago cave, significant changes may have accelerated around 350,000 years ago. The reason for this is that the influx of genes from heat-adapted hunters from Africa may have ceased entirely. Europe was in the midst of a 40,000-year-long cold period, which also affected northern parts of Africa. Many anthropologists assume that migrants from Africa to Europe would not have been able to cross the inhospitable Sahara Desert. This probably put an end to visits from their African relatives. They would now develop into a people well adapted to Europe's changing climatic conditions. Europe became Neanderthal land.

PART II

The people who will hunt reindeer for the next 200,000 years are the true Europeans. They represent the only human species that evolved on this continent. As true-born children of African ancestors but adapted to a harsh and highly variable European Ice Age climate, they will evolve into formidable hunters during their time on Earth. The reindeer, on the other hand, continues to be a reindeer. It does what it does best. It wanders, seeking shelter in areas where living conditions are most favourable, as it always has. Previously, humans rarely followed in its hoofprints, but now traces of hunters are increasingly found in the reindeer's territories.

THE SECOND HUNTER AND THE REINDEER

Europe 250,000 – 40,000 years ago

They had learned much from their ancestors, the people now gathered around the fire inside Lazaret Cave, just a stone's throw from where their forebears had sat by the life-giving fire in Terra Amata over 200,000 years earlier. The placement of the fire in the cave was not chosen randomly. Inside the 40-metre-long and 15-metre-wide cave, there was plenty of space; a fire could be kindled almost anywhere.

French researchers who calculated how smoke from fires placed in 15 different locations inside the cave would affect its inhabitants had a clear conclusion: cave dwellers had chosen the place where the smoke caused them the least inconvenience. The hunters had kindled fires inside the cave about 30 times, and each time the fire had been placed in the best spot An apparently trivial piece of knowledge but considering how much time they spent around the fire and its function the knowledge was important enough.

The fire had become a focal point, a place where they formed social bonds, prepared their meals, and where the meaty parts of prey were smoked to extend their shelf life, making them better prepared for times of food scarcity. And they needed a lot of food. To maintain the right body temperature during winter, reindeer hunters would require between 3,400 and 4,500 kcal per day, or just over a kilogram of fatty meat, nearly double what modern hunters need. But compared to their ancestors, they were much better adapted to the conditions of the cold continent.

Much has happened since Europe's first reindeer hunters gathered around the fires in Arago Cave. Several cold periods have come and gone in Europe. Four times tundra and ice have crept southward, large ice caps have formed, sea levels have fallen, risen, and fallen again. The North Sea was first drained and became Doggerland, later returning to the seabed. Four times large deciduous forests have come and gone. New animal species have followed the forests, and hunters followed in their tracks.

In green meadows, the human population grew. When new cold periods arrived, landscapes, animals and humans were restricted to where conditions were liveable. Waves of climatic and ecological upheaval have swept over people and animals, and the world has changed many times. Fortunately, handling changes is something our kind is quite good at. Previously, scientists' favourite hypothesis was that upright walking on two legs and the use of stone tools were linked to a drier climate, where forests disappeared and people had to spend large parts of their lives on grasslands – the so-called savanna theory.

The theory was that the first humans adapted to a specific environment, the African savannah. This view is now completely abandoned. For our kind – the *Homo* genus – environmental instability is, on the contrary, the most significant driver of evolution, and our ancestors increased their ability to handle changing environments rather than specialising in a specific type of environment. Results from researchers using methods developed by Nicholas Shackleton and Cesare Emiliani show that climate variations on Earth have become increasingly significant over the past 2 million years, while it has gradually become colder.

And it is the climate variations that have triggered change. In very stable environments, such as on the ocean floor, very little has happened, and the organisms living there are ancient and unchanged. The ancestors of the *Homo* genus began walking upright when the forests disappeared about 6 million years ago and were replaced by grasslands. Lucy – the famous fossil over 3 million years old found in the Awash Valley in Ethiopia – had developed a pelvic structure and knee joints indicating that she spent most of her time on grasslands, while her long ape-like arms and fingers showed she still mastered climbing trees. In other words, she had exceptional flexibility to exploit both forests and savannahs.

Stone tools were made 2.6 million years ago, opening up opportunities to exploit new and different forms of food. Meat could be cut, bones could be crushed to access marrow, plants could be ground, nuts could be crushed. When environmental variations on Earth increased in strength about 800,000 years ago, the *Homo* genus responded quickly. The brain grew! Over the first 4–5 million years, those who occasionally moved on two legs had a small increase in brain volume. Now, coinciding with the strong climatic fluctuations, the changes in brain size were dramatic. The increased brain size enabled our ancestors to find creative solutions to various challenges, while also being able to process and store information.

Those now sitting around the fire in Lazaret Cave are therefore the latest in a series of people with a remarkable ability to change and adapt. An ability to change to such an extent that they are now considered an entirely different species from those who hunted in Arago Cave. Both facial and body shape have changed. The nose has a completely different shape. A larger and longer nose now allows for warming and moistening of the cool and dry air before it enters the lungs. The increased nasal volume also allows for the transport of a larger volume of air, which is necessary given the increased energy needs of the new hunters. The body has also become wider, the chest is bell-shaped, the pelvis wider, and the arms and legs relatively shorter. All these traits are further adaptations to the colder climate we saw hints of in the first reindeer hunters. Around the fire, some very pale hunters can also be seen. Red-haired hunters with freckles have also taken their place near the warmth. Light skin is an adaptation to life at northern latitudes.

It is truly a different hunter now hunting in the mountains and forests of Europe. The reindeer they hunt apparently remained unchanged throughout the long period of dramatic climate variations. Where hunters adapted to different environments, the reindeer employed a different strategy. While hunters changed both body shape and physiology, along with taming fire, improving clothing and constructing simple huts, making the environment more liveable, the reindeer responded to changes in its habitat by migrating to areas where it found the most favourable living conditions.

The adaptations the reindeer has made to survive cold and limited access to both sunlight and food during the winter are unique. Compared to over forty other ruminants, it is a master at overcoming tough climatic conditions. Like all mammals living north of the 35th parallel, reindeer need to produce Vitamin D during the summer. Parts of the ultraviolet rays from the sun (UVB) stimulate the formation of Vitamin D, which reindeer need a lot of when they are growing antlers. In ruminants, nearly 30 genes are involved in the production and use of Vitamin D, and in reindeer there are specific changes in two of these genes that make the process 20 times more efficient than in other ruminants.

A similar adaptation has not been found in the humans who will hunt reindeer for the next 200,000 years. On the contrary, studies of these hunters show that they suffer from chronic Vitamin D deficiency. The vitamin, which is actually a hormone, is involved in the formation of more than 3,000 different proteins, and a deficiency in the vitamin can even affect fertility. Some have speculated that this could be the cause of their disappearance.

Unlike reindeer, hunters did not have large fat reserves to rely on during the winter. It is considered highly unlikely that they were able to build up such reserves. The reindeer, however, is a master at it. Once again, changes in a specific gene are the cause. A similar change has only been found in polar bears and Adélie penguins, and it affects both the build-up of fat reserves and the transport and use of fat. However, when it comes to adaptations and changes in the nasal area, they follow the same pattern, the hunter and the prey, although the reindeer's solution is more efficient. The dry and cold air breathed in must pass through a large area of warm tissue and become saturated with moisture before it enters the lungs. The warm and moist air breathed out must pass over large areas of cold tissue and cool down, while the water condenses. This way, both heat and water are preserved in the body. In the climatically very unstable period we are now in, the reindeer will need both its adaptations to cold and its unique ability to migrate. But unlike before, the hunter has increased its ability to follow the reindeer even to areas with very harsh climates. Compared to those who inhabited Tautavel near the Mediterranean and the Spanish mountainous regions south of the Pyrenees, this hunter has made significant technological and cultural advances. But they were not exactly received as a technological and cultural people the first time around.

The valley of the new man – Neanderthal

Neanderthal is named after the German pastor and composer Joachim Neander, who in the 17th century drew inspiration for his compositions from the beautiful limestone valley with its many caves. Neander is a Greek translation of his original family name, which was Neumann, both meaning 'new man'. It was here that the first Neanderthal was found on an autumn day in 1856.

As often happens with fossil discoveries, this one too was a coincidence. The occasion was blasting work to extract stone for building material. The bone remains that were found were initially interpreted as remnants of a cave bear. At that time, the idea that other species of humans could have existed was unthinkable. Fortunately, the bone remains, the top of a skull, parts of an arm, some ribs, and parts of the pelvis, were preserved and eventually ended up with William King, who was a professor at Queen's College in Ireland.

He argued that these were remnants of an extinct human species and proposed the name *Homo neanderthalensis*. He believed that the difference between this fossil and modern human was so significant that it represented a separate genus with greater similarity to chimpanzees. The newly discovered Neanderthal did not receive a warm welcome and was described in the most disparaging terms. A professor of anatomy at the University of Bonn, Hermann Schaaffhausen, described the Neanderthal as 'deformed in a way unknown even among the most barbaric tribes', and English colleagues followed up with 'some poor idiot or dwarf' – statements that have not stood the test of time very well.

The man who would later be found in Dordogne, and given the somewhat impersonal name La Ferrassie 1, would refute the earlier descriptions. He might not have been particularly tall, only about 5 feet 7 inches, but definitely not a dwarf. Deformed? Yes, a little, but this was due to arthritis in the spine, as well as having a mild form of scoliosis – curvature of the spine. Age had weighed on the 50-year-old man.

Inside the cave with him, now bearing his name, lay an older woman and five children, as well as a nearly fully developed fetus. At least one of the children was given a decent burial. Barbaric, hardly. Idiot? Difficult to say. But if there were a correlation between brain size and an individual's intelligence, perhaps we would expect the theory of relativity to have been developed inside the Ferrassie cave 50,000 years ago. The Ferrassie man had a brain size of 1641 cm³, which is significantly larger than Albert Einstein's 1250 cm³. It is this people who will now have the European continent as their hunting ground.

Life in Neanderthal land

The exact point at which the Neanderthals became Neanderthals is a subject of debate among scholars. However, what they can agree on is that this hunter is the only human species to have evolved in Europe, and when one species evolves into another, it doesn't happen overnight. The gradual changes in body shape have led posterity to describe about thirty different variations of the Neanderthal, all with different characteristics. If we consider the period starting 250,000 years ago and ending 40,000 years ago, it covers the time when the 'true' or classical Neanderthals more or less had the entire European continent to themselves.

More or less, because they are not entirely alone. Farthest east in what we can call Eurasia, in the Altai Mountains in the southernmost parts of

Siberia, another group of people has settled. Archaeologists working inside Denisova Cave had previously found stone tools they believed were made by Neanderthals, but in 2008 they found a couple of bone fragments from a finger, and genetic analyses of this would fully demonstrate the power of the new techniques geneticists had at their disposal. Two years after the finger was found, geneticists could confirm that the people who had inhabited the cave represented a previously unknown lineage of our species; they were called the Denisovans. A rather random choice of name considering Denisova Cave was named after the hermit Denis who had stayed there in the 18th century. Although a few teeth and bone fragments from a foot or arm have recently been found, there are still no fossil remains that can tell us about their appearance. Therefore, they are the first human species to be uncovered solely through genetic analyses, and as long as physical descriptions of this human species are lacking, they have not been given their own Latin name – but they are definitely part of our genus.

It has now been revealed that the genetic lineages that gave rise to both Neanderthals and Denisovans diverged from the lineage that became modern humans between 550–765,000 years ago. At the same time, geneticists have found that Neanderthals and Denisovans split between 380–470,000 years ago, and that there was as much genetic difference between the two human species as there is between Neanderthals and modern humans today. But even though our two relatives evolved into separate species, there has been contact between the two peoples.

It's hard to hide things from geneticists. Give them a tooth, and they can confirm that a wandering Neanderthal woman had made the journey to Denisova Cave in Siberia and entered into a relationship with a Denisovan man. The result of the relationship was the hybrid girl, Denny. As a teenager, she died inside the cave, but left behind a tooth. Analysis of this not only revealed the relationship but also showed that the girl's father himself was a mixture of Neanderthal and Denisovan.

Like the Neanderthals, the Denisovans were also big game hunters. Inside the cave bearing their name, bone remains of Siberian roe deer, deer, Irish giant deer, two different species of horse, bison, and woolly rhinoceros have now been uncovered. Fossil remains of reindeer have not been found, but it is unlikely that a lack of interest in reindeer meat is the cause; most likely, the reindeer were not present in the area. Common to our two close relatives is that they are good hunters, and life in Neanderthal land is characterised by two factors: hunting various large game species and adaptations to constantly changing climatic conditions, because it must be allowed to claim that the classic Neanderthals were not lucky with the climate. Until they disappear around 40,000 years ago, they will experience the climate shifting between relatively warm and very cold periods nine times.

Although it starts relatively well in what is referred to as an interglacial period between 250,000 and 190,000 years ago, the climate was not favourable for poorly dressed hunters. It is therefore impressive that small hunting groups managed to travel as far north-west as Wales. It must have been the cold period that the British call Wolstonian, preceding the interglacial, that allowed them to walk dry-shod from mainland Europe, across Doggerland, and west to Wales because much of the water from the sea was bound in land ice. The stay in Pontnewydd Cave 225,000 years ago must have been challenging, but at the same time gave them a taste of what was to come. Whether they made it back to mainland Europe before a new ice-cold period covered large parts of Wales with ice is uncertain. What is certain is that some stayed and left behind 19 teeth and parts of an upper jaw.

How well-prepared the Neanderthals were for the climate that was to come is uncertain. There are few indications that there were innovations that would have improved their living conditions in the next 60,000 years, which must be considered as a very long stay in a freezer. There seem to have been no major changes in the production of clothing, and the weapons also do not seem to have been improved, but they had control of fire. The life-giving fire must have been absolutely essential in this ice-cold period. Until about 190,000 years ago, the glaciers covered areas all the way down to present-day London and Düsseldorf. Neanderthals who had previously found their way to present-day Netherlands would now see that the hunting camp they had established near Amsterdam lay under metres of ice, and in the Alps the glaciers spread over all proportions and now covered the Neanderthals' former hunting grounds in the areas around Munich, Vienna and Bern. The small and few hunting groups were gradually pushed into small ice age refuges where conditions were still bearable.

While apparently there have been few changes in clothing and tools, the hunters' body shape has changed. They have become more compact, with shorter legs and a stronger chest. Whether the changed body shape is an adaptation to a colder climate or a life characterized by great physical activity is difficult to ascertain. Compared to today's Inuit, who clearly have a body shape adapted to cold, analyses show that Neanderthals have a significantly larger body surface area than the Inuit. Based on body surface area, calculations can be made of how much energy is required to keep the body metabolism going. Based on this, it is clear that Neanderthals must have a daily intake of between 3,500 – 5,000 kilocalories. In the cold periods they are now in, the reindeer is undoubtedly the most important prey. One kilogramme of reindeer meat contains just over 3,000 kilocalories, while bone marrow and fat contain twice as much. A hunting group of around 20 people must therefore have daily access to over 30 kilogrammes of meat and fat from reindeer or other large prey, usually horses and bison in the cold periods.

However, securing a stable supply of meat must still have been challenging, and surely increased the motivation to hunt the truly large herbivores – mammoths. Archaeologists estimate that successful mammoth hunts are rare, but in cases where they find traces of Neanderthal campsites associated with mammoth bones, it appears that the hunting technique has been to chase the animals off steep cliffs. Transporting such large animals to a more permanent camp is impossible, and if they only brought with them the meat they could carry, the rest of the dead animal was left to cave lions and cave hyenas. The solution in most cases seems to have been to move the camp to the dead animal.

Our perception of Neanderthal cognitive abilities, that is, the brain-based skills they had to solve and perform both simple and complex tasks, has changed dramatically in recent decades. Despite this, there was great surprise when it was discovered what Neanderthal hunters on the plains north of Toulouse had been up to in the ice-cold period about 175,000 years ago – they had created artwork! A monumental artwork. A group of Neanderthals had travelled 330 metres into Bruniquel Cave. There they had broken off 400 stalagmites – the icicle-like stalactites that form in limestone caves, and collected the 2.2-ton heavy material into a circular sculpture. Why they made this artwork, and what function it served, we may never know, but traces of fires and remains of marrow bones show that they spent a lot of time there. Letting the imagination run wild, one can also easily imagine that long-forgotten rituals took place within the circle of stacked stalagmites.

So, after 60,000 years in the freezer, a 60,000-year period of much more favourable climate begins 130,000 years ago. Seen as a whole, the temperature is still 3–4 degrees cooler than today's normal temperature, but at the beginning of the period the temperatures are significantly higher than what we have today. Chilled Neanderthals will over the next 10–15,000 years, experience temperatures up to 2.5 degrees higher than today's. The changes are enormous. The permafrost disappears, and the previously plain land is covered by forests, not only in the southern parts of Europe. Small stands of hazel and oak find good growing conditions far up the coast of Finland, and even up at North Cape, forested areas are found, and in southern Europe, the former reindeer land becomes habitable for deer and roe deer. From their small ice age refuges, small groups of Neanderthals follow the retreating glaciers northward, westward, and into the Alpine regions.

Archaeological finds show that the Neanderthals' hunting grounds expand enormously. Along the entire Odra valley from Poland and far down into Germany, finds of settlements with bone material testify to great hunting success. Initially, they had followed the reindeer northward, but, as temperatures increased, the reindeer were replaced by red deer and roe deer. In north-west Germany, Neanderthals even succeeded in killing the largest of all game: the straight-tusked elephant. A male elephant of this species is estimated to have weighed up to 13 tons, and in the warmest period 125,000 years ago, hunters with settlements around Gröbern and Lehringen managed to kill such an animal. Hunting success is also documented further south and east. In Bolomor Cave near Valencia, Spanish Neanderthals apparently lived good lives. Access to Irish giant deer seems to have been good, and in addition they exploited a variety of new heat-loving plant species that had found their way to Spain. In Asolo, north of Venice, archaeologists uncover that Italian Neanderthals have had great success in hunting an incredibly large mammoth.

At the end of this favourable climatic period, the number of Neanderthals is probably higher than ever before. Over 60,000 years, life had been good for the Neanderthals. They had occupied increasingly new areas, and child mortality had decreased. The attempts made to estimate the population size are based on the number of reproductive women in the various hunting groups. In total, it is estimated that there were nearly 3,500 of them spread around Europe during this period, which estimates that there were about 20,000 individuals in total. Over the next years, there would be far fewer of them.

For now, life would take a new turn. The forests that were once teeming with life are in full retreat. Firewood for the life-giving fires that they had previously found around the camp was suddenly scarce. While they previously did not need to move far from the camp before they had enough game, they now had to rely on long hunting trips again. And again, it is the reindeer that will keep them alive in the approximately 15,000-year-long cold period that lies ahead of them.

FIG 2. During periods of cold climate, reindeer migrated south and were humans' most important prey for long periods. The thin line illustrates average temperature, the thick line shows the proportion of reindeer in bone material from a number of different settlements. Until about 45,000 years ago, these were the settlements of the Neanderthals.

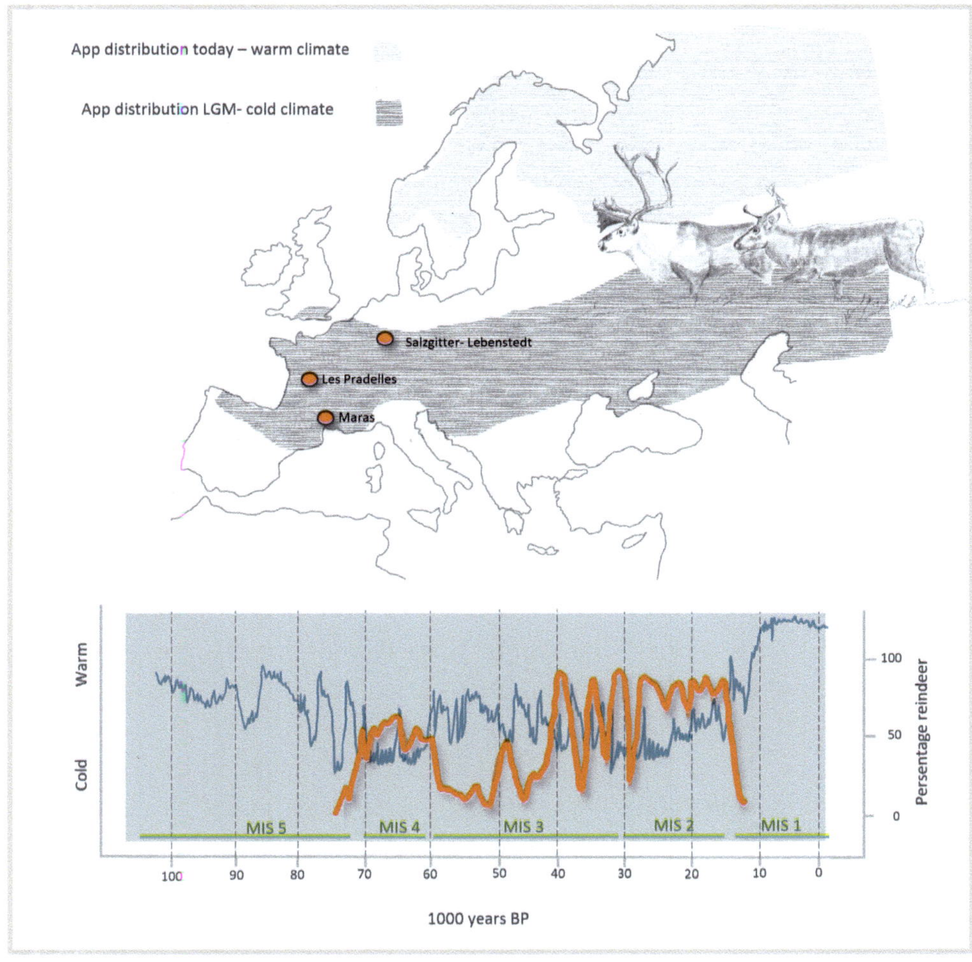

THE ART OF SURVIVAL

Dordogne, France 70,000 years ago

Seventy-thousand years ago, we can imagine three men from the Combe-Grenal cave in Dordogne making the final preparations before embarking on a hunting trip. Their need to acquire more food was great. The group inside the cave had grown, and the hunting luck hadn't been good lately. The hunters were well acquainted with the area. For hundreds of thousands of years, their ancestors had resided here, and much experience had been passed down from one generation to the next, but the hunt for reindeer had almost been forgotten. On the trip, the lead hunter accidentally makes a discovery that will ease the equipment of future reindeer hunters and provide the hunters with opportunities to cover larger areas on their trips.

They had been three in the group until yesterday. For four days, they had been searching for prey. Four days with no results. First, they had searched the best areas in their known hunting grounds. Then the scattered groves down in the valley. Later, they had tried in the hills and up in the mountains and along the borders of the neighbouring clans' territories. The same result there: nothing to be seen, not a single promising trace. The two who had joined the lead hunter were already uncertain about being there; they wanted to turn back, to return to the valley, to the families waiting. They were in a desperate situation. The people had been starving for a long time; they were pale, weak and disheartened. The land that could be so generous had become a greedy land, a cold and dead land sucking the life out of people. The leader had stood his ground: they could not give up now. They had to continue searching; it was their duty, wasn't it? There was no one else. Entering the neighbouring clan's territory, uninvited and unprepared, was unheard of, but because the need was so great, they had to seek help there. Perhaps they had food, perhaps the reindeer had come there? It was a fragile and desperate hope born of necessity, but they had to try.

In the end, his two companions gave in and joined him. Then they had set course to here, a long day's journey from their own dwelling place, although, in recent times the clan had been on constant wanderings and no longer had a fixed abode in a cave. The search for prey that was not to be found had forced the clan on constant wanderings. It was a heavy life to live like that. Everything had to be carried: hides, the smallest children, an elderly person who needed help, weapons, tools, and materials for new tools. Granted, the material for tools was already roughly hewn up on the cliff where they found the best flint, but they were still heavy to carry. They had tried to use other stones, but it was the flint from that one quarry that yielded the best results; other types of stone did not produce the same edge and could not be shaped as well. It mostly resulted in them carrying materials for new tools and struggling with the old ones for as long as possible.

Then they had come here, initially filled with a burgeoning hope that relief could be found among the neighbours to the north – a hope that would be replaced by sorrow and horror. The three had come from the south and had followed the heights on the edge towards the valley. There they had a good view, but they found no traces of reindeer or other large animals. It was easy to walk up there in the heights, where there was little snow and solid ground. Nevertheless, they eventually turned down into the valley. Perhaps there was small game to be found down in the valley bottom and in the thickets along the river.

They followed a steep pass to descend into the valley bottom and had to cross a large pile of stones to get down. Just as they were almost down, the unthinkable happened when walking in such terrain: the leader stepped awkwardly on a round stone, the stone tipped over, and he fell off it and went tumbling down the last metres over rough scree. He heard the others shouting out, in vain; the next thing he remembered was lying on the ground, dazed, but still whole. It was only afterwards that he noticed the knife tucked under the straps holding the foot skin in place was broken. A broken knife was almost a catastrophe. The three hunters each had their own, and no one could do without this tool. They had no materials to make new ones; flint was too heavy for a trip like this, and they hadn't seen any since they left their own valley. The leader didn't say anything to the others about the knife. It was both clumsy and irresponsible to destroy such a vital tool like that.

The suspicion that something was wrong had grown as they approached the cave where the neighbouring clan had resided for generations. There were no traces of life to be seen: no one had been down by the river, no paths leading up to the cave. No smoke. The unease they felt was confirmed at the entrance, where they had to dig through the snow to get in. Then there was suddenly no doubt anymore – all life had gone from here. The neighbours had had even less success with their hunt. Scattered around on the floor were the remains of those who had lived here. Reindeer-gnawed bones showed that it had been weeks since the people here had given up.

There and then, the leader's two companions had had enough. For generations, they had taken their mates from this clan and from the neighbours further south. The remains on the floor were what was left of that family. Now they wanted to go home to theirs.

They discussed it for a long time, weighing the need to find the reindeer against the hopelessness and concern of those awaiting news and needing food. Then they noticed the first change in the weather – at first just a slight breeze in the air, a rustling of coarse snow grains moved by the first gust of wind. The others suddenly became busy; they wanted to cross the valley and get up to the pass before the storm hit. There was a cave up there where they could find shelter from what was coming. From there, they would have half a day's walk before they reached the cave where their families were gathered.

Suddenly the leader was alone. The others left him an extra fur skin. He gathered the bone remnants on the floor into a pile at the back of the cave. Sharp cuts and scratches on one of the thigh bones spoke of the end for the poor souls; here it wasn't just wolves and carnivores with sharp teeth that had helped themselves. The traces of flint knives were all too clear. He hastily covered the misery with snow – it was best to avoid the sight.

After some struggle, he covered the cave entrance with snow blocks and lit a fire. He took out the knife, or rather what was left of it – it had broken in two and was almost unusable. He turned and examined the two flint pieces, a thought gradually forming. What if he removed part of the stone where the break had occurred and added a new curve backward, then he could also remove part of the dull edge. Maybe it would be possible to salvage the stumps of what he had after all? Tentatively, he picked up a piece of reindeer antler from the floor and pressed it against the edge where he wanted to remove some of the stone. With a sharp click, a small chip flew off. He was startled. That was a bit too much – he needed to work more delicately, more skillfully. The danger was that he would ruin what little was left of the knife. In deep concentration, he continued the work, chip by chip removing small fragments, and gradually managed to shape a new and functional tool from something that had been broken and would normally just have been discarded.

With a satisfied grunt, he found the other part of the broken knife and started working on it. As the fire burnt down, he finished his task. Now he had two knives, small and unfamiliar, but both with new and razor-sharp edges. In his concentration, he had forgotten time and place and didn't notice the storm raging outside. Snow flurried through the opening he made for the smoke, and he had to seal it again as best he could. When he had done that, he piled the remaining firewood onto the fire; it would have to do. There was no thinking of going out again in such weather. He wrapped the fur skins around himself; whether he fell asleep or fainted is hard to say.

Outside, the north wind had risen to insane fury; the cautious rustling of frozen snow on the move had gradually turned into a steady roar that had only increased in strength. Now it showed itself in all its power and threw its primeval forces against everything living.

But even after the worst night, there always comes a new day. He lay as if dead. A fine dusting of snow had settled on him, hair and beard covered with frost. A faint frosty mist from mouth and nose was the only indication that he was still alive. He awakened to a dark world; the fire had long since burned down, and only a faint half-light seeped in between the snow, blocking the exit and the cave's roof. During the night, a large drift had built up, and snow almost filled the entire space between what was once a warm fire, the cave entrance, and the world outside. Eventually, he came to, threw off the fur and snow, and began to dig. Outside was a new world – quiet, blue sky and sunshine. There was still enough wind to blow snow along the ground like small transparent rivers. It was a new day, but also a day when he must risk everything, hungry and ravaged as he was by the hardships of the past few days. Dressed in skins, with two spears of wood, two fur skins, and an alien and new knife, he would face the day. His people had lived in this land for countless generations; wind, snow, and cold had tempered both him and his people. Now all this would be put to the test; a man's courage and strength would be tested against nature's whims and occasional mercilessness.

He eventually got going and headed towards the gravel ridges further into the valley. He followed these as best he could. He couldn't walk quickly, but managed to maintain a steady pace and eventually reached the point he had picked out from the view up at the cave. The valley curved here, and a new view appeared: new mounds, eskers, and small patches of willow bushes. It was almost unbelievable, but down by the river less than a kilometre away, he saw a small herd of animals. There weren't many animals, only eight to ten, but still an incredible wealth in the form of meat, fat, blood, and warmth in this empty land. At first, he doubted, unsure of what he had seen; could it really be reindeer? But then they move closer and the variations of gray far away become moving dots. He stopped doubting: reindeer were grazing over there on the edge between bare ground and snow.

Two hours later, he arrived at the stones; if everything went well, the herd would come here. He huddled up by his stone, wrapped the skins better around himself, and tried to find a position where his body could rest. It wasn't easy; the excitement of finding animals and the last hundred metres of crouched walking to avoid being seen had taken their toll. The tension had settled like a locked spring in his entire strong body. But he managed to get here unseen; the herd was still unaware of the hunter waiting.

Then he heard the animals, a crunching sharp sound of hooves against snow. Otherwise, it was silent, completely silent. He tightened his grip on the spear, forcing himself to be calm, to breathe, to become like the stone and part of the landscape. With his senses, he desperately tried to 'see' the herd, following their movements outside his field of vision. He imagined them grazing, digging, walking a few metres. Was that an animal breathing? It was silent again, no new steps in the snow. Then they emerged down by the snow edge, first a cow, then a calf, then another calf, and then another cow, smaller than the first.

The first cow came closer, and the distance from the hunter was finally less than 10 metres. He threw the spear, which entered the reindeer's body right behind the front leg; it was a good throw and a deadly hit. The cow jumped and took a few leaps before tumbling over and lying down. The rest of the herd were startled and ran away, suddenly out of reach. The hunter stayed still again and waited. It might be futile, and he longed to run down, drive the knife into the animal he had felled, taste the blood and warmth, but he waited, as still as a stone.

Then the calf returned; in its language it called to the cow and ran forward with its head held high and its tail stub sticking straight up – a clear sign that it sensed danger. It trotted back and forth out of reach of the hunter. The calf smelt the cow, but something wasn't right. It stopped, stood with legs astride, hesitant. The man by the stone grunted, making a sound that mimicked the reindeer, and the calf was fooled. He threw another spear, and in a matter of a few minutes, he had achieved what he had struggled to do for many days.

THE NEANDERTHAL KITCHEN

Not many decades ago, academic circles were vigorously debating whether Neanderthals were capable of effective hunting. The prevailing theories in the 1960s still suggested that the Neanderthal diet reflected what the large predators around them managed to kill, implying they were reliant on leftovers from cave bears, cave hyenas, wolves, and European lions. Now, there is no longer a discussion about their ability to procure food, but well into the 2000s, academic circles remained focused on just how effective and specialised they really were. It was long assumed that Neanderthals were inefficient and had to settle for the easiest prey available. Specialisation in a particular prey species was thought to be reserved only for hunter-gatherer societies that were well-organised, had developed language, and generally consisted of individuals with cognitive abilities enabling strategic thinking and problem-solving. Neanderthals were not attributed with these qualities.

Today, we know better. A detailed study from the south-western parts of France has largely provided insight into why Neanderthal kitchen middens look the way they do. A compilation of material from nearly 40 settlements with a total of 148 different cultural layers reflects the Neanderthal diet during the period from 130,000 to 40,000 years ago. This period experienced significant climatic variations. Therefore, it is understandable that even though remains of 12 different ungulates are found, their presence varies from being completely absent in periods to occasionally appearing, and then becoming very common. In fact, only four species were present at any given time: bison, horse, deer, and reindeer.

The variation in the diet could, of course, be attributed to individual Neanderthal groups having different preferences for dinner. Some might have preferred only horse steak, while others could not imagine anything other than reindeer roast. Far more likely, however, is that the kitchen middens reflected the environment around the settlements, and the climatic variations during this period provided highly variable living conditions for the prey animals.

Good climate data has now confirmed this. Analysis of sediment cores taken from the seabed in the Bay of Biscay has revealed the type of pollen deposited during different periods. Additionally, the sediment cores contained various foraminifera – small single-celled organisms with calcareous shells. Analysis of these has uncovered the sea temperatures and salinity levels. Lastly, dating of sediments deposited on the seabed after drifting icebergs had melted and left behind gravel and stones attached to the undersides of the icebergs, together provided a detailed picture of the climatic conditions.

By combining findings of bone material from different species with the climate at the time the animals were consumed by Neanderthals, a very clear picture emerges: the Neanderthal diet mirrors the prevailing climatic conditions. During the warmest periods, deer and roe deer are captured and eaten; in cooler periods, roe deer disappear, and reindeer and deer are brought to the settlements, while during the most climatically challenging periods, only reindeer are on the menu.

This means that reindeer have been not only the most important prey for Neanderthals over periods of tens of thousands of years, but in many cases also the only prey. In a climatically very challenging period around 65–60,000 years ago, Neanderthal kitchen middens consisted of 100% reindeer. Without access to reindeer, the small and vulnerable Neanderthal communities could not have existed.

During this period, we also see changes in Neanderthal technology. The difference from earlier times was that the new tools were made so that they could easily be reworked into new types of tools that could be reused as they wore out. The technique used when a tool needed to be reused – retouching, as archaeologists call it – was to use a piece of wood, bone or antler and press it against the edge of an item to shape a new tool or to make a sharper edge on a tool that had become dull, exactly as we have imagined the Neanderthal from Combe-Grenal working on his broken knife. Hunting reindeer likely involved a changed and at least partially new way of life that also required these people to move over larger areas. A light and flexible set of hunting tools was therefore important for these hunters.

The vital reindeer

Archaeologists' relentless work at Neanderthal settlements has provided valuable insights into how this people survived through the last two ice ages in Europe, where there were significant climate variations. Previous assumptions that this hunter-gatherer folk wandered around their hunting grounds and only randomly encountered their prey and raw materials for their weapons and tools have now been abandoned.

It is now accepted that the hunter groups had delimited hunting grounds where they established settlements with various functions. Some settlements were solely used as stone workshops where raw materials were transformed into weapons and tools, some settlements bear the marks of being used for specific seasons over a long period, while others clearly served as regular 'hunting camps' where prey was brought in for further processing. Inside the last ice age that the Neanderthals, perhaps also our own species, would experience, such specialised hunting camps were established in several places in Europe.

Les Pradelles, a collapsed cave in the calcareous areas of Charentes, 100 kilometres north-east of Bordeaux, is one such typical hunting camp. Here, archaeologists have painstakingly excavated through a five-metre-thick cultural layer, uncovering Neanderthal activity through a climatically tough period. The large amounts of bone material show that nine out of ten prey brought into the camp are reindeer. Bone material from horses and bison make up the rest.

Estimates show that approximately 30 tons of reindeer meat were brought to the settlement, mainly consisting of the large meaty parts of the animals taken for further processing. Rib bones and large spinal bones are almost completely absent. This is interpreted as evidence that Neanderthals were able to anticipate and intercept the reindeer's migration from summer areas in high-altitude mountainous regions down to lower-lying winter areas along the coast. If the interpretation of the material is correct, this means that Neanderthals conducted specialised reindeer hunting that required cooperation among many hunters and the ability to plan ahead, as the yield from such hunts in the form of meat and bone marrow was preserved for use in periods of poorer access to prey.

Neanderthals in Germany followed a similar pattern. The northernmost known Neanderthal settlement, Salzgitter Lebenstedt in northern Germany, is located at the southern end of the European tundra that stretched towards the ice edge. To the south and south-west, the Harz mountain range rises to about 1,000 metres above sea level. From these summer grazing areas, the reindeer had autumn migrations down to the winter areas on the tundra. Detailed studies show that the settlement was mainly a hunting camp used only in the autumn. Most of the approximately 80 reindeer brought to the camp were killed in the month of September.

In a hunting camp so far north, access to combustible material must have been very limited. Although they did not consciously hunt mammoths in this area, they had access to bone material from dead animals. This material was evidently used as fuel in place of wood. Much of the bone material from here is therefore heavily burnt. This is a resource usage we also know from more recent times among people living in landscapes with little access to firewood and combustible material.

Further south in France, the bone material from this cold climate period is more diverse, but, even here, all the way down to the Mediterranean, four out of five animals brought into the camp are reindeer. Detailed examinations of the bone material from the Maras settlement, on the plain north of Avignon, show that the reindeer catch took place in the autumn, likely in connection with the reindeer's annual migrations from areas further north and west near Lyon and the eastern parts of the Massif Central. The excavation at Maras shows that parts of the animals were transported here for butchering. The actual hunting took place in the surrounding areas. Some bones are missing from the excavated material, leading archaeologists to believe that the animals were butchered out in the field. At the settlement, they cut the meat from the thighs and shoulders, and the marks from the stone tools that cut long longitudinal scratches in the bones are still clearly visible. The large marrow bones are almost invariably crushed to extract the nutritious bone marrow. After the hunt and butchering, the meat and likely the hides were transported further. The Neanderthals hunting in these areas evidently had knowledge of the seasonal migrations of the reindeer herds. Therefore, there was organised mass hunting of reindeer limited to a specific season.

Recently, other surprising finds have been made at the settlement. The hunters developed a fibre technology! From the inner bark of a hitherto unknown tree species, the hunters extracted fibres and made 3-ply ropes used to lash stone tools to wood. Researchers assume that once the knowledge and ability to make ropes were in place, it is natural to think that they would have used the same technique to improve their clothing and make bags, and nets for hunting. Additionally, knowing that they used tar extracted from birch bark as glue, engaged in some artistic activities, and made jewellery from shells, it's clear that this is not a species entirely lacking in cognitive abilities, and they were soon to face a new challenge. The Neanderthals in a settlement a short day's march north of Maras will be the first to face it.

PART III

What a tumultuous period in Earth's history it must have been! In Eurasia, three different hunter-gatherer peoples exchange experiences related to hunting various prey, technology and genes. Over the next couple of tens of thousands of years, two of them, along with the first immigrants of our species, will disappear. After a period of climatic chaos, volcanic eruptions, and the invasion of foreign viruses and bacteria, the Neanderthals leave us.

THE SPECTACULAR INTERLUDE

Eurasia 60,000 – 40,000 years ago

Recently, archaeologists working inside the Mandrin cave in the Rhône Valley made a groundbreaking discovery, and, as so many times before, it was the finding of a tooth that set it all in motion. A small unassuming milk tooth emerged among a multitude of worked stone tools strewn across the floor inside the cave. What was special was that the tooth had belonged to a *Homo sapiens* child, and it was found between cultural layers clearly bearing the imprint of Neanderthal activities.

The Mandrin cave was discovered in 1960, and a series of excavations have uncovered more than 60,000 different stone tools made by Neanderthals. The first Neanderthals seem to have moved into the cave, which with its modest depth of 8 metres should rather be called a rock shelter, almost 120,000 years ago. For nearly 70,000 years, Neanderthals had exclusive access to the limestone cliff where they had a good view of the area around the eastern banks of the Rhône River flowing in the valley bottom a hundred metres below them. Now they were apparently no longer alone.

Dating showed that the tooth loss must have occurred between 51,700 and 56,800 years ago, providing clear evidence that the first anatomically modern humans, *Homo sapiens*, had entered Europe much earlier than previously thought. A few months or years earlier, Neanderthals in Bacho Kiro Cave in Bulgaria and Grotta del Cavallo in Italy had the same experience. A new type of hunters had entered the hunting grounds.

If they had known that the new hunter-gatherers 15,000 years later would contribute to their own disappearance from history, perhaps the encounters between the two human species could have had a different outcome.

For what does one do when meeting a new human species for the first time? Probably very little. One stares. Observes that the newcomers have darker skin than themselves, and that their long, slender limbs give them a weak, almost sickly appearance. The Neanderthals would surely have speculated whether the newcomers were starving. They would also see that over the narrow shoulders sat heads that were significantly smaller than their own, lacking the robust eyebrows they themselves had. Their eyes are also much smaller than their own, so they could surely speculate whether these newcomers could hunt effectively under poor lighting conditions.

In the years that followed, the dark and slender newcomers and the Neanderthals shared the use of the Mandrin cave. Never at the same time, though. The number of hunters was few and the areas almost endless, making it easy to keep a distance both in time and space. There are good indications of shared use of campgrounds elsewhere too. Finds from Israel show that Neanderthals and anatomically modern humans on their way through the Middle East to Europe shared both residential areas, technology and genes. For it is the latest genetic research that really gives us new insights into what happened in this spectacular period in Europe's history.

As if the Earth didn't have enough with one human species, there are now three different human types exploiting the same hunting grounds. In the east, the Denisovans have taken on the role of the Neanderthals. Migrating anatomically modern humans finding their way to Asia and Oceania exchange genes with the hardy Denisovans, and 3–6% of their genes continue to live on today among the people of New Guinea and among the Australian indigenous people – the Aborigines.

Also, the people living on the Tibetan Plateau high in the mountains today can thank the Denisovans for most of them having the special EPAS1 gene, which improves oxygen transport in the blood and prevents altitude sickness. We still know little about the Denisovans themselves, and estimates of when they disappeared for good vary. Some suggest that they may have persisted until as recently as 20,000 years ago in Asia. In Europe, it is also, in every way, a turbulent period the actors are now going through, the most unstable and violent climate period in over one million years is approaching. In the aftermath of the climate's ravages and over the next 15,000 years, one human species will die out and an entire culture associated with the first sapiens in Europe (Châtelperronian) will also disappear.

Even though the first anatomically modern hunters enter Europe at a time when the Earth is in an interglacial period, this is an extremely variable period with rapid and brutal shifts between warm and cold climates. By analysing pollen deposited at the bottom of lakes, a series of shifts can be seen from a forest landscape, through savanna to treeless steppe. And the changes are rapid. Treeless steppes are turned into forested landscapes in just

140 years! The ecological upheavals created by these climate shifts must have been directly chaotic for both people and animals. There are no longer genetic traces of the newcomers who had used the Mandrin cave in periods; only their tools and weapons remain – and the tooth.

What became of these newcomers, and why did they disappear? No one knows for sure, but there is speculation that the very rapid climate shifts caused the new hunters to return south-eastward in search of warmer and more stable conditions, or, alternatively, that they failed to compete with the Neanderthals for access to the best settlements and hunting grounds. Another possibility is that there were simply too few of them and that they died out for that reason. The Neanderthals could not have been unaffected by the conditions either. Perhaps the surviving Neanderthals were given hope for better times when they again noticed that new hunters had entered the hunting grounds. For 5,000–6,000 years after the first meeting at the Mandrin cave in the Rhône Valley, the slimmer and taller hunters are back. Is it now their turn to outcompete the Neanderthals?

What happens when experienced reindeer hunters meet beginners?

It was certainly well-deserved that the 70-year-old archaeologist Paul Mellars was knighted by Queen Elizabeth in 2010 for his formidable contribution to 'services to scholarship', but there were probably some of his French and American colleagues who were not on the guest list. Mellars had spent much of his professional life working in the south-western parts of France, focusing on the period in European history when two human species meet and compete for the same resources. His theory was that the anatomically modern humans who had now entered Europe were better and more specialised hunters than those who had inhabited the same areas for more than 200,000 years, and that this specialisation gave them a competitive advantage that ultimately led to the disappearance of the Neanderthals.

He faced strong opposition from many of his colleagues, and at times the discussions were loud and intense. The opponents argued that the Neanderthals were as specialised hunters as the newcomers, and therefore the reasons for the disappearance of the Neanderthals must be sought elsewhere. For us outsiders, it may seem strange that analyses of the same type of archaeological material yield such different conclusions. Yet the available amount of material is substantial. Within a limited area in the south-western parts of France, researchers have had access to the remains of prey left by the two groups of hunters at a large number of sites. When the discussions began, the analyses were based on 125 sites; later, the amount of material increased, and researchers could ultimately compile material from a total of 202 different sites, 161 of which belonged to the Neanderthals.

It is tempting to quote the author Mark Twain when, in his autobiography, he claims that 'figures often beguile me, particularly when I have the arranging of them myself', and later gives credit to the British Prime Minister Benjamin Disraeli for the phrase 'There are three kinds of lies: lies, damned lies, and statistics.' Depending on the type of sites included in one's calculations, the result varies. Excluding material from hunting camps in the open air yields a different result than if these are included. And, equally important, as long as the bone material at the sites reflects environmental conditions, comparisons of sites used during different climatic periods can lead to peculiar conclusions.

In the initial analyses, it was found that out of the 30 sites used by the new hunters, reindeer dominated in 23 of them. The same type of reindeer dominance was found in 'only' 31 out of a total of 95 sites belonging to the Neanderthals. Counts showed that on the new hunters' sites where reindeer dominated, bones of a total of slightly over 11,000 animals were left behind, of which nearly 9,000 were reindeer. Corresponding figures for the Neanderthals' sites were just under 11,000 animals, of which 7,300 were reindeer. Statistically, this is different, but whether it is enough to distinguish specialists from generalists is doubtful. Just as doubtful as saying that the new hunters are specialised reindeer hunters would be to claim that the Neanderthals are specialised aurochs/bison hunters (archaeologists cannot distinguish these based solely on bone material), even though these prey animals completely dominate on a dozen sites.

What is common to the sites is that there are four prey species that dominate: reindeer, deer, goats, and aurochs or bison. Based on the species composition at the sites, it is not possible to distinguish between the two groups of hunters. They have both been formidable hunters with a varied meat diet. The disappearance of the Neanderthals can hardly be linked to their inferiority in hunting the animal which, as the last ice age approaches its maximum, will completely dominate the diet of those who survive in the central parts of Europe.

Why do Neanderthals disappear?

In Grotte de Renne – the reindeer cave – far north in the Rhône Valley, preparations for a feast were apparently underway. In cultural layers clearly indicative of Neanderthal activity, decorative items are now appearing. These have never been found with Neanderthals. In scholarly circles, discussions naturally revolve around whether the material is accurately dated and whether the cultural layers may have been disturbed in any way before excavation. But the fact that Neanderthals had so much contact with the newcomers that they also adopted and copied some traits from them is highly probable. Based on age determinations of bone material from the two hunter-gatherer groups and their remains at the sites, it is now assumed that Neanderthals and anatomically modern humans overlapped in parts of Europe for a period of between 3,000 and 5,000 years.

In the reindeer cave, both teeth and small worked bone fragments pierced through, evidently intended for use as ornaments, have been found. One can speculate whether it was Neanderthal men who were the craftsmen, intending to offer gifts to the sapiens women, or if it was Neanderthal women who wanted to adorn themselves before meeting the slender and straight newcomers. There is no doubt that interaction between the two hunter-gatherer groups was extensive. Several geneticists now believe that there was a continuous assimilation of Neanderthals into sapiens hunter groups, and that this may be one of the reasons why Neanderthals eventually disappeared. Genetic studies now show that as much as half of the individuals examined from this period are hybrids between the different human species. The renowned Swedish geneticist Svante Pääbo therefore believes that the people who lived at this time hardly distinguished between 'us' and 'them' when it came to sexual relations. Due to their modest size, Neanderthal hunter groups were initially very vulnerable, and the migration of productive men and women to hunter groups belonging to the new hunters could be fatal for the survival of the group.

The assimilation of Neanderthal women into the hunter groups of the new hunters does not seem to have led to an increase in population. Although Neanderthals and modern humans had sexual relations with each other, unfortunately, sexual intercourse between Neanderthal women and sapiens men was not reproductively successful. When a woman gives birth, the genetic material she carries in her mitochondria – the cell's energy powerhouse – is transferred nearly unchanged to the child's cells. The fact that geneticists have not found traces of mitochondrial DNA from Neanderthals in modern humans suggests that only hybrids were produced, which were themselves not fertile. Neanderthal men's relations with sapiens women, however, have yielded interesting results and may explain why archaeologists working on sites of our own species have often unearthed human bones with distinct Neanderthal features, and surely in frustration asked higher powers for help in clarifying the discrepancy. Whether they were heard is doubted, but geneticists have come to their rescue, including through genetic analyses of a skeleton from Romania.

His real name was Oase1, but he is now known by the more colloquial name of Jon from Anina. He was found inside the cave complex Peştera cu Oase near the town of Anina, south-west in Romania, in 2002. Alongside two other hunters, surrounded by skeletons of deceased cave bears, he had passed away approximately 42,000 years ago. Undoubtedly, he was a sapiens, but he had many morphological traits from Neanderthals. Although the preservation conditions inside the karst cave were not the best, geneticists have recovered enough of his genetic material to ascertain that he had between 6 and 9% of Neanderthal genes. In fact, half of his 12th chromosome was characterised by Neanderthal genes. This provides geneticists with evidence that there had been sexual intercourse between a sapiens woman and a Neanderthal man a few generations back, and they go so far as to suggest that Jon from Anina's great-great-grandmother may have encountered a Neanderthal man whom she found particularly attractive.

In retrospect, it has been speculated whether both the death of Jon from Anina and the disappearance of the Neanderthals can be linked to a massive volcanic eruption just west of present-day Naples. It is estimated that 200 km³ of magma spewed out, leaving tephra – volcanic deposits – over large parts of south-eastern Europe. In addition, the volcano emitted between 50 and 250 million tons of sulfur dioxide, which in the stratosphere reduced solar radiation. The climate deteriorated significantly, and it is assumed that the temperature of the surface water in the Mediterranean dropped by as much as 5°C. Dating the time of the volcanic eruption now shows that it occurred about 40,000 years ago. Jon from Anina's cause of death cannot therefore be attributed to the volcanic eruption.

There is greater uncertainty about its effect on the already hard-pressed Neanderthals. Previous assumptions that Neanderthals persisted until about 30,000 years ago have proven to be incorrect. New dating techniques have shown that the youngest fossil material of Neanderthals is now between

44,000 and 40,000 years old. This coincides with both the time of the volcanic eruption and the disappearance of traces of Neanderthal habitation in the south-western parts of France. It is reasonable to assume that Neanderthals persisted longer in some areas than in others, but it can be concluded that Jon from Anina's great-great-grandmother did not have a wide selection of Neanderthal men to choose from. For Neanderthal groups were both few and small, and they rarely visited each other; even rarer were visits to the new hunters' sites. Perhaps the social structure of the Neanderthals also played a role in their disappearance. Detailed examinations of genetic material have provided glimpses into how these people lived and how they were organised.

Farthest east in their distribution range, at the Altai Mountains on the border with the Denisovan people's territories, genetic investigations show that Neanderthal groups were small, probably no more than 20 individuals. This is not particularly surprising, since such group sizes are typical for hunter-gatherer societies even today. Resource availability and the need for fairly large hunting areas usually set an upper limit on how many people can live together. It is more surprising to find that they were significantly inbred. For example, one of the individuals had a father who was also their grandfather. The analyses also showed that new people entered these groups only about every tenth generation. The overwhelming norm was therefore that the vast majority found a partner within their own small group, and, when new people did come in, the results showed that women were more likely than men to move, or be moved, between groups.

And it's not only in the far east that Neanderthals stuck to their own. After the first *Homo sapiens* left Mandrin Cave and the Rhône Valley, Neanderthals moved back in. One of these was the boy archaeologists have named Thorin, and, once again, tooth analyses yield surprising results. It turns out that Thorin is part of a small clan that has actually not left the Rhône Valley for more than 50,000 years! It's no wonder that some archaeologists have previously suggested that the Neanderthals in the Rhône Valley seemed to have their own tool culture. External impulses were completely absent, and they show no kinship with Neanderthals in neighbouring areas. Surprisingly, Nana, the nickname for the Neanderthal woman found in Gibraltar, is the one Thorin is most related to.

So far, no one has managed to point to a single cause for the disappearance from the face of the Earth of the only human species developed in Europe. The highly variable climate would have affected both hunter-gatherer groups, but while Neanderthals showed little innovation, there was in the period immediately after the eruption in Italy, almost a technological revolution among the new hunter-gatherers. They evolved into formidable competitors who likely adapted to a hostile Europe. Sapiens groups were no larger than Neanderthals', but they visited each other! The larger networks are reflected in the transportation of stone materials in tools over greater distances, as well as shells and molluscs used in amulets and jewellery. Larger and denser networks also provided greater opportunities for the exchange of ideas and faster dissemination of knowledge between groups, which undoubtedly was an advantage when the climate and environment changed rapidly. Greater contact and exchange of hunters between the different groups also led to a very low degree of inbreeding. Transfers of diseases may also be involved in the disappearance of Neanderthals. While sapiens have 'preserved' genes from Neanderthals that provide immunity to many infectious diseases, it is highly likely that Neanderthals were not well-prepared for the disease-causing viruses and bacteria that sapiens brought with them from Africa.

FIG 3. Neanderthals were the true Europeans and are the only human species to have evolved in Europe. During periods of favourable climate, they spread across much of the continent (shaded area on the map). The first anatomically modern humans entered Europe about 50,000 years ago, sharing the continent with Neanderthals for a period of 5,000–10,000 years.

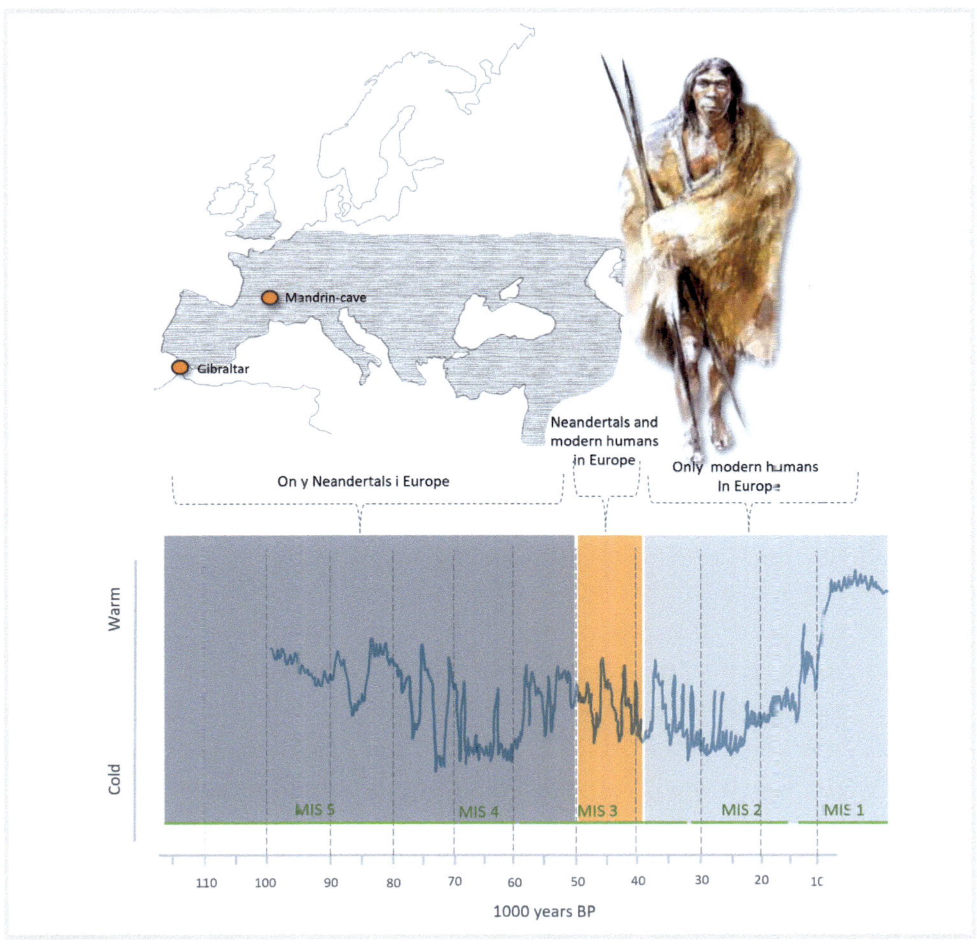

NEANDERTHALS DIE –
LONG LIVE THE NEANDERTHAL!

The new genetic studies show that the number of Neanderthal genes in *Homo sapiens* decreases over time, from containing up to 11% Neanderthal genes in individuals 45,000 years old to only 2% in individuals 7,000 years old. This means that we have 'gotten rid of' genes that were not advantageous for us, but at the same time retained beneficial genes, such as those associated with immunity to certain diseases. Apart from those living south of the Sahara, all humans today still retain about 2% of the genes inherited from Neanderthals and Denisovans. The Swedish Nobel laureate Svante Pääbo even claims that Neanderthals largely define who we modern humans really are, and he is of course right. Now, 2% may sound modest, but, as we've seen so often before, the information lies in the details. Your genetic material consists of DNA and is composed of two strands of nucleic acids containing genetic information. Some comes from your father and some from your mother. But your genetic material is not exactly like what came from your mother and father. There is a recombination of genetic material during reproduction, creating a unique combination of genes for each new individual. This means that siblings, unlike identical twins, do not have identical genes. This is also the explanation for why different parts of the total Neanderthal genetic material have been passed on. We all have some Neanderthal DNA, but not necessarily the same! Estimates from geneticists suggest that together, as much as 40 to 50% of Neanderthal genetic material may be preserved in present-day humans.

Whether Neanderthals themselves chose to spend their last years in what is called Gorham's Cave complex in Gibraltar, or whether it was the only place free from the new hunters who had taken over their hunting grounds, is not known. Regardless, they could not complain about the view. The caves in the steep limestone cliffs on the east side of the Gibraltar rock cover an area of 280 acres and rise more than 400 metres above the Mediterranean Sea. For more than 125,000 years, they have resided here.

An engaged reporter from The New York Times described that 'from the 40 m high cathedral-like opening, the cave narrows asymmetrically inward like a crumpled wizard's hat'. Far inside the 'wizard's hat', an international group of archaeologists recently found a work of art made by one of the last Neanderthals. More than 40,000 years ago, an artist showed that Neanderthals were capable of abstract thinking. The artwork 'The Hashtag' is a network of eight intersecting lines carved into stone. To create such a pattern, researchers have calculated that it would take 317 clearly deliberate strikes with a suitable tool.

We may never know the purpose of the stone carving, but it shows that Neanderthals were far more advanced than they were initially thought to be. Regardless, in the climatic Ragnarök, building up towards the last glacial maximum, the very last of their kind disappear. The same happens to the Denisovan people who reside further east. The ravages of the climate seem to have been too much for the hunters of our own species as well. Clan after clan vanished, and only the remains of past hunts, tools, and the fossilised remains of these people's bones testify that they once lived here. After several hundred thousand years, the *Homo* genus that had resided in Europe is now in ruin and decay.

But amidst the climatic Ragnarok of this period, new cultures emerge – they are artists par excellence. But they too shall face great challenges. The salvation shall come from the east, where a people there will achieve the incredible; not only do they survive the Ragnarök, but they will spread westward and lay the foundation for cultures that will dominate Europe for the next 20,000 years. One of their great innovations was the sewing needle.

PART IV

Europe 40,000 – 11,700 years ago.
They ruled the hunting grounds alone now. The true
Europeans – the Neanderthals – were gone. Small groups of
anatomically modern hunters, eventually called Cro-Magnon,
had adapted to a challenging European climate. They crafted
ivory statues and painted on cave walls. The earth was now
approaching its most recent ice age maximum, and while
reindeer had previously been crucial for human survival, they
now became the very lifeline they had to cling to.

REINDEER HUNTER
FOUND IN A RABBIT HOLE

Aurignac, France Year 1858

Had they known what they had found on that autumn day in 1858, this could have been the headline in the local newspaper in the small village of Aurignac, at the foot of the Pyrenees. It would have been an entry into history that would not have been worthy of this hunter-gatherer people.

During the construction of a new road into the small town, road workers found some bone fragments in a rabbit hole. After further excavations, a cave was revealed. Here, skeletal remains of a total of 17 people were found. When some claim that these are remains of very old people – our ancestors – 'all hell breaks loose'. 'Déloyal tricherie' – 'dishonest cheating' – declared the local magistrate, and ordered all the bones to be buried in the local cemetery. Excavations in the cave itself two years later uncovered flint and bone tools, along with bone remains of long-extinct animals, which the archaeologist and geologist Édouard Lartet believed must stem from the 'most remote antiquity'. It would be another 50 years before archaeologists would define this culture, and name it after the first discovery site – Aurignac – despite the fact that the first traces of this people were later found further east. This was to become a tradition: cultures emerge in the east, but the naming is taken care of by French archaeologists. The same happens when the ice age hunter is to be given a name.

The naming itself takes place in Les Eyzies, the village also referred to as the world's prehistoric capital. Here, the houses line up along the polished white limestone cliffs that surround the Vézère River. This was where young Louis Lartet came in 1868. He had followed in his father's career path and was already admitted to the prestigious Société géologique de France at the age of 23. After a stint in Palestine, where he mapped the geology around the Dead Sea, he returned to France, where he would soon receive a very interesting assignment.

During the construction of the railway through Les Eyzies, some workers found a considerable amount of animal bones, flint tools and skulls of indeterminate age. Louis, who had already established himself as a skilled paleontologist, was immediately summoned. Under the overhanging cliff, Louis quickly unearthed skeletal parts belonging to four adults and one child. In addition, he found perforated shells and teeth for use in necklaces, an object made of ivory, and a worked reindeer antler. These had never before been found together with fossil remains of Neanderthals. A relevant question therefore arose: were these people something different?

Dating of the bone material showed that these people had lived in the Dordogne area almost 30,000 years ago, but both the high forehead, absence of pronounced brow ridges, and their slender bone structure clearly indicated that these were not Neanderthals, but indeed represented findings of the modern hunter. That we would get the name Cro-Magnon is a coincidence. Like many of his compatriots born in the southern parts of France, Louis spoke Occitan, the language that Louis XIV tried to ban in the 17th century. Cro means hole in Occitan, and Magnon was the name of the man who owned the property where the discovery was made. The name would stick with us, and to this day Cro-Magnon is used as a collective term for 'early modern humans' throughout Europe.

Cro-Magnon and the world of reindeer
Europe, south of the glaciers

There are three factors that particularly define the period that began around 40,000 years ago and lasted until the end of the last ice age about 11,000 years ago: humanity's tremendous dependence on reindeer as a resource, dramatic and often very rapid climate changes, and, during the most extreme climate conditions, the emergence of an almost incomprehensible artistic activity that continues to impress the world. What were the living conditions like at that time, and what paved the way for such development?

The steppe tundra, often called the mammoth steppe, which stretched from Beringia all the way down to the Mediterranean, bringing reindeer into the European continent, was, of course, not a uniform continuous environment. The local climate, the topography of the areas, and especially the distribution of loess influenced both which animals the hunters had access to and where the hunters could establish settlements. In cold, low precipitation periods, dry soil influenced by the wind, consisting of organic material, quartz, limestone and other minerals, was carried by the wind and accumulated in large quantities. This is loess. While today's grain chambers in Ukraine and Russia are characterised by thick layers of loess that have provided good growing conditions for plants, only the areas north of Paris and southward to the Massif Central in the west have similar conditions.

Parts of the Arctic mammoth steppe therefore consisted of a mosaic landscape with grasslands, shrubs and small clusters of trees. The amount of lichen, the reindeer's winter forage, was modest in large parts of the area. East of the Alps, all the way down to the Crimean Peninsula, there was a landscape where small hunting groups hunted mammoths, horses, bison, and saiga antelopes as often as reindeer. In the south-western parts of Europe, the amount of loess was modest, and there were many and large lichen mats. This is where most of the hunters resided during this time.

This period in many ways defines the Europe we have today. A new hunter – *Homo sapiens* – would establish itself on a continent that was now going through a new ice age, the most recent so far. The climate was once again testing humans, but they showed a formidable adaptability. Not only did they develop new weapons and toolsand more heat-insulating clothing, but they also changed themselves. Those who were now facing the last ice age maximum were therefore physiologically and aesthetically different from those who first found their way out of Africa. But they were few, and in the climatically toughest periods, all exchange of knowledge, technology and genes, between small groups of hunter-gatherers seeking refuge in delimited ice age refuges, ceased. Subsequent periods of disappearance and re-establishment of various hunter-gatherer cultures largely explain the genetic composition of today's European population. The hunter-gatherers who survived in the south-western parts of Europe would not meet their relatives east of the Alps until they stood together in northern Europe preparing for immigration to a Scandinavian peninsula that was about to shed its burden of three-kilometer-thick ice sheets. But before that happened, much would occur. At least four different hunter-gatherer cultures would develop, but they were all Cro-Magnon – ice age hunters, only distinguished by their different ways of making their tools and weapons. The first we meet are the people who were first found in the rabbit hole in Aurignac.

One can wonder what prompted the Aurignac people to migrate westward in Europe; it could not have been the climate. The beginning of their stay in Europe was tough. Analysis of ice cores from Greenland reveals that they had to endure two especially cold and dry periods, the first lasting 1000 years, the second 600 years. Formerly forested areas were now gradually transformed into species-poor and unproductive steppe areas. The hunting groups became fewer and smaller, and in western parts of Europe the hunting of bison and aurochs was almost exclusively replaced by the hunting of reindeer. The hunters accustomed to hunting in forested areas had to change their strategy to survive. Some succeeded. Surveys of 30 settlements show that reindeer were the dominant prey on most of them; 8 out of 10 bones unearthed by archaeologists are from reindeer.

Adapting to an environment where changes occur gradually over a long time is one thing. Dealing with the violent and rapid climate changes that would follow posed significant challenges for people, animals and plants. In some cases, the changes in the environment were so dramatic that adaptations to the harsh climate were not possible. The hunters who moved northward during warm periods and hunted both in Germany and Belgium experienced the forested areas being transformed into steppes with permafrost within just a few decades. It is clear that not everyone managed to return to the areas south of the permafrost. For in the south-western parts of France and in the Spanish areas around the Bay of Biscay, south of the permafrost, not everything was fine either. The population decreased drastically. It is estimated that at times there were only a few thousand hunters residing in caves and rock shelters in this area. For a long time it was believed that the Aurignac people, the reindeer hunters who entered Europe with flint spearheads as sharp as razor blades, Venus figurines, and ornaments made of bone, antler and ivory, suffered the same fate as the Châtelperronian people and disappeared from history. But that was before an anthropology professor made a spectacular find in a cave in the Rio Asón valley in Cantabria, Spain.

From when the highly esteemed professor, now emeritus, Lawrence Straus started his excavations in the cave of El Miró in 1996 until he made his spectacular discovery, would take 14 years. By then, archaeologists had already demonstrated that Cro-Magnon hunters had lived in the cave for 40,000 years, periodically, but without finding fossils from these people. In 2010, the archaeologists decided to excavate the difficult-to-reach area behind a collapsed limestone block. There they found what they had been looking for, for many years – a skeleton. It was evident that the deceased had been buried by her contemporaries, not only from the way she was laid to rest but also from the fact that the bone remains were covered with a red layer of ochre, the iron-based pigment often used by the artists of the time in their cave paintings, which earned her the nickname the Red Lady.

The woman had been between 35 and 40 years old when she died about 18,700 years ago. Further examinations showed that both the limestone block and the deceased had been covered with ochre. After a while, predators got to the dead and removed both the skull and the tibia, while the jaw and the other bones remained intact. These had then apparently been sprinkled with ochre again. What caused such a special and very rare burial, we will probably never know, but the Red Lady had more surprises in store.

First, examinations of the Red Lady's teeth revealed that she had eaten mushrooms just before her death. Remnants of both cap mushrooms and porcini mushrooms were found. However, it is doubtful whether she had mistaken the cap mushrooms for champignons and red mushrooms, and whether that had caused her death.

The real surprise came when geneticist Svante Pääbo and his team analysed the genetic material of the Red Lady and 50 other Cro-Magnon skeletons from all over Europe, ranging from 45,000 to 7,000 years old. The studies showed that the first Cro-Magnon to come to Europe, the Châtelperronian people, had not left any genetic traces in the population. This confirmed that the people who had left the decisive tooth in the Mandrin Cave in the Rhône Valley had not mastered the demanding conditions. It was long believed that the Aurignac people had suffered the same fate, but the Red Lady showed that this was not the case. Her genetic material showed that she was a descendant of a 35,000-year-old Aurignac man found in Belgium. The genetic material of this people is still present in today's population, so some of us can safely say that we have an ancestor from Spain – El Mirón's Red Lady.

But it really almost went wrong with the Aurignac people. As the climate worsened in the period between 29,000 and 25,000 years BCE, traces of this hunter-gatherer people disappeared in England, Germany and Belgium, and only a few survived in the areas south of the permafrost, spreading their genes further to the Red Lady of El Mirón and her people. In other areas, caves and rock shelters slowly filled up with dust and sand. Tools and objects carved in ivory were covered and disappeared. Caves with paintings of lions and reindeer were forgotten, and these people's lives and victories were in danger of suffering the same fate as the Neanderthals and the Châtelperronian people. And while the Aurignac people clung to life in the south-western parts of Europe, a people further east appeared who had adapted to life on the tundra. These people now came westward, spreading optimism, hunting skills, and genes into a frigid population. The harsh climatic conditions on the mammoth steppes had forced new innovations, and these would eventually be used further west in Europe.

RULERS OF THE
MAMMOTH STEPPE

north-west of the Black Sea 30,000 years ago

We can easily imagine a golden eagle soaring high in the sky. To the two below, it appeared merely as a small black cross against the vast blue vault enveloping a rolling landscape that faded into unknown horizons. It was almost evening, and the slanting warm light enhanced the yellow, brown and gray hues adorning the world of land animals. From the eagle's perspective, the landscape appeared faint with barely discernible topography. A small stream carved through the land, gentle elevations now casting shadows on the eastern side, a few willow thickets along the creek banks, but no trees; it was a treeless undulating landscape. For hours, the eagle had been tracking two elongated dots moving steadily forward in a near straight line. These dots were two people, scouts on a vital mission.

The people crossed a stream and started ascending a long, gentle slope. They paused briefly at the stream, drank water, nibbled on dried meat and fat mixed with berries, then hurried onward. Everything about them exuded purposeful movement – not hurried, but controlled and deliberate. They neither walked nor ran but glided through the landscape as swiftly as possible without overheating or expending unnecessary energy. They were clothed in leather – light leather garments meticulously sewn from carefully selected reindeer calf hides – scraped clean, treated with the brains of the animals they once belonged to, rendering them soft. Later, they were smoked over fire to become durable and waterproof. These were simple clothes, but the cut, the even and tight seams, and a couple of small amulets indicate meticulous craftsmanship. The seams in their clothes primarily revealed their identity.

Never before had people in Europe had such waterproof and windproof garments. They were warm as well, a clear necessity for surviving on the steppe tundra. They were stitched with thread made from reindeer sinews – dried and later pounded so that individual sinew fibres loosened. When moistened, these made for fantastic sewing thread, still used by indigenous peoples in the northern regions – a thread that withstands great stress and swells when wet, ensuring that the clothes were wind and waterproof. The delicate needles, made from reindeer leg bones, split and carved into thin needles, became one of their most important tools. It enabled them to make clothes that functioned well enough in a landscape where cold and strong winds impose absolute limits on those who dare to live out there. The shoes were also made of reindeer hide, from the shanks of bucks, tightly stitched and nearly waterproof. As for equipment, they had little – some long arrows with flight feathers from golden eagles and tips made of reindeer leg bones fastened with soft sinew thread.

Additionally, they had an *atlatl* (a throwing stick), crafted from reindeer antlers, a tool that enabled them to throw their arrows more than twice as far and more accurately than the spears used previously. They carried a hunting bag slung over their backs containing dried meat and fat mixed with berries, a flint knife, a small flint awl, some leather, sinew thread, a couple of needles, and equipment for making fire. That was all they need, along with their own skills and endurance.

They had been on a search for eight days, and that morning they found what they had been searching and longing for. The reindeer herds were on the move; they had arrived late that year, and they came much farther north than usual. The two, a man and a woman were the clan's scouts, specially chosen for this task; their duty was to travel far and sustain themselves for extended periods. In addition to spotting the herds from afar, they must also possess the perseverance required to find them over time. Moreover, perhaps most importantly, they needed to be able to navigate in this formless landscape, foreseeing how the herds would move, which demanded a formidable capacity for abstraction. Last but not least, they needed the physical capability and range to return to the camp in time and direct the hunters so that they would be in the right place when the reindeer arrived.

They both knew that the people in the camp had been waiting anxiously. It was already late in the year, and they hadn't hunted reindeer yet. The meat caches buried in the permafrost beneath the camp's huts were nearly empty. The summer clothes the people had worn since spring were starting to wear out, and the winter clothes needed to be replaced with new ones. This was the big autumn hunt they had been waiting for. This was the time when the hides were most suitable for clothing, sleeping skins, tent canvases, bags, and all the other things this leather-clad people needed hides for.

They needed food, a lot of food; there were 120 people in the camp, big and small, an unheard of number of people considering this was a hunting and gathering society that usually consisted of no more than 20 people, but the resources out on the steppe tundra, the vast herds of animals from which large harvests could be taken, allowed for such large societies. That is, if they could exploit these resources. Like all others embarking on a long journey, the two also had plenty of time to think. We can imagine that the first thing on their minds was the upcoming hunt, where the reindeer would roam over the next couple of days before the hunters arrived. One thing was to 'see' where this would be; another was to convey this information to the others. They had long since created a mental map in their heads, with landmarks in the landscape that could be communicated to others who had barely been there before.

Unbeknownst to them, they were some of the world's first cartographers, creators of maps that were drawn in sand or with charcoal on a piece of skin, ensuring their people would thrive through the next half-year, the time it would take before the herds returned, but then on a migration in the opposite direction.

Then there was the thought of the others in the camp. For days, they had been scanning the horizon, waiting and preparing. They had inspected and prepared the weapons. They had cleaned the meat caches, and had perhaps made a new one in case the hunt proved to be particularly abundant. Then they had checked knives, leather pouches, straps, dog harnesses, and ropes – everything they needed for an effective hunt. Tents were packed, and food prepared for those who would accompany the hunters onto the plains to take care of hides, meat, sinews and antlers. Not a part of the animals would go to waste. The two think the same, smiling at each other with the certainty that they had succeeded in the task of being the tribe's most crucial scouts.

Soon, they were on top of the ridge, and from there they could see what the eagle saw: a cluster of round houses, constructed with mammoth tusks and hides, partly dug into the ground. Together, it was a society that had progressed further than any other hunter-gatherer people in Europe. It wasn't a single thing or invention that set them apart. It was a combination of the technology they had developed, the collaboration of many, and the opportunities for specialisation that had allowed the Gravettians to conquer the steppe tundra, the vast land with its abundant resources. Those who managed to adapt to this harsh, featureless and demanding landscape faced challenging conditions, but the rewards were great.

The bustling activity down in the camp began. First, a group of about twenty people set off at a brisk pace, armed with a map and a goal. Later, there was a long line of people, young and old, with dogs carrying packs. From the eagle's perspective, they looked like a line of dots in a landscape without horizons. These people fetched meat, hides and bones to become new weapons and needles – perhaps the most important tool this people had in the battle against the elements. They may not have known it themselves, but they had solved the puzzle and had refined the knowledge inherited from their ancestors.

They had developed increasingly lethal weapons. They could throw spears farther and more accurately than their forebears, thanks to the *atlatl*; these spearheads were more effective, causing larger and quicker bleedings in the prey; the dogs they brought with them had proven able to locate game from a distance, affording them opportunities for good preparations; and the needle had allowed them to make the warm, waterproof and windproof clothes they were utterly dependent on. But perhaps most importantly, they had refined the characteristic that defines modern humans – *Homo sapiens* – being able to trust and cooperate with people we are not related to.

Craftsmen and flint makers could make tools and weapons for everyone in the group; childcare could be entrusted to someone other than grandparents; the fires they tended provide warmth for the group, and the best hunters distributed the meat to everyone in the group.

Now, some of these people were heading westward in Europe, where they would soon encounter a resilient hunter-gatherer people. They would not meet the descendants of those who remained in the east until they meet on the coast of Finnmark in northern Norway after the ice age they were in was over. And they had no way of foreseeing that the encounters in Northern Norway would result in their genetic material still being present in nearly half of Norway's population.

The innovators from the east save the hunter people in the west

Those coming to the rescue of a frostbitten hunter people in the west are the Gravettian people. Named by French archaeologists after finds at the La Gravette settlement in Dordogne, but it is in the east where they developed their skills. Early on, archaeologists noted significant differences in where the hunter-gatherer peoples from the east and west of Europe chose to establish their settlements. In the west, all settlements were located outside areas with continuous permafrost. At that time, the tree line ran straight through the Franco-Cantabrian region, and it was south of this line where the majority of the Southern European population resided.

In contrast, in the east, most settlements were located north of the tree line and north of the boundary with continuous permafrost. These were the settlements of the true big game hunters of the last ice age. Here they developed the innovative capacity that characterises the people who would dominate Europe up to the last ice age maximum. They entered a Europe where the ice masses were at their maximum and the living conditions were the toughest in European history.

This hunter-gatherer people reached their peak during the period 35,000 to 24,000 years ago, emerging as the great innovators of the ice age. In addition to the use of the sewing needle, contributing to warmer clothing made from multiple layers of skin, we see for the first time the use of animal pits and traps. Bows and arrows were also believed to have been used during this period. Several studies suggest that this people were able to produce simple woven products and baskets for storing various food items. Findings from the Czech Republic show imprints in clay of 4 mm thick ropes, indicating that nets were used as a hunting technique by this people. These were probably used to catch small game and likely contributed to a more stable food supply.

These people are most famous for their spectacular settlements in eastern parts of Europe, where mammoth tusks (probably also ribs) were used as frameworks for skin-covered tents. In addition to the creative use of mammoth bones, findings at settlements indicate that wolves, red foxes and arctic foxes were utilised in various ways: canine and incisor teeth for decorations, bones from the forefeet used to make fish hooks and small harpoons, and, from wolves, both leg bones in the hind feet as well as the thigh bone have been used in making various types of tools. Common to both tools and weapons made by this hunter-gatherer people is that they are very elaborate and delicately crafted. As we say today, those with the most experience with knives have the smallest knives, and the Gravettian people followed the same tradition. Both the design of weapons and tools differs from those used by the people in the west, and bison, horses, mammoths – and of course reindeer, were all killed by smaller but more effective arrowheads. In addition, they may have streamlined hunting through the use of dogs, as many attribute the Gravettian people with taming the wolf. This probably occurred in several areas, but it is very likely that those now entering the reindeer lands in the west were accompanied by dogs.

Life on the tundra in the east must have required very mobile hunters. Resource availability in such areas is low, and hunter-gatherer groups must have utilised large areas to obtain enough food. High mobility would, of course, also reduce the chance of inbreeding, but at the same time, such small hunter communities would be highly susceptible to both social and climatic 'disturbances'. And there is much evidence that many of these small hunter-gatherer communities that chose to stay disappeared during the last ice age maximum. However, some must have survived, for in south-eastern Moldova and parts of Romania, there is evidence of activity throughout this period. But just before the last ice age maximum, it seems there was 1000 km of uninhabited land between hunters west and east of the Alps. Archaeologists have found almost no traces of settlements in this area from this time, and it was therefore long believed that this prevented any exchange of hunters, and thus ideas and culture, between east and west. But now much suggests that the 'mammoth people' in the east managed to transfer weapon technology from east to west even during this period. This period is probably the most critical for the further development of the European population. Those who have estimated the lowest viable population of humans, estimate it to be around 1,500 people, half of whom must be of reproductive age. Based on the number of archaeological finds and expected group size, it is assumed that we were not much more in Europe. It is therefore no exaggeration to say that during this period Europe's hunters were on the brink of extinction.

Surprisingly, the next period from 24,000 to 20,000 years ago, a period many experts call the last ice age maximum, had a milder climate than the previous one. The climatic conditions were still tough, and the vast majority of hunters were within delimited areas, so-called refuge areas. The most important was the Franco-Cantabrian area in the south-western parts of France and northern parts of Spain. The total population seems to have increased somewhat, and of a total European population of between 1,400 and 6,300 hunters, between 1,000 and 4,000 hunters are within this area. In small ice age refuges in southern Spain and the lower parts of the Rhone Valley down to the Mediterranean, several hundred hunters had shelter, and a somewhat similar number had residence in Portugal and the upper parts of the Seine Valley.

In eastern parts of Europe, there were fewer than a hundred hunters in each region, which means that each hunter had exclusive access to about 1,000 km². A small group of hunters also attempted to survive in the area between the Adriatic Sea and the Alps in Italy. Access to big game was obviously limited. While excavations of settlements in France and Spain testify to reindeer meat being on the menu daily, similar surveys in Italy show that hunters had to make do with rodents! A typical settlement from this period is Grotto del Clurantin. Here, archaeologists found that out of over 500 bone remains that could be identified, 90% belonged to Alpine marmots. How long one can survive on marmots is uncertain, but two bones from moose, three from deer, and two from wild boar testify that these hunters could also gather around a good roast occasionally.

The innovative Gravettian culture was eventually replaced by two new types of toolmakers. This cows not necessarily mean that the Gravettian people disappear, but innovative hunters found new ways to make weapons and tools, allowing creative archaeologists to rename them. The ones who succeeded the Gravettian people were the Solutrean people. Strangely enough, they are named after the town located near a spectacular rock formation in eastern Burgundy between Lyon and Paris. At Roche de Solutré, as the French call it, thin laurel leaf-shaped arrowheads and spearheads made of flint, characteristic of this people, were found. The approximately 500-meter-high limestone formation that gave the culture its name is now most famous for being the mountain former President François Mitterand used to 'climb' annually but also for the occurrence of 'horse magma'!

Archaeological surveys show that the mountain and the surrounding areas have been used in hunting horses. The so-called 'horse magma' that has accumulated over a period of 20,000 years is up to two metres thick in some places and is formed of fine sediments and horse bone remains transported by the wind. Hunting for horses in this area must have been extensive. It is estimated that to form a cubic meter of magma, about 11 horses are needed, and it is believed that between 30,000 and 100,000 horses were killed in this area by ice age hunters.

The horse-hunting Solutrean people were replaced by those who, after the last ice age maximum, were truly to dominate Europe – the Magdalenian people. From their settlements in the south-western parts of France and northern parts of Spain, we can trace their tracks northward up to present-day Poland. This people were, of course, also named after a settlement in France, specifically La Madeleine, a settlement under a 60-meter-long overhanging rock formation near the village of Tursac, just a few kilometres from Les Eyzies. Here, our old acquaintances Édouard Lartet and the Englishman Henry Christy began their excavations in the mid-1860s. Their findings of reindeer bones were so extensive that when they presented their findings in 1875, they gave the publication the name 'L'âge du renne' – The Age of the Reindeer. A representative of this entirely reindeer-dependent people would make headlines on the other side of the Atlantic.

The Magdalenian woman

In a cave on landowner Jacques Grimaud's property on the north side of the Beune River in Dordogne, the remains of one of France's last reindeer hunters were found in 1911. The remains, quickly determined to belong to a woman or girl, would, after creative marketing, trigger a migration to the Field Museum in Chicago 16 years later. However, over the subsequent century, she would become most famous for her missing wisdom teeth, and her designation would change from Magdalenian Girl to Magdalenian Woman.

Excavations of the Le Cap Blanc rock shelter had already begun in 1910. Eager and strong excavators used rough tools, and early in 1911 one of the excavators struck the ground hard with a pickaxe, uncovering parts of a buried human. The pickaxe had perforated the skull of the buried individual, which would create extra challenges for those who, a hundred years later, would model how the deceased actually looked.

Archaeology experts from Paris were called in, and in a more professional manner the entire find was removed as a block consisting of soil and bones, and transported to Paris. Blasé French archaeologists conducted what they believed were the necessary analyses, and the skeleton was then somewhat surprisingly returned to landowner Grimaud in 1915.

Grimaud's further plan was to sell the remains for a handsome sum in the USA. As it was not legal to export such material out of the country, this was deftly circumvented by classifying the package as remains of an American soldier! The package was addressed to the American Museum of Natural History in New York, but they were far from willing to meet Grimaud's asking price of USD 12,000, which today would be equivalent to 230 000 GB pounds.

For ten years, the package lay stored in New York. Then Henry Field entered the stage. He was a curator and cousin of the owner of The Field Museum in Chicago. Assuming that the French landowner Grimaud was now desperate to get some money back for the remains, Field managed to negotiate the price down to USD 1,000. The skeleton was immediately transported to Chicago.

From the French archaeologists, Henry Field had received assurances that the skeleton could be up to 20,000 years old and that it had once belonged to a teenage girl. This must have meant that he now owned the oldest skeleton in America. He gave the skeleton the designation 'The Magdalenian Girl', named after the archaeological epoch in Europe between 12,000 to 20,000 years ago. The Magdalenian period is called L'âge du Renne – The Reindeer Age by French archaeologists. In addition to being skilled reindeer hunters, the Magdalenian people also produced the finest examples of cave art and hunting tools made of mammoth ivory. And Cap Blanc is known for its fantastically beautiful rock engravings of a multitude of horses, bison and reindeer, in addition to finely crafted hunting tools.

When Field learned that the remains were found only 60 cm below the hooves of the largest engraved horse in Cap Blanc, and that an engraved heart was also found nearby, he had the sales pitch for his upcoming exhibition ready; in a clever mix of jealousy and romance, Field speculated whether the 20,000-year-old Magdalenian girl was the daughter of the artist behind the fantastic cave art, and that the ivory harpoon which Field had conveniently placed next to the skeleton in the exhibition was the hunting weapon of her lover, which a jealous woman had used to kill her rival. The fact that landowner Grimaud had assured the museum that no hunting tools were found in connection with the skeleton did not make much of an impression on Field.

The newspapers jumped on the story and made their own speculations. Had the brother of the deceased sought revenge? Was the girl killed in battle? The stories made headlines in all newspapers and contributed to creating an indescribable level of interest. The influx to the museum was enormous. A total of 22,000 visitors got a glimpse of 'Miss Cro Magnon', as some newspapers had named her in their headlines, on the opening day of the exhibition. Guards had to be called in to keep order around the main attraction. In his diary, Henry Field writes that he fell asleep with a smile on his face after that opening night.

It wasn't until 2004 that new analyses of the skeleton were carried out. Bone samples were sent for dating to the University of Oxford, and the entire skeleton was X-rayed. Both examinations yielded unexpected results. From Oxford came feedback that the two samples varied in age from 14,200 years to 16,600 years. A new sample was sent. The result was even more confusing: 12,100 years. The case was eventually solved when it was discovered that parts of the skeleton had been treated with ambroid, a cellulose-nitrate-based cement, which had contaminated the skeleton with more modern radioisotopes.

After information about the treatment of the skeleton was taken into account, the skeleton is now considered to be between 13,000 and 15,000 years old.

The X-ray examinations also provided interesting information. Based on the fact that the girl's third molars – the so-called wisdom teeth – had not yet appeared, her age was estimated to be around 20 years. However, the X-rays showed that the wisdom teeth were greatly reduced and would never emerge. This made sense to those who had previously analysed tooth wear. They believed that the girl was much older than previously thought. She was probably an adult woman close to 35 years old. The Magdalenian girl was overnight upgraded to the Magdalenian woman.

The lack of wisdom teeth had never before been detected in such old skeletons, leading to speculation that the Magdalenian people had a different diet than previously thought. A rough diet requiring a lot of chewing activity would strengthen the muscles in the jaw area and make room for wisdom teeth, was the theory. The lack of wisdom teeth was therefore taken by some experts to suggest that the Magdalenian people had a more easily digestible diet.

Today, the original remains of the Magdalenian woman are still in Chicago, but at the very impressive visitor centre established at Cap Blanc, there is now a sculpture where data from CT scanning of the skull has been used to reconstruct facial features. The woman, named after the last cultural period in Ice Age Europe, has prominent cheekbones, decorative beads in her hair, and a Mona Lisa-like smile that does not reveal the missing wisdom teeth.

A 30,000-YEAR HUNT
FOR REINDEER

It's difficult to imagine. Large parts of Europe's population were entirely dependent on access to reindeer to survive during the last Ice Age. In the most climatically challenging periods, it was the reindeer that kept us alive. An Ice Age Europe without reindeer would have left a continent without hunter-gatherers, and the land would have remained untouched, waiting for farmers to arrive 30,000 years later. There are probably still a few who think this sounds good.

When French and North American archaeologists tried to describe the daily life of Ice Age hunters a couple of decades ago, they assumed that the hunters' exploitation of reindeer was similar to what we find today in some Arctic regions: large herds of reindeer making long migrations between their summer and winter ranges, and hunters having to find good hunting locations along the migration route in spring and autumn, or trying to follow the wandering reindeer herd as best they could. The conclusion today is quite different. It turns out that in most areas, reindeer were present year-round. A nomadic life, with constant movements, was unnecessary. The hunter groups could thus establish settlements that could be used for long periods of the year. Archaeologists often find that the hunter groups occupy the same settlement from early autumn to well into spring, then move to a higher settlement in the summer – almost like a 'seasonal pasture strategy'. Compared to a nomadic way of life, a more or less permanent settlement pattern would provide the basis for a completely different social structure and cultural expressions.

The Aurignacian people's dependence on reindeer as a resource from 45,000 to 30,000 years ago has been well documented before. For the entire period, eight out of ten prey animals brought to the settlements were reindeer. Now, detailed studies of over 250 settlements used by hunters up to 15,000 years ago show that the dependence on this animal has been very significant. More and more archaeologists now claim that the 'L'âge du renne' – the age of the reindeer – extends over 30,000 years. In the Spanish areas around the Bay of Biscay and up to the Cantabrian Mountains, and large parts of France, life seems to have followed the same pattern throughout the period. When French archaeologists are asked what differentiates the exploitation of reindeer by the various hunter-gatherer cultures, they answer, 'nothing'. They certainly have weapons of different designs, use different techniques, and are probably organised in different ways, but their main survival strategy is the same.

The new knowledge about hunter-gatherers' exploitation of reindeer began with the analysis of the material found in La Madeleine, the settlement that has given its name to the Madeleine people. More than 12,000 bones and antler fragments from two different cultural layers were thoroughly examined. Almost all the material was from reindeer. In one cultural layer, 87% of the remains were from reindeer, in the other, as much as 95%. By looking at the development of antlers in adult individuals, the development and wear of cheek teeth in reindeer calves, and the length of the long bones in unborn calves, researchers could determine the time of year the animals were killed. The results were clear and surprising! Contrary to previous beliefs, it turned out that reindeer were hunted in all seasons. This must mean that the reindeer herds did not make long migrations between summer and winter ranges, but actually stayed within the same limited area year-round. Subsequent studies of four other settlements in Dordogne yielded the same result. Could this apply to other areas as well?

The answer is yes. In nine out of ten areas, hunters had access to reindeer year-round. Admittedly, there is variation in the proportion of reindeer between the different areas, depending on the availability of lichen in winter and the extent of areas with permafrost. In the two areas with the least permafrost, Dordogne and Lot, reindeer have accounted for 82% and 72%, respectively, of all prey animals brought to the settlements over a 15,000-year period. In only one of the ten hunting areas is reindeer not the most important game. The hunter-gatherers residing at the mouth of the Gironde, not far from present-day Bordeaux, have hunted saiga antelopes and bison. Only three out of ten prey animals brought to the camp are reindeer.

Another, not very surprising, result is that the proportion of reindeer varies with the climate in all areas. In the coldest and driest periods, the proportion of reindeer is clearly higher than in the brief milder periods. A female elder among French archaeologists, Françoise Delpech, together with an American colleague, conducted detailed studies of the settlement Grotte XVI in Dordogne, which show that the composition of prey animals reflects the climatic conditions in different periods. This settlement has been used by hunter groups for over 20,000 years, and the bone remains they leave behind show that they have hunted 9 different large prey animals. The pattern is clear; the colder the climate, the higher the proportion of reindeer found at the settlement.

During the last Ice Age, there were several marked warm periods when the climate improved. During a relatively favourable climate period 37–28,000 years ago, reindeer make up 42 to 58% of all prey animals. In the period of gradual worsening of the climate towards the Ice Age maximum, the proportion of reindeer increases to between 71 and 81%. The last cultural layer is dated to be 12,000 years old. The Ice Age maximum was over at that time, but a dramatic deterioration of the climate during the period called the Younger Dryas, means that reindeer now account for a whopping 94% of all bone material. In the following years, the climate becomes increasingly milder, and archaeologists assume that the last reindeer left France 11,500 years ago. Cro-Magnon's over 30,000-year hunt for reindeer is over in Southern Europe. How have they lived their lives during this period?

Ice age hunting camps

Winter camps seem to have been a time of leisure for the inhabitants. This was the period when the group's toolmakers and artists were active and they produced a large number of artworks made of what archaeologists call portable art. Elaborately crafted tools made from reindeer antlers and bones, as well as mammoth ivory, feature incised figures of prey animals. The same can be found on larger and smaller stones at the campsite. Communication and interaction among hunter groups must have been good, not only locally but also regionally. Raw materials from hunters settled on the coast frequently made their way inland. Recently, it was discovered that a 15,000-year-old arrowhead was made from bone of a gray whale. The bone must have made the 350 kilometre journey from the Bay of Biscay, eastward through the Pyrenees, to end up in Dordogne.

Skin preparation also seems to have taken place during the winter. During this time, it appears that mainly adult female reindeer were hunted. Some believe this is related to the fact that female reindeer at this time are in good condition and have fully developed antlers that can be used in tool production. In the summer, campsites are generally located higher up in the terrain and are not used for as long as winter campsites; therefore, the mobility of hunter groups is higher. In the 'good season', as archaeologists call it, reindeer do not have fully developed antlers, and their fur is unusable. The sole purpose of hunting is to provide food. By autumn, the bucks have fully developed antlers and are in good condition before the rutting season begins. Therefore, there is a clear predominance of adult bucks in the hunting material from this time of year.

Only in one of the surveyed areas have hunters not had access to reindeer year-round, and that is the region archaeologists call the Paris Basin. Here, reindeer apparently made long migrations from their spring and summer ranges up to the Massif Central in the south, to autumn and winter ranges in the areas around present-day Paris in the north. The campsites of these hunter groups are often established in the open air, providing insight into the hunters' social organisation. The Pincevent site on the western bank of the Seine, 60 kilometres south of Paris, is a prime example. Fourteen fireplaces have been registered at this site, with three locations where tents have been set up, similar to the tipis associated with the first North American inhabitants. Reindeer account for 98% of the bone material. Based on the age composition of animals and dietary studies through remnants of plant material found on jaws, archaeologists can determine that the hunting occurred in the autumn.

Detailed excavations of the campsite clearly show that the camp is divided into different zones. Around some fireplaces, there has evidently been significant activity associated with meat processing and flint tool making, while around other fireplaces, there is an absence of both bones and flint. Archaeologists believe this means that although the hunters spent most of their time around a communal fireplace, several members of the hunter group had the opportunity to withdraw to private spaces with their own fireplace. This may also indicate differences in social position among individuals in a hunter group. Other findings support such an assumption. At the La Madeleine site, a buried child was found in 1926. The approximately three-year-old girl had been buried over 10,000 years ago, at the very end of the Magdalenian people's epoch. The burial itself is not unusual, but the circumstances surrounding this burial have sparked discussions and speculation.

The deceased child had been sprinkled with ochre and buried with a very elaborate garment. The clothes had long since rotted away, but on and around the child, 1,275 shells made of molluscs of the dentalium genus, belonging to a group of animals called tusk shells, were found. The 6–7 mm long perforated shells had evidently been sewn onto the garment along with a dozen or so perforated teeth, either from reindeer or deer. It must have taken a very long time to sew such a garment; how could they even find the time to make such a garment? Perhaps daily life was not simply a constant struggle to obtain enough food? And how had such quantities of marine animals found their way to Dordogne? It is likely to assume that the hunter-gatherer society was class-divided, and that the child belonged to the group's upper class.

How did the hunter-gatherers manage the quantities of reindeer meat brought to the campsites? The scholars disagree! Some argue that Ice Age hunters had good access to fresh meat year-round and, therefore, did not have traditions related to drying and storing meat. Others believe that to satisfy the energy needs of hunter groups, estimated to number between 50 and 100 individuals, they had to store food when access to meat was particularly good. They argue that it is obvious that the meat would have been cut from the bones and hung to dry over fireplaces.

Recently, interesting studies have been conducted that could support such an assumption. By analysing and comparing tooth material from Neanderthal children and Cro-Magnon children, it has been found that very few Neanderthal children suffered from vitamin A and D deficiency, while 70% of Cro-Magnon children had low levels of these vitamins. This surprising finding is explained by the fact that a diet consisting of a certain amount of fat is necessary for the absorption of these vitamins. Among Neanderthals, there is no evidence of food storage, so the children ate fresh meat rich in fat year-round, while Cro-Magnon children had a diet consisting of dried meat for long periods, where the fat had disappeared during the drying process, leading to a deficiency in vitamins A and D. Dried or fresh, access to reindeer meat has been good. So good that the scholarly communities have found another topic to discuss.

Did Ice Age people domesticate reindeer?

That the wolf was the first mammal to be domesticated is hardly a matter of debate. However, discussions arose when some archaeologists in the late 1960s suggested that reindeer and horses could have been domesticated by Ice Age people 20,000 years ago.

One of the fundamental questions posed was: could animal husbandry and the control of large herds have been a gradual process, not just introduced to Europe through the migration of farmers from the land between the rivers

Euphrates and Tigris – Mesopotamia? Isn't it equally likely that some Cro-Magnon hunters, who for thousands of years had employed a strategy of 'hunting what is hunted', came up with the idea of taming some of the species they hunted?

The hunt for evidence began. Not surprisingly, the search started where the quantity of archaeological finds is greatest: in the Franco-Cantabrian refuge area of the Magdalenian people. Throughout the 1970s and 1980s, the archaeological literature was flooded with publications indicating that Ice Age people had had control over some of their former most sought-after prey. By analysing rock carvings of horses, some believed they were able to identify both harnesses and neatly trimmed manes and tails. Additionally, the discovery of a reindeer that had survived for at least two months with both its upper and lower jaw broken, was believed to indicate that the animal had been cared for by humans. Likewise, findings of antlers from castrated reindeer, deer killed with blows to the skull, and horses with tooth wear that could result from crib-biting, were taken as indications of human control.

However, this fascinating theory of early animal herd control does not seem to withstand critical scholarly scrutiny. The very few rock carvings that some interpreted as harnesses or bridles around horse heads, others interpret as highlighting the animal's musculature. A detailed examination of 335 horses carved into the rock in the Lascaux cave shows no signs of bridles. This would have been expected if Ice Age people controlled large herds of horses. The defenders of the theory rightly point out that there are also only a few rock carvings and cave paintings that clearly depict hunting scenes, without concluding from this that they were not hunted, but this argument does not carry much weight.

Nor can the reindeer that survived months with a broken upper and lower jaw, with signs of healing in the upper jaw, be taken as clear evidence that humans cared for the animal. It has now been shown that healing of fractures in deer species occurs rapidly. In humans, we can see that fractures start to heal after a week, and the process is even faster in deer species. The reindeer had shed its antlers, indicating that the animal was injured in late autumn. At this time, fat reserves are built up, and the animal could have survived for a long time with little or no food. At the same time, it can be argued that if there had been human control over animal herds, fewer examples of healing of these types of injuries would likely be found than in wild populations. A wounded animal that cannot eat would probably be quickly put out of its misery.

Three deer skulls with holes in the skull found inside Abri Pataud, three stone throws from where the first Cro-Magnon were found, cannot be taken as evidence that the animals were under human control either. It is just as likely that injured animals were given the coup de grace – the mercy blow – by the hunters. Likewise, a single antler from a castrated reindeer cannot be taken as evidence of human control. From excavations in Stellmoor, Germany, 1,020 reindeer antlers have been examined. Only five of these could have belonged to castrated animals, and are believed to have resulted from injuries the animals could have received during the rut. Also, the finding of worn teeth in a horse cannot be exclusively interpreted as crib-biting. It has now been shown that horses in difficult winter conditions with a lot of snow graze a lot of bark, and that this results in the same type of tooth wear.

Most archaeologists have now realised that the discussion about whether Ice Age people domesticated reindeer and horses should cease. They were hunters, and that's what they would prove again when they found themselves north on the continent, south of the retreating glaciers. But before that happened, they would leave behind artworks that will amaze the world.

Reindeer hunters and artists

Imagine today you were offered to participate in the reality show 'On Your Own – A Year in French Mountain Areas.' You would be stripped of your newly purchased Gore-Tex hunting suit, as well as your mountain boots. The anatomically designed frame backpack would also stay at home, along with the cooking equipment, matches, down sleeping bag, the lightweight inflatable sleeping pad and your rifle. Instead, you would be dressed in leather clothes and handed a spear with a stone tip and a knife, also made of stone. Additionally, you would be assigned a couple of suitable dwellings, caves and rock shelters in areas where reindeer graze. The task is simple: stay alive and ensure that a couple of the children you've brought into the world survive for a year. You might still say yes, and, if you're of the right temperament, you might even manage the task. But would you have the time, energy and inclination to decorate the cave in a way that would leave Pablo Picasso speechless, while at the same time carving decorative objects from antler material and ivory with your stone knife, so beautiful and delicate that world famous sculptors would turn green with envy? No! Not a chance!

But that's what they did! Ice Age reindeer hunters left behind inexplicably beautiful artworks. In our story of Cro-Magnon, you encounter four different cultures. While the horse-hunting Solutrean people are best known for their delicate arrowheads, the Aurignacian, Gravettian, and Magdalenian peoples have left behind artworks that still astound the world today. UNESCO has designated World Heritage sites related to the ancient reindeer hunters' artistic activities in France, Spain and Germany, indicating that these are areas worth visiting.

Perhaps the earliest Cro-Magnons, the Aurignacian people, created the most spectacular artworks.

Chauvet – the sensation in Ardèche

On his previous trips to the magnificent Ardèche Canyon between Lyon and Marseille in France, Jean-Marie Chauvet had felt a faint airflow coming out of a small opening in the cliffs just above the majestic Pont d'Arc, which forms a natural bridge over the river at the bottom of the valley. The area is very rich in limestone and, over millennia, water has carved out large cavities inside these mountains. On this Sunday afternoon, December 18, 1994, he had brought two of his friends – Christian and Éliette, and was determined to find out if it was possible to penetrate into the mountain. With the help of digging tools they had brought with them, they managed to create an opening large enough to enter the mountain, but only a few metres into the passage they suddenly found themselves on the edge of a sheer drop. They had to turn back. Even though it was close to midnight by the time they returned to the car, where they had the necessary equipment to continue exploring the cave, they immediately returned to the cave. Using a rope ladder, they proceeded further and found themselves inside a large chamber inside the mountain.

'They have been here,' Éliette suddenly exclaimed. The beam of her flashlight had captured a drawing of a reddish-brown mammoth on a small protrusion on the cave wall. Within minutes, the beams of light revealed hundreds of other drawings and engravings in the rock, in addition to the skull of a cave bear strategically placed on a large boulder in one of the large rooms they entered.

The discovery was unique. In the southern parts of France, there are dozens of known caves where our reindeer hunters have painted the fauna around them, but in the Cave Chauvet – now the official name – two things are special. The first is the age; datings show that the oldest artworks are

37,000 years old, while the youngest were made in the period between 31,000 and 28,000 years ago. This moves cave painting art 10,000 years back in time, as it was long believed that the famous 24,000-year-old 'dotted horses' in the Pech Merle cave were the oldest artworks.

The second is the incredibly fine paintings of the animal that constituted the main resource for the artists. In one of the rooms, among paintings of long-extinct mammoths, cave bears, wild horses, Irish giant deer, lions and aurochs, there are beautiful lifelike paintings of the animal that kept the European population alive for 30,000 years – the reindeer. Over 30,000 years ago, a reindeer hunter, using charcoal from the fire, stood inside the cave and carved a fantastic reindeer male. And the artists did not stop with this single artwork of their most important prey animal. Inside the same cave, there is what has been designated 'the reindeer panel'. Here, on a large scraped stone surface, charcoal drawings of 11 reindeer have been made, while isolated images of bison and horses play minor roles.

Equally spectacular is the artwork showing five reindeer swimming. Only their heads are drawn, and the way they hold their heads leaves no doubt; they are swimming across a river or a body of water, and the artist must have seen this countless times to be able to capture the situation so well. One cows not need much imagination to see that locations where reindeer have to swim across rivers or bodies of water can be good trapping spots, and this type of trapping technique will later be well documented among indigenous peoples both in Scandinavia and North America.

Cave Chauvet can be said to be somewhat atypical when it comes to the number of reindeer artworks, as cave paintings of reindeer are rare. In France, where we find the largest quantity of cave paintings, representations of reindeer make up less than five per cent of the artworks. Archaeologists' peculiar explanation that artists do not often paint 'their daily bread' is difficult to accept. What we must accept is that most of the wild species depicted inside Chauvet are now gone for good. The mammoth, the European lions, cave hyenas, and cave bears are gone, the aurochs held out the longest, but in 1627 the last individual of this species was also killed. But the reindeer is still here.

Europe's jewellery designers

We've encountered them before, then as well-adapted mammoth hunters from eastern parts of Europe. Some of these fortunately venture westward and come to the aid of a declining Aurignacian population with new tool cultures and new genetic material. Just as famous for their tent-like dwellings with frame structures made of mammoth tusks, the Gravettian people are now to be known for their fantastic abilities to create various types of jewellery and small statues – Venus figurines.

These 4– to 20-centimetre-long statues depict female bodies with oversized breasts, large round bellies, and wide hips. Often depicted with small featureless heads, most of them lack hands and feet. The female genitalia are often prominent, so when aristocrat de Vibraye found the first statue in Dordogne in 1864, he called it Venus Impudique – the immodest Venus. Although there is far from any agreement on the purpose of these statues, many interpret them as representing women's fertility, sexuality, or even luck in love, childbirth and marriage. This is a direct parallel to the role of the goddess Venus in Roman culture.

So far, more than 200 such Venus figurines have been found within the Gravettian people's living areas from Russia in the east to France and Spain in the west. The most famous depictions are probably the very lush Venus of Willendorf, the atypical Venus of Brassempouy made of ivory and with a detailed face, and the approximately 35,000-year-old Venus of Hohle Fels in Germany. However, the Gravettian people have recently become relevant again. Now examinations of their jewellery production, combined with detailed DNA analyses, have provided new insights into what life in Europe was like just before the last glacial maximum.

For a long time, it was believed that the Gravettian people were a fairly homogenous group of people who dominated Europe in a 10,000-year period from 34 to 24,000 years ago. Although it is still accepted that this group is characterised by having the same tool culture and the same distinctive tradition of making various types of jewellery, the diversity in both kinship relations and jewellery design is great. Now, the genetic material of 356 ancient hunters scattered across the European continent has been analysed. What is found is that Gravettian people residing in eastern and central parts of Europe do not have genetic material from the first reindeer hunters – the Aurignacian people, but Gravettian people residing in western parts of Europe do.

Detailed examinations of jewellery production from 134 settlements, on the other hand, show that there are 9 different types of 'ornamental cultures', from the Russian steppes in the east to the Iberian Peninsula in the west. Geographically close settlements largely have the same 'ornamental culture', and one might think that people with the same kinship background share the same type of ornamentation when it comes to jewellery. But surprisingly, that is not the case! Reindeer hunters in south-western France and north-eastern Spain have the same kinship background, but have very different 'ornamental cultures'.

At the same time, the 'French' reindeer hunters are not closely related to Gravettian people residing in present-day Belgium, but they share the same 'ornamental culture'. What significance it would have to belong to different 'ornamental cultures' is now being discussed in academic circles, of course. Clear conclusions are difficult to draw, but today we clearly see that people who divide themselves into different cultures share the same beliefs, customs and behaviours.

Culture is a powerful social tool that can create a high degree of belonging, contribute to carrying out large common projects, and survive the toughest conditions. But culture can also contribute to opposition to those we consider different from us. Whether there have been hostilities between groups belonging to different 'ornamental cultures' we do not know. But what we do know is that the Gravettian people from the south-western parts of Europe give rise to the Solutrean people, the horse hunters, who after the last glacial maximum for 19,000 years gave rise to the Magdalenian culture. It is the artistic activity of this people that will first become known to a very skeptical population.

THE GIRL FROM ALTAMIRA

Spain Year 1879

While the discovery of the Chauvet Cave made headlines, it pales in comparison to the media attention the first findings of Ice Age hunters' artistic activity would receive.

To understand the story unfolding, we must grasp the worldview of the time. The year is 1879, and Charles Darwin's books on the origin of species and human descent had not yet gained general acceptance. For much of the population, including a large portion of the academic community where many professors also had a religious education, the theories of the creation narrative by the Bishop of Dublin, James Ussher, as presented in his magnum opus *Annals of the World* from 1650, still held sway – that the Earth was created on Sunday, the 21st of September, 4004 BC. Even though many were aware of the discoveries of human remains that had lived in Europe long ago, it was by no means acceptable that these cave dwellers had abilities comparable to those of modern humans. The idea that they could express themselves through fantastic artworks was unthinkable.

A discovery made by a 9-year-old girl in the hills above the Bay of Biscay near the town of Santillana del Mar in Cantabria in 1879 would therefore have significant consequences, and not only for her immediate family at the time. Later, the discovery would create deep divisions in the contemporary academic community for nearly a quarter of a century, and even the Spanish King Alphonso XII would play a significant role.

Nine-year-old Maria was the daughter of Don Marcelino de Sautuola and grew up in the family's castle in Altamira, but the story actually begins the year she was born, 1869. That year, a dog vanished from the face of the Earth. Like most counts and castle owners, Don Marcelino also had his own employed hunters. One of them was out hunting with his dog when it suddenly disappeared in the middle of a meadow. The hunter searched and soon found a hole in the ground. After some digging, he made contact with the dog, which seemed to be inside a large cave. Don Marcelino was informed, and together they entered the cave.

The lack of light and low ceiling height made the visit brief, and in the following years the cave received little attention. The exception was, of course, adventurous village children, but they were sternly warned by their parents to stay away because the cave was inhabited by spirits that should not be disturbed.

Don Marcelino's visit to the World's Fair in Paris in 1878 would give the cave renewed relevance. In Paris, he saw some of the latest archaeological finds. There were harpoon points and bone needles, arrowheads and tools made of flint, but, most interestingly, flat stones with engraved drawings of bison and mammoths. The scientist who had found most of the tools told Don Marcelino that he had also found bones of both bears and humans side by side in many of the caves he had examined.

The count's interest in caves was awakened! Equipped with a pickaxe and other digging tools, he quickly made his way up to the cave upon his return from Paris. It didn't take many days before he came home to the castle one evening in a very excited mood, showing arrowheads of the same type he had seen in Paris. His conclusion was clear; the Ice Age people had lived their lives and fought against ice and wild animals in the same area where he now had his castle.

From then on, Don Marcelino had daily trips to the cave. Often Maria accompanied him. She liked sitting in the light of the candles and watching her father eagerly examine the many clumps of earth he dug up from the ground. One November day, it was particularly cold inside the cave. While her father kept warm with his digging, Maria began to freeze. She took one of the many candles and walked around the cave, letting the light warm her frozen fingers. She entered one of the cave's side chambers and let the light play over the ceiling.

That's when she saw them! 'Toros! Toros!' Her excited cries made her father drop his digging tool and bend down to enter the side chamber. Was the girl sick? Was she seeing things, was she feverish? 'Do you see oxen?' asked her father. 'There!' Maria lifted the light towards one of the rocks on the ceiling. 'They're only shadows,' said her father. 'You shouldn't be afraid.'

'Next to the shadow is a red ox,' said Maria. 'No, it's probably the dim light that makes it look like that,' said her father. Maria persisted: 'There are many oxen, and they're all red.' She fetched one of her father's pickaxes, gave him the light, and pointed with the handle of the pickaxe at a large red animal huddled as if wounded. Then Don Marcelino saw it too.

A bison in mortal combat. The animal looked at him with its large eye, and in the flickering light it seemed like the animal was breathing. He hugged Maria and let his gaze wander from one rock projection to another. On each of them, he saw a bison. In the days that followed, Don Marcelino examined the walls and ceiling of the cave. In many places, he had to crawl on his back because of the low ceiling height, but he continued to make new discoveries.

In the end, he had recorded over a hundred paintings. Not only of bison but also of reindeer, wild boar, and deer. And what paintings! The artists – Don Marcelino deemed it impossible that only one artist could have made all these artworks in his lifetime – had exploited the cave's rugged shape so artistically that in the flickering light, the paintings came to life – it was as if the cave ceiling in some places was covered with living animals. From Madrid, Spain's foremost expert on earth exploration – Professor Vilanova – was summoned. The trip into the cave left the professor in an almost shocked state.

When he regained his composure, he began to question Don Marcelino. 'When was the cave found?'

'Almost ten years ago,' was the answer.

'Do you know everyone who has been inside the cave since then?'

'I do,' said Don Marcelino.

'No painters?' asked the professor. Don Marcelino shook his head.

Together they explored parts of the cave where Don Marcelino had not been, and they continuously found new paintings, charcoal drawings, and animals carved directly into the porous rock. Even in the innermost parts of the cave, nearly 300 metres from the entrance, they made new observations. Some paintings had faded, while others the professor had gently touched, regaining fresh red, yellow, and brown colours on his fingertips. They also observed that many of the paintings were crossed by cracks that had formed in the rock, apparently after the painting was made.

The professor's conclusion was crystal clear: 'These artworks are made by people who lived here many thousands of years ago.'

'Is that your firm conviction?' asked Don Marcelino. The professor nodded. 'Then I must make a confession! There has been a painter in Altamira for the last ten years. He lived with me while painting the picture hanging in my study, at the same time repairing some of the castle's paintings that had been damaged over time. But I can assure you that he has never visited the cave!'

'I have seen those paintings,' said the professor. 'The man who painted the castle's paintings has nothing to do with the cave paintings! Such paintings are made only a few times in a century!'

As a highly respected scientist, Professor Vilanova had access to the Spanish royal family. His compelling description of the fantastic discovery led King Alphonso XII to immediately want to visit Altamira. It became a triumphant tour. The king spent a long time inside the cave, and when he emerged visibly moved, he delivered a speech to the villagers and the many journalists gathered outside. During the speech, he singled out Maria, took her hand, and said, 'You, little Maria, we have to thank for a great discovery! Spain is proud of the girl from Altamira. Next year, professors from all over the world will come to Lisbon to report to each other on the most important discoveries. I will invite them to Altamira because this is the greatest of the recent discoveries!'

'Long live Maria! Long live the King!' shouted the crowd.

The professorial meeting in Lisbon would mark the beginning of a quarter-century of disputes in the academic community, casting the Spanish king, Professor Vilanova, Altamira, and Don Marcelino into deep embarrassment, and, somewhat less important, turning Don Marcelino's dark mane of hair snow-white within a week. Professor Vilanova's presentation of the discovery at the professorial meeting in Lisbon fell on deaf ears, and he realised that his reputation as a scientist was at stake. It was him against the rest of the assembly.

Where is the progress if man was capable of creating perfect artworks already 20,000 years ago, asked a Swiss professor. That Ice Age humans painted in the same way as the best painters in Paris today is simply too incredible, argued another professor from Paris. A Spanish nobleman is not a scientist; a nobleman can be mistaken about a scientific question. Both you and the Spanish king have been deceived, claimed a professor from Portugal.

Then came the death blow. A professor from Madrid stepped forward. This was one of Professor Vilanova's colleagues. They have told me that Don Marcelino has had a painter as a guest in his house. Even a mute painter. Perhaps Marcelino had a reason to choose a mute painter, or he has made the painter mute – with money? There was a tremendous uproar. The battle was lost!

Leading up to the professorial meeting in Lisbon, all Spanish and Portuguese newspapers, and most major newspapers around the world, had headlines like:

FAMOUS SCIENTISTS VISIT THE ICE AGE.

PROFESSORS FROM ALL OVER THE WORLD COME TO ALTAMIRA

But no scientists came to Altamira, and newspapers worldwide featured headlines of mockery and suspicion:

SPANISH NOBLEMAN AS A MAJOR SWINDLER.
BISON BREEDER FROM ALTAMIRA

and in some newspapers, one could read:

THE MYSTERIOUS GUEST AT DON MARCELINO'S
THE PAINTER WITH THE SEALED MOUTH.
WHO WAS THE ALTAMIRA PAINTER?

Don Marcelino first received a telegram, then a letter from Professor Vilanova, stating that he had fought for Altamira as long as he believed that the paintings were from the Ice Age, but under the weight of the evidence, he could not maintain his claim. Don Marcelino continued his fight for vindication. But in vain. He met nothing but ridicule and pity.

The old man from Altamira, a fool, thought the scientific communities. After his death, the scientific communities eventually began to come to a new understanding. Knowledge of human evolutionary history increased, but it would be 23 years after the infamous professorial meeting in Lisbon before one of the greatest opponents – the professor from Paris – finally visited Altamira.

The girl from Altamira, now a young countess, welcomed him and led him to the cave. In the cave lay the pickaxe she had used 23 years ago when she pointed to the bison in mortal combat. 'My father worked until his death with this pickaxe. He was sure that one day one of his opponents would come here and say – "I was wrong." I was given clear instructions to give this pickaxe to the first one who came.' When the professor from Paris received Don Marcelino's pickaxe, he was so moved that he momentarily lost his ability to speak. The girl from Altamira understood what the silence meant: her father's enemy had now become his ally. The following year, the professor from Paris published a paper where he admitted his mistake to the whole world. The year was 1902, the beginning of a century that would give us entirely new knowledge of how modern humans and their ancestors lived their lives in Europe over an almost unimaginably long period – 1 million years – under changing climatic conditions.

HUNTERS AT THE EDGE OF THE ICE

15,000 – 11,700 years ago

About 15,000 years ago, the over 3,000-metre-high ice cap that extended southward from Scandinavia had retreated enough that the northern parts of Germany were inhabitable for the Magdalenian people who came from the south. Meltwater from the glaciers had shaped valleys in the terrain and left behind long, narrow lakes. Additionally, remnants of ice had remained, forming so-called pot holes. It was in these, and the now dried-up lakes, that the electrician-trained boy from Hamburg, Alfred Rust, would make his discoveries that would earn him honour in the form of an honorary doctorate from the University of Kiel in June 1940, but unfortunately also little honour.

The Nazi party believed that his discoveries provided strong support for the superiority of the Aryan race and offered Rust a job in the party, which he accepted. He was exempted from mandatory military service and could continue his work uncovering the lives of Ice Age hunters at the edge of the ice.

Even as a young boy, Alfred had found flint material on his trips in the forested areas east of Hamburg. He believed that some of the flint pieces must have been crafted by humans, and this was confirmed by the archaeology professor who led the evening courses he attended at the Folk High School. In 1933, he went out to his childhood areas and conducted several soil samplings with soil augers. Encouraged by findings of cultural layers 4 to 8 metres deep, he initiated more extensive fieldwork. The work was demanding.

Groundwater penetrated the excavation area and was initially attempted to be removed with buckets by the workers. This was ineffective, so Rust had hand-operated water pumps installed, which took both time and effort as the water continued to flow in. It wasn't until Rust had diesel-powered water pumps installed that the working conditions for the archaeologists became somewhat tolerable. At a depth of 6.5 metres, the first discovery was made; a reindeer antler clearly crafted by humans. This was the first, and, for most, very surprising evidence that there had been Ice Age hunters in Germany over 14,000 years ago.

Further excavations revealed more discoveries, not only bone material but also flint spearheads, flint scrapers for removing fat and meat residues from the skin, and roughly hewn stone axes for crushing large bones. The shapes of both weapons and tools resembled those previously found among the Magdalenian people, supporting earlier assumptions that it was the people who had survived the last glacial maximum in the south-western parts of France and north-western parts of Spain who had now migrated northward.

The discovery of a crafted reindeer antler with incisions of human-like figures with animal ears showed that the artistic abilities of the Magdalenian people were still intact. Pollen analyses showed that the area had been a steppe landscape, with grass, willow and juniper, and smaller areas of birch and pine. In such a landscape, it would be problematic to sneak up close to the animals. It is assumed that the hunters had spears as their main weapon, and, even with the use of atlatl, hunters had to get within 30 metres of the prey for the hunt to be successful.

The archaeologists' theory is that the hunters must have had extensive knowledge of the reindeer's migration routes and utilised all hiding places along the route to get close enough to their prey. The hunting techniques of the Hamburg hunters will likely be further discussed in academic circles. Recently, there have been reports that indications have been found that the first Cro-Magnon hunters who used the Mandrin cave (remember the cave where the tooth shedding took place?) had used bows and arrows.

Neither the arrow nor the bow has been found, but several stone projectiles that are assumed to have been arrowheads have been found inside the cave. Regardless of the weapons used by the Hamburg hunters, they must have been well acquainted with the reindeer's migration routes. Recent isotope analyses of bone material from reindeer found during the excavations show that the animals primarily had an east-west migration, with the eastern areas being most utilised in late autumn and winter, while the large contiguous areas including Doggerland and present-day England were used in spring and summer. The fact that the many river valleys in the landscape served both as travel routes and as good hunting grounds is evident. The archaeologists have found remarkably many settlements for reindeer hunters in connection with the river valleys formed by the rivers Oder, Elbe, Weser, Ems, and Rhine. At the same time, reindeer hunters were active in England and Wales. Here too, it is clear that they had their most successful hunts in river systems connected to the Thames, which was a tributary of the Rhine at that time.

Rapid climate shifts at the end of the Ice Age

Reindeer hunters at the edge of the ice likely noticed that warmer times were approaching. Increasingly larger areas were covered by pine and birch, rapidly evolving the landscape into a subarctic forest, similar to those found in the northern regions of Scandinavia today. New species entered the areas previously dominated by reindeer. Hunters now had to learn to hunt elk, Irish giant deer, and beaver. The forest provided them with better cover, and hunting techniques changed. Hunters could now manage to sneak up on their prey. The spear, which had been their ancestors' main hunting weapon, was now replaced with bows and arrows. This was well documented by Alfred Rust, who himself found over a hundred arrows during the excavations in 1935–36. Unfortunately, all of these were lost during an Allied bombing raid in 1944.

These forest hunters who came after the Hamburg hunters, and whose heyday was 14,000 – 12,800 years ago, formed what is called the Federmesser culture. They were named after the shape of the flint arrowheads they made, resembling a penknife previously used to split feather quills.

In the camps of the Federmesser people, the atmosphere was likely good. The use of bows and arrows allowed them to kill prey from up to 50 metres away, and abundant pine and birch provided life-sustaining fires. However, a colder climate would quickly make itself felt in the northern hemisphere.

From one generation of hunters to the next, hunting conditions changed dramatically. Forested areas with elk and giant deer were transformed into a steppe tundra within a few decades, similar to what can be found in the northernmost parts of Siberia today. And now history repeats itself. For as we have seen several times over the past half-million years, it is once again the reindeer that provide the people with the necessary resources. The period known as the Younger Dryas, named after the Latin name for the beautiful pink mountain flower that covered large parts of Germany and Scandinavia during this period, had begun, and over the next thousand years hunters would again see the glaciers in the north grow larger, and the previously forested lands replaced by tundra and steppe landscapes.

What triggered this cold period is actually uncertain among experts, but the idea that freshwater access could be a key is not unlikely. Initially, it was believed that cold meltwater from the large ice cap over North America prevented warm water from the Gulf Stream from reaching the northern parts of Europe. Another theory is that warm Atlantic water, rising sea levels, and the opening of the Bering Strait caused the thick sea ice that covered the Arctic Ocean before the Younger Dryas to drift into the Norwegian Sea, thereby dampening or stopping the Gulf Stream.

Alfred Rust, who continued his excavations, found traces of the culture that would dominate this cold period 4 metres down in the sediments in the dried-up meltwater areas near Ahrensburg. The settlement of Stellmoor was apparently used by hunters in the autumn, and here Rust found more than 30,000 objects related to the new hunting culture named the Ahrensburg culture. Reindeer were completely dominant. Bone remains of as many as 650 reindeer were found at this settlement, including some complete skeletons, including one where flint arrowheads were still lodged in the animal's sternum. Additionally, wooden poles were found, with the head of a reindeer buck adorned with a magnificent antler placed on top. A motif we find reflected in the 'city coat of arms' of Ahrensburg today.

While the diet of the hunter-gatherer people south of the glacier appears to have been quite meat-based, their relatives further west seem to be transitioning to becoming fish eaters.

'The Doggerlanders' had a taste for surf 'n turf

Those of us who have lived for some time will likely still remember the regular segment on NRK radio, 'Fishing Report', where the average radio listener would hear about the fishing conditions in various fishing grounds. One of the areas Norwegian fishermen went to was the Dogger Bank. If we had been told that our ancestors 10,000 years earlier had used the Dogger Bank as a habitation area, and that their diet was largely dominated by freshwater fish, NRK's seriousness as a state channel would surely have been thoroughly debated. However, this has now been confirmed as solid documented fact.

For a long time, we have known that Doggerland – this large submerged landscape between the Netherlands, Denmark, and the British Isles – at the end of the last ice age was the habitat for both woolly rhinoceros and other mammals, including reindeer. More recent are the findings Dutch archaeologists have made in the submerged area. Based on isotope analyses of 56 bones from humans who resided here, they can document that our ancestors in the period from about 11,500 to 8,000 years ago increasingly shifted from being meat eaters to a diet dominated by freshwater fish.

The study is based on analyses of so-called stable isotopes, primarily carbon and nitrogen. Isotopes are atoms of the same chemical element with the same number of protons but a different number of neutrons in the atomic nucleus. Two atoms with the same number of protons and different numbers of neutrons are therefore two isotopes of the same chemical element, and it is the distribution of stable isotopes of the same chemical element that creates a kind of fingerprint that can say something about the origin of foodstuffs, as in this case.

The trend of increasing freshwater diet over time is believed to be related to the fact that Doggerland gradually flooded after the last ice age, and it is assumed that the sea level rose about 2 metres per century. The lowest lying parts of Doggerland were then flooded. While it has previously been assumed that this would lead our ancestors to either move inland and seek meat resources or out to the coast for a more marine diet, isotopic analyses show a different scenario. Instead of leaving their residential areas, our ancestors adapted to the lush and nutrient-rich wetlands that formed in the delta areas of the Rhine, Meuse, and Thames.

So, while some hunters continued as fish eaters in Doggerland, others continued their migration northward as the ice receded, for the end of the Younger Dryas 11,700 years ago marked the end of the last ice age, and the end of the Ahrensburg culture – the last Ice Age hunters who were entirely dependent on reindeer. Warmer summers are now accelerating the melting of the inland ice over Scandinavia, and the hunters see opportunities in the land areas that were previously inaccessible. The hunters have now set course for Norway. They become seafarers!

PART V

Norway 11,700 – 800 years ago
The former land-based reindeer hunters become seafarers and
quickly colonise the Norwegian coast. Far in the north, they
receive surprising visits from hunters from the east. The fusion
of these two hunter-gatherer cultures is struck by Europe's
greatest natural disaster, but over the next 8,000 years, they
continue as hunters, fishers and gatherers. Invasive farmers do
not gain the same dominance as in southern Europe, and the
reindeer hunting culture continues, and in the north and
south-east of the country domestication of the
reindeer spreads.

INTO THE LAND BEYOND

For over half a million years, various hunter-gatherer groups in Europe had been land-based, with most activities occurring on solid ground. Although the last ice age hunters, Cro-Magnon, had fished for salmon in the more than sixty salmon-bearing rivers in France, and had likely felt the icy glacier water when hunting reindeer crossing the great rivers, which from their sources in the Central Massif made their way down to the Bay of Biscay, they were not accustomed to the sea. Now, standing at the edge of the retreating ice sheets, they looked upon a tempting land further north on bright, clear days.

The reindeer had for a long time populated the northern land, being adept swimmers with their air-filled fur. The animals had visited the land several times before during the many short warm periods of the last ice age. Some as long as 40,000 years ago, but now the reindeer were finally here to stay. For the hunter-gatherer people, the Norwegian Trench was a problem. The deep, 50-mile-wide open sea had been formed by ice erosion during the penultimate ice age and now acted as a barrier to further travel north.

Even though the reindeer had been the main prey during the Younger Dryas, the 1000-year-long cold period marking the end of the last ice age 11,700 years ago, many of the hunters along Doggerland's and Skagerrak's coasts had likely seen the sea ice that formed in winter as an interesting hunting ground. The ice was almost an extension of the flat landscape they used in the summer. Out on the sea ice, they gained experience with marine mammals. They quickly discovered that seals were easy prey when they surfaced from their breathing holes in the ice, and that, in many ways, seals provided them with the same raw materials as they got from reindeer and other land mammals. In addition to meat, blood, bones, bladders and tendons, seals also had large amounts of blubber, which worked excellently as fuel.

Another important product was seal skin. We do not know how quickly the hunters discovered that processed seal skin could be used as a shell for waterproof vessels, but it is undeniable that creative hunters over a millennium developed knowledge and experience related to boat building, as evidenced by the seafaring people who left the first traces on both the Swedish and Norwegian coasts. The most seaworthy and daring hunters likely made shorter reconnaissance trips to the land they glimpsed to the north and returned to Doggerland in late autumn, full of stories about the land beyond their own. For they probably saw themselves as Doggerlanders, while 'the land beyond' was foreign and unknown, beyond the direct experience of the hunters. They surely gave it a name; we can follow archaeologist Ingrid Fuglestvedt's designation and call it the Beyond Land. The stories of those who returned from the Beyond Land would have given many hope for a good future there. The increasing temperatures and the spread of birch forests had reduced the reindeer population they had previously hunted extensively in the tunnel valleys near Stellmoore. They had tried all possibilities to change their hunting luck. The shamans had used their entire repertoire in attempts to appease the lord of the reindeer among the spirits. Some experts believe that the discovery of 12 reindeer calves submerged in a small pool in one of the tunnel valleys were offerings made in a desperate attempt to change their hunting luck. Those with less imagination might argue that these were not offerings, but simply a common way to preserve meat when temperatures are too high. Regardless, the reindeer population was declining, and as so many times before in our prehistory, climate and environmental conditions affect people's ability and desire to move.

The objects left behind at the settlements and the size of the tent-like shelters erected suggest that small family groups were on the move. They were explorers. No settlements bear witness to long stays, and they are all located just above the contemporary sea level, which in the south of the country was around 150 metres higher than today's. Much of the water masses were indeed bound in the ice sheets, but the up to three-kilometre-high ice sheet had pushed the land masses down. Further east, in the Bothnian Bay north of Umeå, the world's highest land uplift is recorded today. Here, the land has risen nearly 800 metres since the last ice age, creating a dramatic coastal landscape. But along the Norwegian coast, small and large islands protrude, providing opportunities to navigate in calm waters.

The pioneers surprisingly take a short time to explore the entire Norwegian coast. There are not many centuries' difference in age between the oldest settlements along Oslo Fjord and settlements on the Varanger Peninsula in Finnmark. This is a common feature found on other continents as well; when hunter-gatherers first take to the sea, colonisation of new areas occurs very rapidly. There are at least two important reasons for this. Firstly, it is faster to transport families with small and large members by boat than on foot. Another equally important reason is that when pioneers arrive in new areas, they encounter prey that has no experience with humans. This means that most prey animals have not developed a flight or fear response associated with the sight of humans. It is well documented that prey animals growing up in predator-free environments lose their original behaviour towards predators in just a few generations. This means that access to prey animals for those who are travelling northward along the coast for the first time may have been good.

On their journey along the coast, they likely encountered their familiar prey. The oldest bone findings of reindeer in Norway are approximately 14,000 years old, and typically these are found in Øygarden in Vestland. For the reindeer, the coastal area was likely their habitat for the first 2–3,000 years, and the coastal strip was dominated by an arctic plant community that provided good grazing for the reindeer. Several thousand years without contact with humans likely made the reindeer naive and easy prey for the seafarers. The same can be assumed for marine mammals. Archaeological material from the Kattegat – Skagerrak area after the last ice age shows that many 'ice-dependent' species were still present, similar to the species composition we find today around Svalbard and Greenland. This means that the pioneers had access to a variety of seal species such as Greenland seal, bearded seal and walrus, in addition to polar bears. The flightless great auk bird probably also provided a reliable food source on the journey along the coast. Therefore, we can assume that the country's first pioneers did not spend much time obtaining the resources they needed on their journey from island to island northward along the Norwegian coast. For they were island hoppers.

Of the more than 800 registered settlements from this pioneer era, nine out of ten are located on islands. But there are exceptions. In the mountains behind the Rogaland coast, hunters had already been hunting reindeer 10,000 years ago. More than 50 kilometres from the coast, there are settlements that show signs of being used for shorter periods in summer and autumn, but over a long period of time. The characteristic ring-shaped stone structures show where the tents were pitched, and remnants of the fires that were lit provide good dating for when the hunters were there. The hunters who first visited these hunting areas use arrowheads that are exactly like those used by the reindeer hunters on Doggerland.

The first hunters also had good access to flint, as virtually all processed stone material is of flint. Later, it appears that the access to flint decreases, and the arrows are eventually equipped with tips made of quartz. Settlements of the same type as those found around Myrvatn in the mountains of Rogaland soon appear in many mountain areas on the West Coast as well. The people follow the reindeer up into the emerging mountain areas, but it is along the coast where the activity is greatest.

Artifacts left behind at the settlements of the seafarers are now being uncovered along the entire coast. The way flint knives and other tools were made is unmistakable. The fact that the first discoveries of the pioneers' settlements were made at Voldvatnet near Kristiansund, and named the Fosna culture after the trading post Lille-Fosen, does not change the fact that it is the old reindeer hunters from Germany and Denmark who are travelling northward along the coast. The tools and weapons they used were made in the same way as those used by the last ice age hunters.

Farthest in the north, the old reindeer hunters would soon receive visitors from the east! For while the central parts of the Scandinavian Peninsula were still dominated by an ice cap, the northern parts of Finland were ice-free, and the coastal strip in the north-western parts of Russia was navigable. Ten thousand years ago, these areas left traces of a completely different tool culture than the reindeer hunters coming from the south used. How far east they came from is still uncertain, but it is indisputable that the people who lived their lives in the north-eastern parts of Europe were familiar with reindeer and reindeer hunting. The technique these new hunters used to make their flint knives and other tools was completely different from what the south-western reindeer hunters brought with them. These same cultural traces are quickly found down the coast towards the south. A settlement over 10,000 years old for this people was recently uncovered as far south as Vinjeøra.

Fortunately, it is not only stone tools that Norway's first inhabitants leave behind; a small number of skeletons have also been found. This has provided opportunities to find out whether it was the tool culture that was copied by the first reindeer hunters and brought southward, or whether it was indeed the toolmakers themselves who made the journey. Isotope and genetics analyses of seven 6,000–9,500-year-old skeletons from Scandinavia have now been conducted. One of these seven skeletons was found in Steigen north of Bodø. The hunters and gatherers from Steigen turn out to be a mixture of eastern and southern immigrants. All results now indicate that hunters from parts of what is now the north-eastern parts of Russia travelled southward along the Norwegian coast and eventually formed a common hunter and gatherer culture with the southern immigrants. In the time just after the colonisation of Norway, the genetic variation among the population in the northern parts of the country is greater than further south, and actually greater than what is found further south in Europe.

Furthermore, this mixture of southern and eastern immigrants has also developed genetic adaptations to life far north, including light skin and an increased ability to absorb vitamin D. Although detailed investigations in the near future will reveal more precise knowledge of where the eastern immigrants came from, recent genetic studies may indicate that they are descendants of eastern and western Gravettians who, after many thousands of years of separation, meet on the Finnmark coast shortly after the last ice age. If so, it's a fantastic and beautiful story! A cold-adapted, innovative, and highly mobile hunter-gatherer people split in south-eastern parts of Europe, and meet again on the Finnmark coast many thousands of years later.

Despite the fact that several of the genetic combinations we find in this early phase have now completely disappeared, the genetic material from these two immigrant groups of hunters constitutes half of the genetic material of today's population in Norway. They were to become many and make their mark far south in Europe, but initially there were not many of them. Several attempts have been made to determine how many people were present in the ice-free parts of Scandinavia shortly after the last ice age. Various methods have been used in such calculations, and the numbers are surprisingly low. In the few ice-free parts of southern Sweden, some survived thanks to successful reindeer drives at Lake Finjasjøen, but the population in Sweden was only a few hundred people. Not much more had a foothold in the northern parts of Denmark. The approximately 30 different hunter groups residing in these areas count a total of no more than 650 people. In fact, there are more people along the coast of the Beyond Land, the land that eventually will be called Norvegr. The highest estimate is that there are 1,800 people along the ice-free coast. The fewest are found in the Oslo Fjord area. Here, there are only a few hundred hunters present, just under one-third of the population in Northern Norway. The population is largest in the south-west of the country, but estimates vary between 250 and 830 people. In the central parts of the coastal strip, between 100 to 300 'Trønders' manage to find enough resources to survive. Overall, from Finnmark in the north to the Oslo Fjord in the south-east, it is estimated that less than 80 wandering hunter groups are present.

FIG 4. The colonisation of what we now call Norway proceeded rapidly after the first pioneers arrived here about 11,000 years ago. The timeline in the figure shows some of the important events in the story of humans and reindeer in Norway since the end of the Ice Age.

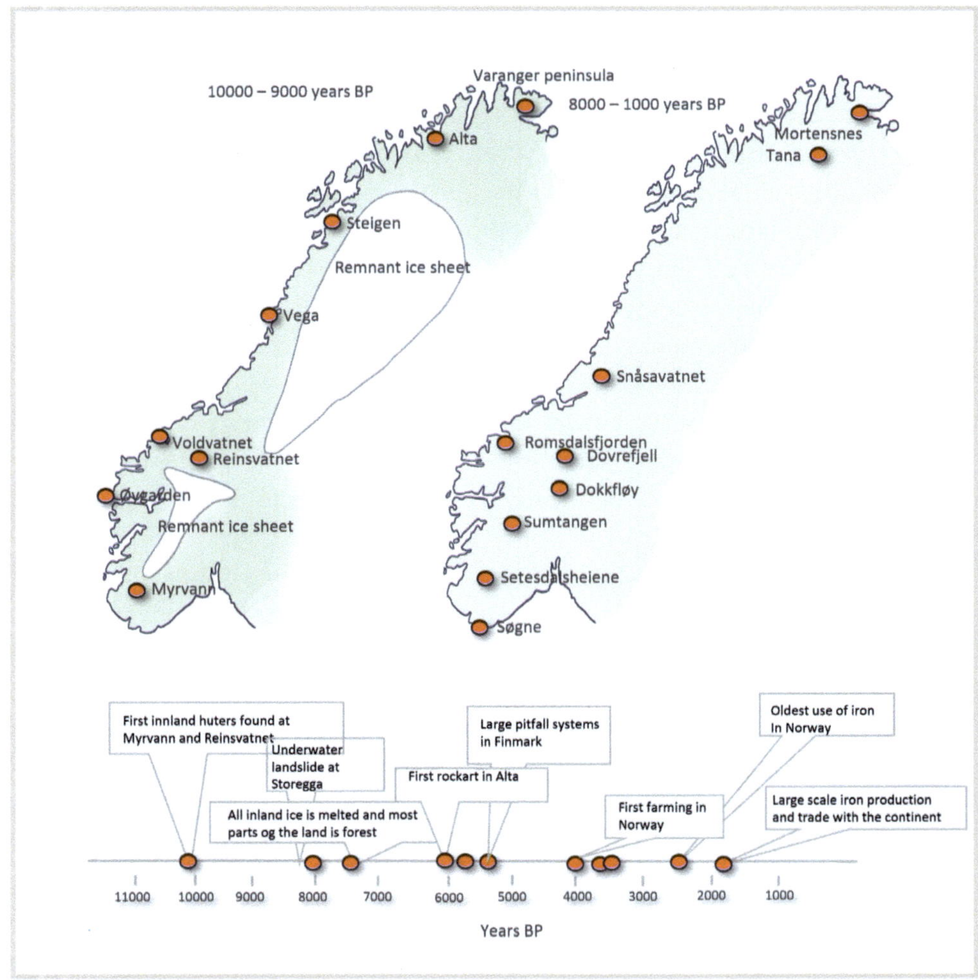

SOL RISING FROM THE SEA

After a millennium marked by rapid movements between simple camp sites, the seafaring people began to establish more permanent settlements. Still, it is the islands that most chose to settle on. On the island of Vega, the oldest permanent settlements are over 10,000 years old. At 'Åsgarder,' there are about twenty house mounds within an area of two acres. Here, the people dug almost one metre down into the cobblestone surface and formed 3- to 4-metre-wide stone pits. Here they lived, and here they harvested from the sea. And what resources they had access to! Only Canada has a longer coastline than Norway. For every kilometre of coastline, Norway has over 30 kilometres of shoreline, and in these productive, shallow seaweed areas, the people could extract most of the food they needed. Not surprisingly, the old settlements are located where the amount of animal and plant plankton is highest even today. Plankton attracts species that feed on it, and these, in turn, attract fish-eating or crustacean-eating species. Now we know more about one of those who settled in such areas.

The child is known by many names. Archeologists call her Sol (Sun), others call her the Lady of the Sea, while those less lively among us simply call her the Søgne Woman. For it was from Søgne, just west of Kristiansand, she emerged from the sea. She lay only a metre deep, and her skull was initially assumed to be an old jar. Those who transported the deceased 35-year-old woman out to what is now called Hummervikholmen to bury her could not possibly have known that she would, nearly 10,000 years later, become the oldest preserved skeleton of the Norwegian pioneers, nor did they have any chance of predicting that the discovery of her would prevent any form of bathing activity in the bay where she was laid to rest for several years while archaeological investigations of the area continued. But that's how it turned out.

Sol has contributed to our knowledge of prehistory in Norway. She probably didn't know the guy from Steigen, but some form of kinship is not unlikely. Just like him, Sol was a great mix of southern and eastern immigrants.

About a third of her genetic material she inherited from the reindeer hunters who came from the south, while the rest came from the people who came from the east into northern Norway and continued their journey southward along the coast. We don't know where she inherited her green or brown eyes from now, but geneticists will surely give us answers to that too, knowing them. Her teeth were without cavities but very worn down. Archaeologists believe that sand in the food and processing of seal skins are the cause. Tanning seal skins required significant chewing activity at the time, which wore down the teeth.

Sol is top-heavy! She is a paddling person, used to using her upper body when navigating in a skin boat between islets and skerries. This gives her a strong upper body and slender legs. Sol is a representative of the world's northernmost settlement, and she has a body shape exactly like that found in people from the world's southernmost population, the Yahgan people, who about the same time crossed the Bering Strait and about 10,000 years ago found themselves in Tierra del Fuego, the archipelago at the southern tip of South America. They are both originally land-based hunters but now master the marine landscape equally well. And it is from the sea they extract almost all of their sustenance.

Structures in the bone material testify that Sol was malnourished for a short period as a child. Perhaps she did not receive enough breast milk when her mother had to prioritise younger siblings, but later in life she got enough nourishment, and a full 80% of Sol's diet was from the sea. The seal was as important to this people as the reindeer was to the Ice Age hunters. She ate seal, was dressed in seal skin, paddled a light boat covered with seal skin, lived in a small house where seal blubber was used for fuel, and, most importantly, she had tools made from seal bone. Someone in the group came up with a technological innovation. Fish hooks and harpoon points were made from bone; daggers and spears were shaped from bone and inset with small pieces of flint that gave a sharp edge. Some apparently also took the time to decorate some of the tools with fine geometric patterns. It is definitely liveable by the coast, but around 8,000 years ago, a nearly 2,000-year-long warm period began that would change the settlement pattern. Unlike today, at that time the Earth was closest to the sun in the summer of the northern hemisphere, and the solar radiation at northern latitudes was more than 10% higher than today. Large parts of the high mountain areas became ice-free, and more and more people settled on the mainland and resumed their ancestors' main activity – reindeer hunting. But for many who had not taken the trip to the mountains that autumn day 8,000 years ago, it would be the last day of their lives.

THE DAY WHEN ONLY THE MOUNTAIN PEOPLE SURVIVED

We can envision a group of hunters heading up into the high mountains. There were five in the group on this early autumn day. For the twins, this would be their baptism of fire in the mountains. Early in the morning, they set out from their dwelling near Måndalen, a place deep into the Romsdalsfjord. Even though the fjord still teemed with fish, and the shallow waters around their home provided them with access to crabs, shells and small fish, they had been spending more and more time in the mountains in recent years. The reindeer that had previously been confined to the narrow coastal strip had now, as the glaciers melted, taken over the mountain areas. And the grazing conditions must have been good, for the herds now occupying the mountains between Storfjorden and their own fjord had grown large.

The people of Storfjord knew this too. Like the group of hunters, they had also spent much time building hides in recent years. Not that it was much work to construct these hiding places; there were plenty of building blocks in the mountains. The vast areas of frost-cracked stone made construction easy. What took time was finding the best spots. Where did the reindeer go when fleeing hunters on foot, and which snowdrifts did they prefer on warm days to escape the worst insect plague? The people of Storfjord knew their stuff as well. Nearly fifty new hides had been erected in the past year, and they seemed to be strategically placed. Some of these they would use today, if the people of Storfjord hadn't themselves ventured into the mountains.

Like the reindeer, the group moved against the wind, steadily climbing higher into the terrain. The strategy was to gain the best possible overview, locate reindeer, decide which hides to man, and send out the nimble-footed 12-year-olds as drivers. They had the most important job today. Not to panic the reindeer herd, but to approach calmly, almost disinterestedly, not to go straight at them, but to angle the marching direction so that the herd moved at a leisurely pace in the right direction relative to the three archers.

Luck was on their side. In the valley below them grazed a herd of fostered reindeer. Almost 50 does, as many calves, and some young. The plan was put into action. The archers needed time to get unnoticed into their hides. The twins would use that time to move around the herd unseen. Everything went according to plan. From several hundred metres away, they made themselves known. The herd stood motionless for a long while, but soon the likely lead female began to move uphill and toward the archers. As there was a wind blowing, the reindeer wouldn't smell the hidden hunters until they were near the hides. They couldn't see the arrow shot from the stone wall, but a reindeer suddenly picked up speed. It was the twins' father who had shot. A reindeer calf stood for a couple of seconds, then was hit by an arrow from the other hide. It dropped to its knees but got back up on all fours. The other animals now swiftly moved away from the two hunters, but one calf came right up to the last hide and was hit by an arrow. What a day! Three animals on a single trip. What joy it would be down by the fjord when they returned fully loaded from the mountain. The twins would be lavished with praise, and the father visibly proud. He took them over to the calf, gave the girl one of his knives, and showed her where to cut. Their knives had become progressively better over the years; not larger, quite the opposite, but more delicately crafted and, most importantly, sharper. The blade sliced through the buckskin; the father showed her how to hold the hand on the inside so that the knife didn't pierce the stomach. After the stomach was emptied, she handed the knife over to her brother. Under expert guidance, the rest of the butchering was done. The other two archers finished the other animals, and the burdens were loaded onto the wooden frames they had brought.

Excited by the good catch, they hurried home despite the heavy loads. Early in the afternoon, they approached the final descent and would soon see their dwelling down by the fjord. Then suddenly, the ground beneath them trembled, just for a short while, then everything returned to normal. They all felt a profound unease. None of them had experienced this before. Was the mountain displeased that they had taken so heavily from its resources? They continued their descent and could now see the small houses below. But what was happening down there? Everyone seemed to be on their feet. The twins saw their mother and younger brother far out on the beach. They were accompanied by the rest of the group. They seemed to be gathering things from the shore. And it was an unusually low tide. There was almost no water in the bay below the houses. What on earth had happened? Where had the water gone?

Then a strong wind hit them, coming in from the fjord. That was when they saw it. A wall of water. They couldn't utter a word; they just stood there gaping. The sight was completely unreal. The wall of water increased in height and rushed inland toward the group still out on the shore. They shouted, but in vain. Before the people could make it to higher ground, the water was upon them. People, houses, and boats disappeared into the immense waters. Trees were uprooted by the tremendous forces; everything was mashed together. The sound was deafening. They saw the wall of water continuing at great speed further into the fjord, leaving behind a lifeless, unrecognisable landscape. They had survived the tsunami but lost everything.

Today we know that the large tsunami was caused by a significant part of the continental shelf collapsing approximately 8,150 years ago. The Storegga Slide is considered one of the world's largest underwater landslides. Along a 290-kilometre-long front off the coast of Møre, 100 kilometres from shore, up to 500-metre-thick sediment masses left by the glaciers slid many hundreds of kilometres down the continental shelf. The first slide, for there were to come two more, involved over 3,000 km³ of mass. The Storegga Slide immediately affected both the position of the Earth's axis and increased its rotation, leading to minor changes in day length (we are talking about microseconds) and the tilt of the Earth. Shortly after the slide occurred, the water level dropped by about ten metres before an equally high wall of water moved towards the coast. The wall of water is estimated to have been nearly 50 metres high inside the fjord areas. People who lived or had their camps in these areas had no chance of survival.

The tsunami also affected people outside Norway. Hunter-gatherers both in Doggerland, England and Scotland felt the power of the water. In Scotland, the tsunami is estimated to have been 20 metres high. Although the physical traces of the catastrophe are clear in many countries, archaeologists have not been able to come up with accurate calculations of how the catastrophe affected the population. But it is highly likely that it caused a significant decline in the number of hunters in the north-western parts of Europe. The extent of the population affected by the catastrophe also depends on the time of year the tsunami struck. From a lake in Bjugn in Trøndelag a layer of soil deposited by the tsunami contains large amounts of small pollock bones. Pollock hatch between January and April, and the findings suggest that the fish were six to ten months old when they died. If so, the catastrophe happened in the autumn. The survivors would then have had little opportunity to build up new stores of food before winter set in. It was probably a greatly reduced population that would continue its colonisation of the country.

THE SETTLERS

There is undoubtedly something mysterious about Sumtangen jutting out into the Finsberg lake beneath the Hardangerjøkulen glacier at the northernmost tip of the Hardangervidda plateau. The glacier, with its ice cap, dominates this landscape, and the rounded ice cap is a sharp contrast to the jagged peaks of Helvetshorgi. Both are clearly visible from the remnants of the three stone huts located on the south side of the promontory, giving the place an aura of ancient history. While the ruins may not be particularly impressive, with walls partly or completely collapsed and what was once a roof now just a lost memory, remnants of bones and bits of reindeer antlers still defiantly protrude from the earth where refuse heaps once were.

The bone mounds surrounding the huts were known in local folklore in Hardanger through tales of ancient large-scale hunting of swimming reindeer. But it was not until a day in late summer in 1838 when two men from Eidfjord docked in Bergen with a Hardanger jekt* that Sumtangen would become known to the science of the time. The two men had a pile of old reindeer bones in their cargo and planned to sell the bones as fertilizer to earn some much-needed cash. The use of bone meal as fertilizer was not a new idea. Both European and American bison had been used for this purpose before, and there are striking images from both Poland and the USA of enormous bone heaps used for that purpose. The cargo carried by the two men from Eidfjord was by no means as extensive as the heaps of bison bones in Poland and the USA, but the effort Ole Medhus and his companion had put into getting the bone heap down from the mountain to Bergen was undoubtedly significant. Whether they were paid for their efforts is not known, but what we do know, and what we will soon see, is that the discovery of the bone remains in the high mountains would spark a discussion about who had left these large quantities of reindeer bones, thus contributing to the debate about who Norway's indigenous people are.

---

* A traditional cargo vessel

After the devastation wrought by the Storegga Slide on people along the coast, a sparse population would now inhabit the land. The knowledge and stories that can now be associated with Sumtangen and the surrounding mountain areas are in many ways representative of how mountainous regions, not only in southern Norway but throughout the country, will be utilised over the next millennia.

Throughout this long period, fragments of history exist in the form of flint flakes, hearthstones, and occasionally arrowheads and tools. In some places, remnants of the hunter-gatherers' dwellings and stone circles indicating where tents once stood have also been found. Ideally, they were located on plains near a mountain lake, by rivers, or on shorelines where the path to the sea and ocean was short. Hunters armed with bow and arrow construct thousands of shooting positions – bågåstø – in the mountain areas, and, at the traditional crossing points of rivers and lakes, leading fences are built to gather the reindeer towards waiting hunters. At Sumtangen, cairns are erected in strategic locations, and these almost human-sized stone constructions also help guide the reindeer towards the hunters. Thus, the people of Western Norway follow, as we shall see later, the same hunting tactics as the Dene people and the Nenets and other indigenous peoples in North America and Russia. Many of the hunting sites testify to continuous use over millennia. The oldest traces of hunting therefore often lie beneath newer and thicker layers of culture, as at Sumtangen, where the oldest traces of Stone Age people lie beneath thick layers of bones and antler remains from both the Roman and medieval periods.

Over 7,000 years ago, the climate was significantly warmer than it is today. The average temperature was 1.5 – 2 degrees Celsius higher than today, and the tree-line was 200 – 300 metres higher than now. Most of the glaciers we have today were completely melted during much of the early Stone Age. Where the Briksdalsbreen glacier now spreads out, there was birch forest. On the Hardangervidda plateau and the Dovrefjell plateau, the pine forest had roots up to 1,200 metres above sea level when the climate was warmest. Later, during the younger Stone Age, the climate was slightly colder, and the tree-line was then about 1,000 metres above sea level. Therefore, the hunters who resided along the major watercourses on the Hardangervidda in the early Stone Age saw a different landscape than what we see today, and the lower parts of the mountain areas were then large forested areas with pine where lichen was the dominant ground vegetation, much like what we see in Østerdalen today. The reindeer herds were large, and they found grazing opportunities in large contiguous areas. And if the grazing conditions were not good enough, the reindeer had no barriers preventing them from doing what they do best – roaming.

It would still be a long way off before these hunters became farmers. From the first settlers setting foot on Norwegian soil until it becomes common to cultivate this land, nearly 8,000 years pass. For 8,000 years, all resources had to be harvested from the nature they were surrounded by, and on smooth stone surfaces all over the country we can still see what the settlers were occupied with. On rocky outcrops now lying tens of metres above today's sea level, stone carvings of halibut and small whales were made. At the now-submerged Dokkfløyvatnet in the Gausdal Vestfjell mountains, what is still a Stone Age people engraved moose cows and calves on their journey down to the summer pastures by Lake Mjøsa, and at Snåsavatnet, which was then part of the Trondheimsfjorden, a reindeer hunter and artist about 5,500 years ago made one of Norway's finest and most famous rock carvings – the Bøla reindeer.

Reindeer hunters in Alta in the north are no less remarkable. At the head of the Altafjord, activity had been high. Assuming that the rock carvings were made on rocky outcrops on the shoreline, on the rock surfaces now located from 17 to 26 metres above today's sea level, hundreds of reindeer figures were carved at 7 different locations between 5,000 and 7,000 years ago. And some of the reindeer are surrounded by fences shaped like gathering enclosures similar to those used by modern-day reindeer herders! This shows that even so far back in time, there were larger groups of hunters who cooperated in a well-organised reindeer hunt.

Soon, thousands of hunting pits also emerged – earth-dug pits for elk in forested areas, stone-walled ones for reindeer in the high mountains. As early as 5,000–6,000 years ago, animal pits were established along the Alta and Kautokeino rivers in Finnmark. A little later, the same happened in Grimsdalen on Dovre. The settlers left cultural traces that would later surprise archaeologists. The perception among archaeologists who examined the cultural traces in Dovrefjell was that the hunting pits in this area mostly dated from the Viking Age and the Middle Ages. But the C14 analyses from the animal pits at Bjørnsgardsætre on Dovre would show that the animal pits here were already in use in the transition between the younger Stone Age and the early Bronze Age almost 4,000 years ago. The new hunting techniques with animal pits would be further developed in the next centuries and have significant consequences for both farming communities, hunter-gatherers and reindeer.

THE COUNTRY BECOMES MULTICULTURAL

Around the same time that the first hunter-gatherer groups arrived in Norway, people began experimenting with grain cultivation in the Middle East. However, it would be many thousands of years before animal husbandry and agriculture became known in Norway. When it finally happened, and the first animal husbandry and farming appeared around the Oslo Fjord and on the southern coast, there was very little resemblance to what we today associate with farming. It is only towards the end of the younger Stone Age, nearly 4,000 years ago, that agriculture began to spread, and it wasn't until about 2,500 years ago, at the beginning of the Iron Age, that farming became common in areas other than along the productive coastal strip.

It is somewhat of an oversimplification to claim that the country first became multicultural when farmers arrived. The first inhabitants of the land were already a mixture of southern and eastern migrating reindeer hunters. But in the centuries and millennia that followed, a number of new cultures would move northward towards Scandinavia. What they had in common was that they were farmers – and often warlike!

Before geneticists gained access to their powerful methods, one could only speculate whether it was only agricultural culture spreading, with hunter-gatherers copying those who had adopted a new way of using the land, or if it was a new people who actually found their way northward. Now we know the answer. It was the farmers themselves who came. Genetic studies show that many from the ancient hunter-gatherers, especially women, assimilated into societies with a way of life characterised by agriculture, while there are few, if any, farmers leaving genetic traces in the predominantly hunting society. Some geneticists have thus drawn the hasty conclusion that a few hunters became farmers during this period, while the farmers who came to Scandinavia remained farmers. However, researchers have now delved into the ceramic pots of the farmers and examined the remnants of the food stored there. What the analyses of the pots show is that the diet of farmers and hunters was not so different. This now suggests that farmers quickly learned to hunt, fish and gather resources in the areas they entered, which provided great resilience to climatic conditions affecting agricultural production.

Recent genetic studies of remains from those who entered Scandinavia reveal a number of exciting stories, where warlike farmers and hunters often stand opposed. The complete picture of the various cultures' activities and behaviours is not yet in place, but we can expect more knowledge in the near future. What we can establish is that the development of agriculture and animal husbandry eventually led to significant population growth, both on the continent and later in Scandinavia, which over time brought about major societal changes. Norway became a patchwork of different cultures, where newly arrived farmers and their cultures lived side by side with the older hunting cultures, because there turns out to be more than one hunting culture.

Parts of the country were now moving out of the Stone Age. Bronze had gained entry, especially in the southern parts of the country. The Bronze Age is considered by many to be the beginning of globalisation, where trade systems were established, and changes in climatic conditions and 'culture collisions' between different ethnic groups led to large population movements. Together, this also results in more mixing of genetic material between different cultures. The European population became more homogeneous. In Norway, during the 1,200-year period leading up to the Roman Iron Age, 500 years before our time, a trading system was established that ensured copper and tin found their way into the country. Several archaeologists are now suggesting that we almost had a Viking Age 2,000 years before the Viking Age! Nine out of ten rock carvings from the Bronze Age depict boats with crews, and in Østfold, Northern Europe's largest rock carving of a boat has been found. The 4-meter-long rock image, called the Bjørnstad ship, shows a ship that could probably carry at least 50 men. It is carved so clearly that one can almost hear the crew's rhythmic paddling and the helmsman's command.

Perhaps ships of this type were used on trips down to the Mediterranean to fetch copper, and, on the way back, they stopped by England to pick up tin. Even though only about 800 bronze objects have been found in Norway from the 1,200-year Bronze Age, isotopic analysis has revealed that much of the copper comes from Italy. It is just as likely that there was a maritime-oriented population in the north capable of bringing back amber from the Baltic Sea area and ivory in the form of teeth from walruses and toothed whales to the Mediterranean, as it is that southern Europeans themselves would make the journey north to fetch material for jewellery production.

We can assume that teeth from walruses and toothed whales mainly come from northern parts of Norway. It is therefore not surprising that while trade networks were established between many European countries, contact between different regions of Norway also seem to have been increasing. Rock carvings of ships from Alta resembling the Bjørnstad ship show that the networks extended along the entire coast up to Finnmark. Some even argue that it will give us a new view of society at this time if we see the history from the north and south in Europe. Because there is no doubt that the mixture of reindeer hunters from the south and east, who first met along the coasts of Northern Norway, left their genetic traces downwards into Europe. Long trading journeys often do.

In Finnmark, trade networks were developed at the same time that went eastward and into present-day Russia, and it is traders in Finnmark who would bring the first signs of a completely new era.

IRON CREATES
'KLONDIKE ATMOSPHERE'

About 2,500 years ago, a group of people arrived in Varangerbotn in Finnmark. Whether they were on a journey or had just returned from a trip to trading posts far to the east is uncertain. They probably had reindeer carrying packs, or, alternatively, they may have driven reindeer with sleds and had skis with them. It is easiest to imagine that it was winter and they came on skis with reindeer pulling sleds. The people of the North, whether in Europe or America, have mostly used winter to their advantage when embarking on long journeys. What we know is that someone who was, or who had been on such a trading journey, brought something entirely new to Finnmark at this time. The items were not large and grandiose; in fact, the small curved knives were quite inconspicuous compared to far older bronze artifacts, but they represented something completely new. They were made of iron.

Somewhat later, traders who paddled across the Skagerrak also brought back goods made of iron. Far more importantly, they eventually brought with them the knowledge of how iron could be made from bog iron ore. At this time, Celtic tribes dominated in Europe. They had already mastered the technique of iron-making 3,000 years ago, and it is likely that knowledge of iron extraction came from the Celts. The significant, or nearly enormous difference between bronze and iron was that iron could be extracted from local resources. This was in contrast to bronze, which required access to copper and tin, often sourced from South Tyrol in Italy and England.

The oldest known iron production in Norway is about 2,400 years old and is documented, among other places, in Fet in Hardanger (which is located a few kilometres from the hunting ground at Sumtangen) and in Trøndelag. But if we go about 500 years forward in time, drastic changes occurred. The Romans dominated in Europe, iron had become common in tools, and was produced on a large scale in central and south-east Norway. Marshes were dug into, and forests cut down on a scale never seen before. In fact, we have to go all the way to the 1900s before iron production reaches the same level in this country again. We have arrived at the Roman Iron Age.

Surprisingly, iron production was mostly limited to southern Norway. Although traces of iron extraction are also found in Troms and Finnmark, much of the iron used there was likely imported to the region. Thus, it was not only southward toward the Roman Empire that the people of Trøndelag sent their iron; there were trade routes going northward as well, and iron was exchanged for other goods that were in demand in the south.

The extent of iron production was large. In Trøndelag alone, more than 680 iron production sites are known, and there is good reason to believe that there were far more than those mapped today. Some of the best-studied areas are in Meråker municipality. In this municipality alone, 40 such facilities have been found, and archaeologists estimate that during the Roman Iron Age, something like 1,750–3,000 tons of iron were produced in Meråker. Knowing that one ton was enough to make about 2,000 axes, and with a total of 680 facilities in Trøndelag, it is clear that the total production was much greater than the local demand. However, it was probably not ordinary people who were behind iron production. It was more likely that a few had the knowledge needed, and that these few also had the resources and opportunities to organise such work.

During the same period, archaeologists have found status items in the form of jewellery, weapons, glassware and clothing imported from Central Europe and the Roman Empire. Many of the hill forts were also built at this time. Archaeologists who have worked on this period therefore believe that iron production and trade with the Roman Empire were important elements in the development towards a much more stratified society, where trade networks between various chieftains laid the foundation for economy and power structure. Iron was likely one of the goods traded, but fur, ivory from whales and walruses, ropes made of walrus and seal, whale oil, skins and antlers from reindeer, and slate sharpeners were some of the goods that were suitable for and used for export.

Iron production was undoubtedly a very demanding process that required many people before bog ore was turned into workable iron. The facilities were located in places where it was easy to find bog ore and where there was enough forest to provide the large quantities of charcoal the ironworks required. The large workforce required to do the work needed to be fed. In many of the areas with extensive iron production, there was therefore a short distance to areas where it was possible to engage in mass reindeer hunting.

There are many known areas like this, stretching from the Setesdal mountains in the south-west, Eidfjord in Hardanger, Aurland and Vik in Sogn, to Trøndelag. Bergljiot Solberg points out in her reference work on the Iron Age in Norway that these power centres likely had one foot in the village and at least one in the wilderness, and that hunting was an important basis for iron production, trade, and the structure of society in the Roman Iron Age.

At the beginning of the 400s, the Western Roman Empire collapsed. In 541–542, a major wave of plagues broke out that ravaged Europe several times. This period was one of great changes and migrations in Europe. In Norway, defensive works were established around small rural communities, and we get descriptions that 'heiner' (Hedmark), 'raumer' (Romerike), and 'ryger' (Ryfylke, Rogaland) were considered separate ethnic groups. Norway entered a period of decline. Luxury items were no longer placed in graves, the long boathouses along the coast fell into disrepair, the smoke from the ironworks disappeared, and the knowledge of extracting iron in this way disappeared. Mass reindeer hunting at Sumtangen came to an end, and the hunting cabin there was left to decay. The centuries around the beginning of our era brought about significant changes, even for a hunter-gatherer people who had settlements inland and northwards in Norway.

THE REINDEER PEOPLE
WHO BECAME SAMI

Christian Magnus Falsen, grandson of the 'Father of the Constitution', wrote a book in 1830 where he claimed that the Finns (meaning the Sami) were the indigenous people of Norway. He easily convinced the assemblyman Wilhelm Frimann Koren Christie, who had heard of 'Piles or Mounds of Reindeer Bones and Horns" on the Hardangervidda plateau, resembling similar findings in Finnmark.

This was not something A.W. Brøgger, the leader of the Antiquities Collection in Oslo, wanted to hear about, described by his friend Francis Bull as a man with "temperament and suddenly changing moods." In Norway, one Norwegian identity had emerged, created by the unique nature and conditions it provided, he believed. Norwegian identity and livelihood had hardly changed since the Stone Age, and cultural continuity was rooted in "the country's own nature," he argued. The fact that Norwegian farmers had engaged in both agriculture and hunting, thus being self-sufficient, versatile, and innovative, became part of the nation's history back to the heyday of the Viking Age and the Middle Ages. Excavations at Sumtangen and other locations on the Hardangervidda plateau would later confirm the presence of a hunting culture there over periods of many thousands of years but also confirm the Norse origin of the hunting cabins and the large bone heaps at Sumtangen.

Almost to support a view that implied a Norse continuity all the way back to the first hunting people, Norway established its own Lapp (meaning Sami) Commission, which was to show once and for all that the Sami's affiliation with Southern Norway was of recent origin. They hired the ethnographer Yngvar Nilsen to lead the work, and it did not fit the ethnographer's theory that the term "Finns" was already used in the first and second centuries by the Roman official and historian Tacitus (fenni) and the Greek geographer Ptolemy (fennoi) when describing a veict people in the north with a lifestyle that contrasted with farmers. Another written source is found in the work "Historia Norvegiæ," also a Latin document probably written in the second half of the 12th century. Here, among other things, the division of Norway into various counties and the natural geographical conditions of the country are described. We are told about three land areas or belts where people can live. The largest is the coastal belt, followed by the inland areas, while the third area is described as being full of forests where "the Finns live without plowing the earth."'.

Written source material is usually modest among people with origins in a nomadic hunting culture, making archaeological finds very important. Unfortunately, many archaeologists have been so frightened by how archaeological finds were abused by Nazi Germany in the lead-up to World War II that they have argued that one should avoid linking archaeological finds to ethnic groups and rather present prehistory detached from the current situation. This has probably greatly contributed to the poor knowledge and understanding of the prehistoric relationship between the 'Norse' and Sami cultures. It was not until the 1980s that Norwegian archaeologists made Sami prehistory a separate field of study.

Claiming that the hunting people we now refer to as Sami had a presence in large parts of Southern Norway more than 3,000 years ago would have been seen as an attack on the very history of Norway and the 'proto-Norwegian', which had been created throughout much of the 19th and 20th centuries. It was not much better on the other side of the border. Archaeologists who showed that there had been activity by a hunting people in the central parts of Sweden for several thousand years were outright silenced. The Sami are still often presented as a people without history. While the Sami are represented and portrayed as an 'ethnographic people' with little development and historical depth, other Norwegians are described as having a continuous developmental history from the Stone Age to the present day.

Now we know better. And it's an exciting story unfolding. While much of Sami culture both north and south in Norway today is inextricably linked to reindeer, in Southern Norway, the moose was the most important animal for long periods. And they didn't just hunt moose.

THE BEER-BREWING SAMI TAKE TO THE MOUNTAINS

Increasingly, archaeological evidence points towards the presence of a people engaging in wild game hunting in large parts of Southern Norway and into the central parts of Sweden. Scattered throughout the vast forest and mountain areas stretching from Østerdalen in Norway into the middle regions of Sweden, archaeologists have uncovered what many now refer to as game trap graves. In many cases, the buried individuals are laid to rest alongside large quantities of moose antlers. This distinctive burial custom cannot be linked to the Norse farming society. These are traces of a hunting people who, over long periods, have exploited the resources found in the wilderness. While it is uncontroversial to argue that there is a continuity in history from the first farmers who began cultivating the land in these areas between the Early and Late Iron Age about 1,500 years ago until today's society, many find it much harder to accept that there is a corresponding continuity in history from the hunting people who hunted moose in these areas to those who today engage in reindeer husbandry. But there is little room for doubt. The people who already in the Bronze Age over 3,000 years ago had moose hunting pits near Lake Femunden are the same ones described in written sources from the 17th century as Sami in the same areas. But now, reindeer is the most important animal.

The pattern seems to be the same in large parts of Østerdalen. Immigrating farmers took over increasingly larger areas in the lower-lying, most productive forest areas during the Migration Period about 1,600 years ago. There was simply not enough space for both a hunting culture and an agricultural culture in the same areas. At Rødsmoen, a few kilometres north of Rena, the hunters were engaged in both moose hunting and barley cultivation. The barley was used in brewing beer, claims archaeologist Jostein Bergstøl, one of those who has contributed new knowledge about the activities that took place in parts of Southern Norway during the Bronze Age and Iron Age. Through many centuries, there was probably good contact between the agriculture-oriented population and the hunters in these areas. Moose meat may have been exchanged for iron, and the beer brewed by the hunters from the barley may have been given as a gift or served when the trade was settled.

At the same time as moose hunting gradually ceased, archaeologists see many signs that the hunting people took to the mountains. The number of arrowheads in the high mountains increased towards the Viking Age, a large number of bow stands were built, and the pitfall traps were found higher up in the mountains than before. The first stone-built reindeer pitfall trap also appeared. Previously, it was believed that the geographical division between excavated moose graves in the forest and stone-built reindeer traps in the mountains represented a division between Norse and Sami cultural affiliation, but there are at least two different reasons why this is not the case. It was not only the hunting people who later became known as Sami and who demonstrably had settlements in south-eastern areas who hunted moose in the forested areas. The same applies to the mixture of the two hunting peoples who first entered the country. And similar to the hunting people in the eastern part of the country, many of these responded to the influx of a belligerent agricultural people by increasing their use of mountain areas.

Soon, traces of mass trapping systems for reindeer originally found in high mountain areas have been found over virtually the entire country. South-east in the country such facilities have been found in Alvdal, Rendalen, and Engerdalen. Common to these facilities is that fences made of stone or wooden logs were constructed, narrowing down into a funnel shape, and they were often placed in such a way in the terrain that the animals would not see the actual trapping enclosure or gathering area until they had been caught. In Engerdal, where the largest trapping system is located, there are also several bow stands and many meat caches for storing the slaughtered animals. The construction, maintenance, and, not least, operation of such facilities would have required cooperation among a larger group of hunting people. It is likely there was an organisation similar to what we see today with Sami siidas, where two or more families collaborate in the operation of reindeer herding. Although the dating of such facilities is problematic, the few dates that have been made suggest that the facilities were in operation in the Viking Age over 1,000 years ago, probably even earlier.

Other archaeological finds in Østerdalen support the assumption of close mutual cooperation between the Norse and Sami settlements. Often, there is a mixture of Sami and Norse objects in the same area. Norse relief buckles from the Migration Period have been found together with bronze jewellery associated with Sami religious practices. Moreover, in Rendalen, one of the strongest Sami symbol markers, a runic drum hammer, was found with both Sami and Norse decoration.

In the northernmost parts of the country, there were also hunting groups entirely dependent on reindeer.

WILD REINDEER HUNTING
IN VÁRJJAT

In Finnmark, Ceavccageađge, Mortensnes, has been a gathering place for hunters, fishermen and traders for over 10,000 years. Perhaps it was here that the pioneers met – both those who came by sea from the south and those who came from the east via Finland and Russia. Few places in the Nordic region have yielded more archaeological finds within such a limited area. The traces of the first tent sites are still visible, as are the stone tools and weapons they used. Later, traces of large peat houses testify that some may have resided here year-round. Over time, the area would be dominated by those who made reindeer hunting a vital livelihood. Three thousand years ago, the Sami began burying their dead in rock crevices at Mortensnes, often wrapped in bark and placed in a sled. Archaeologists would eventually find nearly 300 such graves. Some reindeer were also given a decent burial. For reindeer would soon become the focus in the mountainous areas on both sides of the Varangerfjord.

In these same mountain areas, 25 different trapping systems, three trapping facilities with bow stands and guiding fences, as well as a large net-like mass trapping system, vuopman facilities, for reindeer in Noaidečearru – Kjøpmannskjølen, have now been found. In total, more than 3,300 earth-buried trapping pits have been found. All pits were dug into the ground, the trapping enclosure itself was framed with wooden logs, and it is likely that split logs were placed diagonally from this enclosure and up towards the mound. Thus, the captured animals did not get a foothold for their hooves in their struggle to get out of the pit. Pointed wooden poles or wooden poles with iron tips at the top were set up from the bottom of the pit in some cases, if we are to believe the writings of Utsjok priest Jacob Fellmann, but it was probably more common to keep the animal undamaged until slaughter.

A formidable amount of work was put into this. In total, more than 20,000 cubic metres of material were removed to create the pits. Just to make the wooden frames in the pits, logs with a total length of over 50 kilometres must have been used, and even more timber would have been needed for the cladding of the split logs. In an area lacking large trees, this must have required a lot of work. The trapping systems were, of course, developed over time. The oldest are estimated to be over 3,000 years old. Dating of wood material in similar systems in Karasjok and Kautokeino shows that some of the pits were used between 5,000 to 3,000 years ago.

During the Stone Age, neither these trapping systems nor the hunters were probably large enough to make significant inroads into the area's reindeer population. That would soon change. For although the hunting people residing in Varanger had access to rich fishing resources along the coast, likely also walrus and other marine mammals in early times, it was the reindeer that were the backbone of the economy. The trapping systems were gradually expanded and improved, and the settlements often found in connection with the trapping facilities grew in size. Excavations at some of these sites reveal enormous amounts of bone material. The same is found in settlements right down by the coastal strip, but there are only bones from the meat-rich parts of the reindeer. Obviously, thighs, back, and shoulder would have been transported from the trapping settlement down to a more permanent settlement near the coast.

Similar trapping systems were established throughout the entire North Calotte. Age determinations of some of the hundreds of trapping systems on the Swedish side show that they were in use for over 3,000 years, lasting well into the 13th century. The trapping intensity is high and likely led to a reduced reindeer population. Possibly, the reduced reindeer catches prompted the coastal Sami in Varanger to start keeping both small and large livestock as early as the 12th–13th century, albeit to a modest extent.

WIDE DISTRIBUTION OF
SAMI PRODUCTS

In the north, on both sides of the Kjølen mountain range, Sami products were in high demand and literally highly valued. In Northern Norway, the Sami people were strongly integrated with the local chieftaincies through extensive trading activities. Trade and, most importantly, taxation of the Sami contributed to building up a wealthy upper class. The Sami were specialised hunters and gatherers, and their products were seen as exotic and highly sought after by the European elite. Fur, walrus tusks and hunting falcons thus found their way southward onto the European continent. In many ways, it can be said that the Norse chieftains became dependent on Sami hunting communities. The chieftains' fully laden boats with Sami hunting products ensured access to foreign luxury goods necessary to maintain their own social status, while the Sami received iron, grain and imported goods in return. Thanks to the English royal house, we have written sources confirming this.

At the end of the 9th century, Ottar, a local king from Hålogaland, visited King Alfred in England. At the same time, Alfred had knowledgeable individuals translate Paulus Orosius' classic historical work from Latin into Old English. Whether Orosius was born in Portugal or brought there from England is debated among scholars, but there is little doubt that he was a well-travelled man in the 5th century. Unfortunately, Orosius had little to say about the areas north of the Alps. This is where Ottar sailed in from Norvegr, contributing to an increase in knowledge about the northern regions, the people, and their customs, which warranted space in King Alfred's new literary work.

Ottar's travel descriptions about meeting the Bjarmians, a hunting people at the head of the White Sea, his journey into the Oslo Fjord to Skiringssal a little north-east of present-day Larvik, and further down to Hedeby in Denmark (now Germany), the largest city of the Viking Age, are interesting in themselves, but it is his descriptions of alliances with the Sami that pique our interest.

Ottar could tell King Alfred that he was considered a very wealthy man. Not only did he have hundreds of unsold reindeer at that time, six of these were actually decoy reindeer. These were very valuable animals because they could be used to lure wild reindeer. Alfred was far less impressed that Ottar had only 20 cows, 20 sheep, and 20 pigs.

Ottar's wealth was evidently mostly based on the tribute paid to him by the Sami. According to the account, it is stated that 'this tribute consists of animal hides, bird feathers, whale bones, and ship cables made of whale hide and seal hide. Everyone pays according to their status. The noblest must pay fifteen marten skins and five reindeer skins and a bear skin and ten ambars of feathers and a bear- or otter-skin coat and two ship cables; each of these must be sixty ells (approximately 30 metres) long; one must be made of whale hide (most likely walrus hide), the other of seal hide.'

This type of trade and exchange of products between Norse and Sami settlements continued for nearly 400 years. However, for Ottar and the other petty chieftains along the coast, their power and opportunities for trade with the Sami communities diminished in the 11th century when the Norwegian kingdom gained more power and wanted to handle this type of trade themselves.

On the Swedish side of the Kjølen mountain range, trade followed similar paths. At several Sami sacred sites from the 9th century and four centuries onwards, excavations reveal coins from Germany, Denmark, Norway, England, and even from the Caliphate – the Islamic empire that lasted from the death of the Prophet Muhammad in 632 until the Mongols razed Baghdad in 1258. Such extensive trading activity is not possible without a well-organised chain of intermediaries. And there were several of them. In the Bay of Bothnia, Kvens engage in agriculture and fishing, while also trading with and taxing the Sami on the Swedish side. According to Snorri's version of the saga of Egil Skallagrimsson, one of the Kvens' chieftains, Faravid, is described as having the same status and position as the local petty chieftains on the Norwegian coast.

Over the next hundred years, significant changes would occur, not in the form of glaciers and climate change, but in the form of societal changes. The petty kingdoms eventually coalesced into realms, and a new religion gained a firm grip on people's lives. Norway became a Catholic kingdom where the riches from the hinterlands supported a king's power. Strong entrepreneurs drove development forward, large-scale iron production resumed, and the reindeer catch reached levels best described as industrial.

PART VI

Norway 800 – 100 years ago.
At the beginning of the Middle Ages, activity in the mountain areas was intense. The extraction of iron and the hunting of reindeer became major industries, in which both kings and the clergy played active roles. Even after the ravages of the Black Death had passed, there was still a strong demand for the mountains' resources, and in both the north and south of the country, reindeer hunting was gradually replaced by nomadic reindeer herding. The struggle for access to the outfield resources grew fiercer.

WELCOME TO THE
MIDDLE AGES!

Once again, there was great activity at the trapping facilities, in fact, greater than ever, and reindeer trapping had become part of the legislation. The Norwegian realm was at its most powerful, and the country had long been Christianised. People were generously giving away properties as indulgence gifts to shorten their time in purgatory. Among the wealthiest of the population, it became common to pay the church to commemorate their anniversary, i.e., death day, by placing coffins in front of the altar, burning candles, reciting special prayers for the occasion, and giving gifts to the poor. The church willingly took on such tasks with promises that the nobility's death days would be commemorated for eternity. The payment was land properties, and the church eventually owned more than half of the land area. Whether people were sinners of such magnitude, and whether such generosity was necessary, is uncertain, but the threat of a troublesome time in the afterlife was significant, for sure. But what was this time like, and who were these people who drove the development and contributed to trade and royal power? Not much written information exists, but some things and some people from this time have survived in folklore and legends. One of these is Ragna; according to legend, she lived in Eidfjord and was especially wealthy in land and gold. Much of the wealth comes from iron production and the trapping facilities for reindeer in the high mountains.

Ragna and Dag
Eidfjord in Hardanger, year 1308.

A gray and black-clad woman sat on a rock, observing a work team laying the first stone ring in a wall that would become a new church. There wasn't much to see yet, but already everyone knew it would be a large building. The woman overseeing the construction was Ragna. She often visited, not every day, but more often than the weather would suggest. She was getting older, and her once straight neck was now more bent. Both age and the worries that had weighed on her in recent years were probably to blame. But her gaze could still stop the most rugged man in his tracks. Her nose had also become a bit more crooked over the years, but it was still as long and pointed as ever, at least according to the villagers. She had always been determined and sharp-tongued. Many were afraid of her, the strong-willed woman who walked her own path and seemed to care little for customs and gossip. No, talking wasn't her thing.

◆

Early in life, she grew tired of talk, realising it seldom led to anything, at least not what she wanted. It was better to be straightforward. Her father was a talker, a chatterbox she often thought. His earthly possessions were a patch of land at the end of a fjord surrounded by steep mountains. It wasn't much, but enough to support a family if one was willing. The ironworks on the mountain had potential. He ran it for many years, but there was always something: people who preferred shorter days, people who complained about the food and not getting enough meat and travellers. Running the ironworks was hard work; trees had to be cut, wood dried, bog iron collected and transported. Furnaces had to be built, first for roasting, later for extracting iron. Then the slag had to be pounded out, the iron forged into bars and transported down to the valley. It was heavy work that required many people and a lot of food. They obtained meat from the mountains; there was little or nothing to be had in the village. Reindeer trapping was also sometimes a misery. The reindeer didn't always come, the trappers weren't efficient enough, and there were disputes over profits and sharing of animals. Her father managed somehow, but it wasn't profitable.

She married late in life, to a man from a farm further out in the fjord. A fjord man. Her parents had proposed the match. He came from good stock, and her father got along well with him. At first, it went reasonably well, but the new man on the farm struggled to find his place. And it wasn't easy. Ragna's father did his own thing in his own way, and Ragna controlled everything else. She probably hadn't quite seen the point of marriage; what was she supposed to use a man for? There were labourers if needed, and they did as she asked; a man who tried to voice his own opinions was a heavier burden for her. It went on like that until the day her father, Åsolv, was no more. Her husband, Tyr, couldn't handle the work at all. He was too weak, lacked the will, and even less energy, and he had little opportunity for long trips to the mountains to deal with the labourers. Thus, he lost the respect of those who worked on the mountain, and Ragna eventually began to think of him as useless on the farm. But to be fair, Ragna could have done more to give him the space he needed.

Ragna got up from her rock and gazed towards the fjord – the weather and light were changing. The clouds had parted, allowing slanting rays to fan out across the fjord, lighting up a stripe across it. It was beautiful – the water, hills, ridges and cliffs bathed in hazy light, gaining colour and dimension for a while. It was as if God were in a particularly good mood, taking time to play with His creation, yes, as if He really wanted to showcase what He had created, or perhaps He just wants to remind people that He exists and that there will come a day when earthly life will end for everyone, big or small. It was a serious reminder to receive. Yes, Ragna knew she would have much to answer for when that day comes. She had been warned about what awaits someone like her; there will be punishment in purgatory! The alternative was a pilgrimage to Santiago de Compostela in Spain or something else equally suitable as penance and indulgence. She had heard of Spain, but she had never been farther than Bergen and had no plans to go further. So, it had to be something else, something that really mattered; accusations of murder were no joke, especially when it concerned her own husband. She had thought and speculated for a long time and eventually reached an agreement with herself, and hopefully also with God, that a new church was what was needed to keep purgatory at bay. The old church they had was falling apart, and there was probably still much wickedness from ancient times in those walls. It was decided she would arrange for a new church, and it had to be a grand building with thick walls. One end wall should be more than two metres thick, and finely hewn slate stone edges should be fitted around the windows, gray sills against whitewashed walls. She had finally acquiesced to these thoughts. For a long time, she had resisted and thought that what happened back then was almost justified. But with age came other thoughts and a changed view of life.

It was on a trading trip to Bergen when it had happened. They had gone with a shipment of skins, antlers, and a decent amount of iron bars that had come down from the mountain. Things had improved since she had put the lad, Dag, in charge of the work up there. Dag was a younger man, tall and big, but quick on his feet, soft and strong from a life in the mountains. He had hunted and trapped since he was a boy, first with his father, later alone. Ragna had taken notice of him early on and had taken him under her wing. It was strange how she could bend herself for a man when needed, and with Dag it was exactly like that. So he had started helping on the mountain. First with reindeer trapping, later with the ironworks as well. He took the lead in all the work and had such an effect on the labourers that they followed him in their work. Gradually, there was more activity up there, and the loads that came down to the village were bigger and more frequent. The incompetence she was married to was overshadowed by Dag; so much so that her husband was barely visible to her in the end. She could have lived with that, in a way, but everything changed on that fateful trip. Tyr had had a lot of beer in the city, and more on the way home. A good way out in the fjord, he had to relieve himself; the sea was rough, and the drunken man fell into the sea and sank like a stone. But people talk, and people talked a lot about Ragna, and thus a rumour spread that the man hadn't just fallen into the sea, but that Ragna had put him on a reef that was flooded at high tide.She was aware of many of the rumours that circulated, and the thoughts had also plagued her; could she have done more back then, been more attentive to her husband, or kept him away from the beer? Over time, she began to feel a kind of guilt for what had happened. She also knew they called her Rich-Ragna. She had never cared about wealth; her deed was more about getting things done, seizing opportunities, and with Dag she had achieved that. She, in the village and town, he in the mountains. And so the years passed. The shipments from the mountain came steadily, the boats went to Bergen, and thus they created what people called wealth on a small piece of land surrounded by steep mountains at the end of the long Hardangerfjord.

But then, almost 30 years ago, Dag was taken from her– abruptly and harshly. Together with two other men, each with their own horse and large packs, Dag was on his way towards Sima Valley and was about to begin the steep descent towards the fjord. There was still no fjord or valley to be seen, just the beginning of cliffs on the north side of the valley indicating that the rolling landscape on Hardangervidda had an abrupt end where the mountain ended in an unimaginable drop towards Sima Valley. There was only one way down: a path that led over stone slopes and slippery rocks. They had taken the usual route, up from Sima Valley, into Sumtangen along Leiro. They had stayed a few days at Sumtangen; the men there had already got some animals, but Dag had to spend two days sorting out the troublemakers.

As usual, two of the men had clashed over the division of animals, about how much each should have of skins and meat. It was the same arguing every time; one of the men, the easterner, always insisted that the one who took the animal got too little. And the man from Bergen who was supposed to take care of the skins stuck to his guns and complained and nagged constantly that the skinning was too poor. Dag had mustered some courage this time and pointed out the law that came from Bergen the previous year, and that it was now decided that the one who took the animal should have a hindquarter with the skin on it and compensation if there was no skin on the quarter, a so-called skin fine. The deal they had with Dag was that the hide, heart and liver would act as a fine for the whole skin. The man from Bergen was beside himself with anger every time the issue of taking a hindquarter with the skin on it came up – the skin had to be whole, and woe to anyone who tried something else! There was no point in bringing disfigured skins to town. It was always a hassle with that man. He kept on and on and drowned out everyone and everything; it was as if all the unrest and noise in the whole world resided in that man's head. He could barely keep quiet while Dag spoke. He had been sent here from Bergen to ensure that all skins were properly treated. Most of it was sent to Bergen for tanning, but that was Ragna's affair. He had to keep an eye on the men up here, and this outburst from the city could get on anyone's nerves. He had given them two options, either to accept the arrangement as it was or to leave, immediately. They chose to continue the work, but he had no faith that they would keep quiet about this for long. From the trapping site, the journey had continued down towards the ironworks at the bottom of Bjore Valley. The men who worked there were easier to deal with, and as long as Dag managed to gather enough meat they kept quiet. But if the gruel was less than three meals a day, the peace was shattered. Then there was constant nagging from these men too. So far, the trapping had gone smoothly, and the men at the ironworks mostly kept quiet and did what they were supposed to. Now they had skins and antlers from the bucks and the iron they fetched from the ironworks in their packs. They only had to descend into Sima Valley to complete the round for this time. Perhaps there would be one or two more trips that year before they had to finish for the season. It wasn't possible to stay up there on the mountain when winter began to take a grip; it was only when winter had truly set in that Dag had new tasks up there, and then his focus was on the ptarmigans. To begin with, he liked the big catch and that they could take so many animals at once! It was like an adventure compared to the effort he had made to get one or two animals. It was so easy up there at Sumtangen. Once the animals had entered the trap between the cairns, it was only a matter of waiting until they reached the water. The herd was easy like this, a stone cairn with a grouse wing fluttering in the wind was enough to guide the delicate animals. Once the lead animal had turned, the others followed. Down by the water, the herd sometimes became more difficult, but, most of the time, they wanted to be in the water, and then much was done. The trap they had with the cairns and later the ropes stretched across the water was effective. Once the animals had started swimming between the ropes, it was an easy matter to spear them from the boats they had. Simple, but also a terrible thing to be part of. There were animals that panicked, animals that swam and struggled with wide eyes and panicked breathing. Calves that struggled to stay close to their mothers in the chaos. But they couldn't get over the stretched ropes, and the spear bearers in the boats were merciless; they stabbed and stabbed as long as there was life. The water was teaming with dead and half-dead animals and turned red with blood and foam; occasionally, some poor creatures just waited for the spear bearers. No, it was a terrible hunt. Unlike what he had done. Then there was the slaughtering, blood and gore, the strong smell from stressed animals and dirty men. Flies in black swarms gathered on the carcasses as soon as they came ashore. The pile of offal was out of the question; there, flies and worms ravaged so the whole pile was alive and buzzing. No, Dag had completely lost his taste for reindeer trapping at Sumtangen. He shuddered at the thought. He simply didn't like to see the animals like that. It was different when it was just him and a few animals. Cleaner, fairer, the animals he killed barely knew what was happening. After the activity at the ironworks, there was never enough; no matter how many animals they took, they could have taken more. No matter how many skins and hides they carried down from the mountain, there could have been more. Ragna was good at boasting about the work up on the mountain, but there could always be more; it could go faster next time. Sometimes he thought that's precisely why she says what she does. That it's not to give recognition but more to motivate that next time there should be more, go even faster. Dag and the packers came all the way to the edge of Sima Valley, and Dag cast a last glance eastward and into the mountains. Then it was down the slope, on a narrow and rocky path and over slippery rocks. As they were about to cross the last truly wet and slippery rock, it happened. Dag's horse slipped, the shoes don't catch, and, despite all the warnings he had given all the others, Dag held the reins wrapped around his right hand. He registered that the horse had slipped, then he was jerked towards the edge and he fell to his death. After that time, heavy thoughts about punishment and doomsday came over Ragna. That she should lose Dag like that must be a punishment; she couldn't see it any other way. Punishment for what happened on the sea that time; perhaps she had been too sharp in trade and dealings with silver as well. It could be that, but she thought for a long time that she had also done her duty, achieved things; it wasn't easy to get things done, being a woman. The men had it easier; in everything, they had an easier path in life. There was no talk about a man, whether he got things done or not.

Evening came and a rainstorm approached over the fjord. The sunbeams that had Ragna so well had gone; so too the colours on the hillside where the light had played so nicely just a while ago. Ragna shivered and pulled her cloak and shawl closer around her as she took her staff and began her journey homeward. She would take the trip again tomorrow if the weather improved. He should ensure that – he who controls everything – when they had such a major project underway! But this thing with the merfolk and their easier path in life still gnawed at her; they should only know what she and other women had had to endure of foul smells, laziness and womanly teasing. There should be some indulgence given for such things too! If an opportunity aros on Judgment Day, she intended to bring up just that!

KINGS AND CLERGY DOMINATE THE REINDEER HUNTING ON DOVRE

Before roads and railways contributed to the fragmentation of the continuous mountain areas that today constitute Dovre, Rondane, and Sølenkletten, the reindeer herds had annual migrations between the summer areas in the west and the winter areas in the east. Such established migration routes have been used by hunters for hundreds of thousands of years to ensure good catches. This was also the case in the Dovrefjell area.

The founder of Norway's oldest scientific society, the theologian and historian Gerhard Schøning, undertook a journey over Dovrefjell in 1775 and noted with wonder the large number of hunting pits he saw:

> *'Both on Dovre Mountain, as well as on the other mountains above and beyond Gudbrandsdalen, there are here and there a large number of moose and reindeer pits, located close to each other, and remarkable, both by their quantity and by the diligence with which they are constructed... Large areas on these mountain, are almost completely filled with them.'*

But as in all mountainous areas of the country, it also started small on Dovrefjell – with a few hunters equipped with bow and arrow. From the 5th century, at the beginning of the Migration Period, and for the next 500 years through what archaeologists call the Merovingian period and most of the Viking Age, it was bow hunters who posed the greatest threat to the area's reindeer herds. Even though there are strong indications in the mountain areas south of Dovre that it is the former moose hunters in Østerdalen who are increasing their activity in the mountains, there is reason to believe that in many mountain areas in Southern Norway there is also activity by a Norse population whose main activity is agriculture.

Perhaps the volcanic eruption in the tropics in the year 535 caused failing harvests, and forced a starving population into more intensive exploitation of mountain resources. From the Mediterranean area, there are reports that the sun shone like the moon for 18 months, the fruit did not ripen, and the wine tasted like sour grapes. Grape quality probably didn't concern the people of Gudbrandsdalen, but when it is assumed that the population in Norway is halved, the people of Gudbrandsdalen are also affected. Are there bow-shooting farmers who spend much of their time in the mountains, and eventually learn the reindeer migration routes and understand the animal's behaviour when stressed by hunters? Or is it possible that there is a collaboration with a population group whose main livelihood is hunting and trapping?

Regardless of who the builders were, an impressive system of pitfall traps was gradually constructed over Dovrefjell. Dated studies show a large spread in time of when the stone-built graves were completed. Some were made as early as the Bronze Age, some during the Migration Period 1,600 years ago, but most probably during the Viking Age. The hunters have evidently had detailed knowledge of the reindeer migration routes. The series of graves over the nearly 40-kilometre stretch are not continuous. Some locations, which the reindeer obviously did not use during the migration between summer and winter pastures, lack trapping pits. In other places, the graves are closer together, with only a few tens of metres between each one In total, 1,002 graves covering nearly 30 kilometres of the total length are registered today. This highly effective trapping system is probably Europe's largest cultural monument in terms of area, and is easily accessible today along the E6.

In most mountain areas, we find traces of the hunters, but it is the large mass trapping facilities with kilometer-long guiding fences and trapping pens that characterise the mountain areas around Dovre. In the northern parts of Gudbrandsdalen, a total of 15 such facilities were constructed. But unlike in the east and north of the country, the trapping ends in the mid-1200s, after about 300 years of operation. After that time and towards the mid-1600s, only smaller trapping systems are maintained.

When and how the cooperation and trade between the Norse and Sami populations started, we do not know. The existence of a Sami population in the area at this time is evidenced by findings of settlements. The Sami's characteristic row fireplaces are already found in the Snøhetta area early in the Viking Age. Many will probably argue that the Sami did not play a major role in the increasingly intensive mass trapping of reindeer, while others point out that the cooperation may have been valuable for both parties. One of those who has worked most to map and understand the significance of the mass trapping of reindeer at that time, archaeologist Egil Mikkelsen from the University of Oslo, keeps the door, if not wide open, at least ajar, regarding the possibility that Norse farmers utilised Sami expertise. Perhaps there is also a grain of truth in the story of Harald Fairhair and the Sami king Svåse.

'Snorre Sturlason and other saga writers had a different relationship to historical truth than we as modern historians have. Nevertheless, their sagas are very valuable historical sources, not only because much of what they write must be considered reliable, but also because their descriptions of the political game can tell us a lot about their own time,' argues historian Hans Jacob Orning at the University of Oslo. He points out that the old chieftains built their power from below and that they had to obtain resources and provide effective protection and gifts to local farmers to retain their support. Forming alliances with people who could provide the necessary resources was therefore important. And in the mountain areas, what better alliance could one have than with people who know the art of catching reindeer?

The story of the Finn King (Sami King) Svåse, his exceptionally beautiful daughter Snøfrid, and Harald Fairhair is probably more than a folk tale without historical value, as some historians claimed in the early 20th century. At that time, Sami settlements in the mountain areas south of Trondheim were not widely accepted. Now we know better. Sami had settlements in the Dovrefjell and Rondane areas during the Viking Age. Near the royal farm Tofte, not far from the town of Dovre, Svåse was allowed to build a hut. There he lived with his beautiful daughter Snøfrid. Harald Fairhair became so enamoured with Snøfrid that he immediately wanted to take her to bed with him. Svåse strongly opposed this and demanded that the king marry her first. A wedding was quickly arranged, something the king's first wife Gyda Eiriksdotter was probably not informed about. The saga further tells that Snøfrid gave birth to several sons, each more unruly than the previous.

Such marriages between Norse chieftains and Sami women of high birth were not uncommon. From the Viking Age in Finnmark, this is confirmed by findings of well-equipped graves containing a mixture of Sami and Norse clothing, jewellery, and weapons. In Helgeland, archaeologists excavated an ancient grave in 1942. The woman buried there is buried according to Norse traditions, and she has been given a beautifully crafted axe. Naturally, she is recorded in the museum documents as Norse, but DNA analyses later show that she has a genetic material designated by geneticists as 'samii motif'. This, and several other findings, support the fact that marriages between Sami and Norse populations were not uncommon, especially among people somewhat up the social ladder.

The royal farm at Tofte is close to the large trapping facility at Einsethø, but is also centrally located in relation to several other large mass trapping facilities. In the mountain areas around the upper parts of Gudbrandsdalen, there are a total of 15 large mass trapping facilities. It would require many people and good organisation to maintain the facilities, organise the actual trapping, slaughter, skinning and butchering of animals, transportation, and contact with intermediaries to get the products into a trading system. In Dovre, everything indicates that the Norwegian king is now heavily involved in the mass trapping. Perhaps only the king can mobilise enough people to operate the mass trapping facilities? And it must be permissible to ask the question what was Svåse doing at Tofte? We probably don't stretch the source material too far when we claim that Svåse was more than a bystander when reindeer herds were driven between the kilometer-long trapping arms of the facility and finally ended up in a collection point. So, we can choose not to believe in the story of Snøfrid and Harald Fairhair, but we must accept that there was Sami activity in the mountain areas both in Rondane and Dovrefjell at that time. With the cooperative relationships described between Sami and Norse settlements east and north of the country, it is highly likely the Sami were involved in both the construction of the large mass trapping facilities and their operation. Professionals are professionals: surely both small and large kings understood that during the Viking Age.

Ottar's conversation with the king of England confirms that Sami had served as hunting specialists in his organisation. What could be more natural than the Norwegian king enlisting Sami expertise to lead the work of mass trapping? It is well documented that contact between Sami and the Norse aristocracy became closer during the Viking Age, so we know Ottar was not the only Norse chieftain who became dependent on Sami hunting communities. The chieftains exchanged Sami hunting products at markets in England and other places in Europe, thus exchanging luxury goods that helped maintain their own social status. On their side, the Sami received back iron, grain and imported luxury goods. Archaeological finds confirm that during the Viking Age and early Middle Ages larger social differences developed among the Sami than those we see both before and after this period. This could be interpreted to mean that only a few Sami were associated with the Norse organised mass trapping, and that in areas with a relatively large and well-functioning Norse settlement with farmers, the necessary Sami expertise could be ensured through involvement of a small number of Sami. And as long as they had the king on the hunting team, who could provide king's men to organise tenants and thralls, mass trapping was feasible.

The Archbishop of Nidaros had of course noticed the king's strong involvement in reindeer trapping in the mountains, and that the natural resources from this activity greatly contributed to the extensive trade. The clergy had no less need than the king to increase their access to natural resources, and started what archaeologist Egil Mikkelsen calls a large-scale high ecclesiastical land policy, which eventually resulted in the archbishop having large estates in the Lesja and Dovre areas. While the king had local king's men, the archbishop established local stewards, who helped solve the clergy's various administrative and economic tasks.

In the fishing villages along the coast, the stewards managed the stockfish trade, and in the inland areas they managed the reindeer trapping and ensured that the products were brought to Nidaros. The stewards were privileged men and escaped the leidang – the requirement to provide people and other types of resources to the king when needed. Written sources from Tunsberg in 1277 state that the archbishop should have 100 stewards, and each of the bishops 40. In later sources, we find that the archbishop has at least three stewards in the Dovre area. It is not unlikely that these stewards served as managers of the archbishop's properties in the valley, with the right to use the large trapping pit systems in the mountains, after the use of mass trapping facilities ceased.

While the trapping pit systems were in use for many centuries, the large-scale industrially built reindeer trapping in the sluice-shaped mass trapping facilities stopped at the end of the 1200s, after almost 300 years of use. The reason probably lies in a sharp decline in the reindeer population due to intensive trapping. Magnus Lagabøters Landslov from 1274 provides valuable information on how the resources in the mountains have been utilised. It is clearly stated that the common lands should be as they have been in old times, which we must assume refers back to the Viking Age. Hunting, trapping and fishing are free for everyone, but trapping systems and construction of mass trapping facilities with guiding fences and trapping pens should not reduce the hunting success of other trappers. Then follows a very interesting piece of information: *animal pit fall traps that have not been in use for ten years are owned by everyone.* Any trapping activity that requires more effort than one can expect to get back is not viable at this time. This must mean that the trapping systems have been effective, resulting in such a significant reduction in the reindeer population that continued trapping would not yield sufficient returns in relation to the effort required. The owners of these systems have therefore had to use their labour on other things than trapping reindeer.

The middens found in connection with the large mass trapping facilities consist of large amounts of bones. Giving an estimate of how many animals were caught is, of course, impossible, but that the trapping was extensive for long periods is obvious. The transportation of the catch to a meat-hungry population must have been done on foot or through the use of packhorses. It is therefore natural that much of the butchering and skinning of meat happened at the trapping site. But one type of bone material is missing – the antlers. These have been seen as an important resource and were therefore taken away to be used.

While Cro-Magnon used antler material for making weapons and atlatl – a spear-throwing weapon – and for shaping various art objects, during the Viking Age and early Middle Ages a need arose for a completely different type of tool – the comb – which was highly valued. Early in the mass trapping period, at the end of the 10th century, it seems that travelling comb makers went to the cities and sold their products, but later traces are found of their own comb 'factories' in all the oldest cities in Norway. New techniques have now made it possible to extract genetic material from the old antlers, and in this way find out where the raw material for the combs comes from. Not surprisingly, it is the nearest mountain areas that provide most of the raw material for the old city's comb makers. In Bergen and Skien, most antlers come from the Hardangervidda, but the people of Bergen also receive boatloads of antlers from Dovre and Reinheimen. In Nidaros, antler material is collected from both Dovre and areas further north in Trøndelag.

The products have not only found a local audience. Norwegian combs made of reindeer antler have been found both in Denmark and Scotland, showing the extensive international networks that already existed at that time, and it is precisely trade and networks that will lead to the next epoch in history. Calf reindeer skins were long the most sought-after and best-paid fur in Bergen. Reindeer trapping on the Hardangervidda had been poor for many years, so it was probably not reindeer skins the people intended to buy as they gathered on the quay in Bergen on a quite ordinary day in 1349. Like every other day, the quays and commons were busy trading places, and perhaps it was with a special expectation that the merchants saw the long-awaited ship from England moor. In 1349, the people of Eidsfjord had been using the new church for 40 years. What they thought while they sat and listened to a sermon in Latin, we do not know. Perhaps their thoughts were on the church builder Ragna and the fear of both purgatory and hell if they did not pay their indulgence gifts. We do not know, but we can take it as certain that they did not think of a ship that docked in Bergen, and that this ship actually had judgment day in its cargo.

MY SHIP IS LOADED WITH...

Just a few days after the disease arrived in the country, it spread like wildfire from house to house and from town to hamlet. The disease spread through flea bites. The infection settled in the lymph nodes, causing them to swell and become boils as large as eggs, hence the name bubonic plague. The course of the disease was boils, fever, hemorrhages, and then most people died within one to five days. In a short time, farms, and in some cases entire villages, were laid waste, and we still have many farm names in this country that date back to that time. Ødegård and Aune are both names attributed to farms that were left empty and abandoned. The impact that the disease and all the deaths had on people, we can only imagine.

The legend of Pesta, an old hag who wandered through the villages with a rake and a broom, is a good illustration of what it may have been like. Where Pesta used the rake, some survived, but if she used the broom, everyone died. Historians who have worked on the topic believe that the ravages of the plague are the single factor that has had the most extensive and long-lasting negative effects on the country's overall social development.

Repeated outbreaks of the plague throughout the Middle Ages meant that it took more than 200 years before the population in Norway reached the same level as before the first major plague outbreak. It wasn't until the late 1500s that the waves of plague began to recede and population growth became significant enough that many of the abandoned farms were once again put into use. In Oppdal municipality, which in the High Middle Ages had as many as 80 operational farms, there were barely 20 farmsteads in 1520. Population growth continued into the 1600s, and most of the deserted farms were back in use by the mid-1600s. However, agricultural technology remained at the same level as in the 1300s. Periods of famine due to difficult climatic conditions, along with population growth and inefficient production methods, contributed to periods of hunger in Norway, with people exploiting the wilderness to the utmost. Competition and conflicts over resources increased, leading to conflicts with the Sami population as well.

During the High and Late Middle Ages, significant changes also occurred in the hunting and trapping-dominated Sami culture. One of the truly significant changes is the emergence of reindeer husbandry as a specialised cultural form and, as a result, a nomadic way of life among parts of the Sami population. Societies in Scandinavia also changed significantly during the Middle Ages.

The formation of nations over time meant that the networks from the Iron Age and Viking Age, which were based on a significant degree of reciprocity, were replaced by a more direct taxation of the Sami. In the west, the chieftains had long dominated trade in the north, from Namdalen all the way to the White Sea. The last of these chieftains, the Lade Jarls, lost their rights to this trade during the unification of the kingdom, which was subsequently placed under royal authority. In written sources from this time, Norwegian kings claimed that the Sami in what is referred to as 'Finnmark' were obliged to pay tribute to the king, a tax that was now collected by the king's officials or bailiffs.

On the Swedish side, a somewhat similar system had been built up over a long period of trade activity and was managed by the so-called 'birkarls'. These Swedish traders, named after the trading place Birkö, replaced the Kvens and conducted trade with the Sami from the Viking Age until the 1600s, ensuring that reindeer skins, fur, handicrafts, and probably dried reindeer meat were spread throughout Europe. It was long believed that the ethical and moral attitudes of the birkarls left something to be desired, but it seems rather that they established close and good relationships with the Sami.

In the written sources dating back to the 1300s, there is only one case involving violence perpetrated by a birkarl. In 1547, a birkarl named Hindrik Nilsson from Torne Lapland was fined 8 marks for hitting a Sami. Given the high fine, this was evidently taken seriously. Being a birkarl brought prestige but was not hereditary. When a birkarl needed to be replaced, his successor was recruited from among those who were trained and familiar with the logistical and practical challenges a journey to the 'Laplands' entailed. The Sami trading partners also had a say in the appointment of new birkarls. While the Norwegian royal power quickly and effectively stopped the local chieftains' monopolistic trade with the Sami, the Swedish birkarls were given some protection in an agreement with the Swedish-Norwegian king Magnus Erikson in 1328. This, in practice, led to a kind of monopoly on trade with the Sami here.

Over time, the royal power viewed them as strong opponents to its own economic and political ambitions and eventually gained exclusive rights to trade with the Sami in the 1600s. By that time, the wild reindeer was nearly extinct, and some of the Sami had developed nomadic reindeer husbandry. Farthest in the north and east, there is a third actor who also trades with the Sami and eventually demands taxes. Novgorod had grown during the early Middle Ages to become the most important centre for fur trading.

Towards the end of the High Middle Ages, conflicts over trade and taxation led the various state powers to enter into agreements where they, among other things, divided the Sami areas among themselves. Various trading networks, such as trade in stockfish and contact with the Hanseatic League in Bergen on the north-west coast, and fur trading with Novgorod in the east, contributed to different external influences in the Sami area, and thus also different foundations for changes in the Sami economy. According to Lars Ivar Hansen and Bjørnar Olsen, these differences were important influencing factors in an economy that, in the latter part of the Middle Ages, was still dominated by hunting and trapping, with wild reindeer hunting and fishing as important pillars of the economy. They also point out that the connection to new trade systems probably contributed to a marked intensification of wild reindeer hunting in some areas.

FROM HUNTING CULTURE TO NOMADIC REINDEER HUSBANDRY

The transition to nomadic reindeer husbandry has received considerable attention among various researchers as a subject, yet it is by no means the case that those who have worked on this as a research topic have come to a common agreement on why reindeer husbandry emerged. Most likely, the domestication of reindeer occurred in several places in Eurasia, and various triggering factors may have been involved in the transition to a specialised and nomadic reindeer husbandry. One explanation that many in Norway often cite is that the intensive hunting in mass trapping facilities led to a drastic decimation of wild reindeer. When access to wild reindeer dwindled, the need for larger herds of domestic reindeer increased. However, external factors such as the establishment of stronger royal authority and increased taxation by various kingdoms and nations may also have contributed to the profitability of maintaining larger herds of domestic reindeer, despite the increased workload and a more nomadic way of life.

We have previously seen that large trapping facilities were established in places like the Varanger Peninsula. The same happened in south-east Norway and many other places in Norway. We find large trapping facilities with animal pits, but also facilities with fences and barriers intended for live trapping of wild reindeer. In south-east Norway, this trapping method was most prominent in the early Middle Ages but seems to have ended before 1349. The facilities in Finnmark were likely in operation much longer, and there is documentation that the Sami in this area paid an annual fee in the form of live reindeer to the local lord at Vardøhus Fortress in the late 1600s. The techniques for trapping reindeer in large facilities, whether through animal pits or, preferably, by actively driving the reindeer into live trapping facilities, were steps toward the later emergence of reindeer nomadism. Researchers who have worked on the topic point out that both trading networks and the demand for trapping products provided a basis for individuals to acquire more status and position through trade, which was a significant change from the more egalitarian hunting and trapping society, and it provided opportunities for organising people and labour. The large facilities required organisation and cooperation on a very different level than what was necessary in the hunting and harvesting-based culture. Therefore, some of the basis for the development of reindeer husbandry may be found in the older mass trapping of wild reindeer, in terms of technology, knowledge and societal changes.

How and why reindeer husbandry emerged is another question. There is little doubt that in the older hunting and gathering cultures, domesticated reindeer existed long before, and these animals were used as draught animals and decoy reindeer for hunting wild reindeer. It is also natural to think that milking reindeer and the use of meat and skin were common before specialised reindeer husbandry emerged. However, when they started keeping some domesticated animals and where the domesticated reindeer came from is more uncertain, and, understandably, there are very few written sources to rely on regarding this question. We have already mentioned the merchant Ottar, who according to English writings owned 600 reindeer, 6 of which were decoy reindeer. More tangible evidence comes from Kolafjorden in present-day Russia, where a sled approximately 3,500 years old of Sami type has been found. From other places in Russia, there are known findings of neckbands used on reindeer that are approximately 2,500 years old. Both Sverre Fjellheim and Leif Braset describe in their books how the transition to nomadic reindeer husbandry may have occurred practically. Both refer to Swedish sources describing how a few reindeer were kept in enclosures while wild reindeer were hunted as hard as possible. Both see this information in relation to the oldest documentation of conflicts between reindeer herders and settled communities, which in an early phase were due to conflicts over hunting and taxation of reindeer and moose. Conflicts over land and grazing rights came later. Like much else concerning the story of human and reindeer history, geneticists have also contributed to illuminating this part of the story. Knut Røed and his colleagues compared the genetics in the old populations of wild reindeer with those in reindeer husbandry today and found that domesticated reindeer today have much less genetic variation than the original wild reindeer populations that lived in areas where reindeer husbandry now exists. The analyses here show that much of the original genetic material inherited from females (the genetic material found in the mitochondria – the cell's powerhouses) has disappeared and been replaced with genetic material found in domesticated reindeer, among others in Jamal in Russia. It is therefore not unlikely that reindeer from Jamal largely laid the foundation for later domestic reindeer herds.

Where and by whom reindeer husbandry first developed is a question that has preoccupied many researchers, and not surprisingly there are also many opinions on how this happened. Linguists, geneticists, historians, archaeologists and biologists have all contributed to the debate to varying degrees. Two theories have been proposed. One possibility is that reindeer husbandry originated in one area and later spread to other areas. Alternatively, it originated in different areas independently of each other and at different times. The same research team that studied the genetics of wild and domesticated reindeer in Norway has also looked at the genetic variation in various reindeer populations in 25 areas in Eurasia and found a striking difference between reindeer from Scandinavia and those found further east. This result supports the idea that reindeer husbandry originated in different places independently of each other. In Scandinavia, it seems that reindeer husbandry first emerged in central areas between Sweden and Norway, and specialised reindeer husbandry was established somewhat later farthest north in the country and in Finland. There is still much we do not have secure knowledge about, but certainly today we have a much more correct understanding than before. Nevertheless, most people today seem to agree that specialised and nomadic reindeer husbandry was well established by the end of the 1500s. It is at this time that the first conflicts between reindeer husbandry and other interests were documented in written sources such as tax lists and legal documents.

THE BATTLE FOR THE OUTFIELD

The large trapping systems in Southern Norway fell out of use in the 1200s. The smaller systems and individual animal pits remained in use much longer, but the wild reindeer populations were severely decimated. It is against the backdrop of conflicts over the harvesting of resources from the commons that we find the first documentation of conflicts between those promoting the then-new form of reindeer husbandry and the rest of the population. Much of the documentation from this time is compiled in Sverre Fjellheim's books on South Sami reindeer husbandry in the Røros area.

The oldest documentation of such conflicts in this area dates back to the first half of the 1600s, consisting of several complaint letters from the commoners, and, in one case, from the governor of Herjedalen. All of these are allegations that the Sami are harvesting too heavily from the commons and that they are depleting populations of primarily reindeer but also elk. At the same time, there is also documentation that the Sami in this area have large herds of domestic reindeer. Fjellheim sees the heavy exploitation of the remaining wild reindeer populations as part of the process of transition from a hunting-based reindeer husbandry to a nomadic form of reindeer husbandry. At the same time, in Sweden there is written documentation from this transitional phase showing that it was not only the settled inhabitants and farmers who reacted negatively to the extensive hunting of wild reindeer. The priest Tornæus writes in 1672 that wise Sami in earlier times gathered wild reindeer in enclosures (wuomen), and that this trapping method was so effective that those who practised this form of trapping were hated by other Sami ('hated by other Lapps').

Closer to our own time, we see that these conflicts escalate, but now more often revolve around grazing rights and compensation claims directed against the Sami. One of the core areas for these conflicts was the Røros area. At the end of the 1700s, settlement in this area also increased, partly as a result of mining activities in Røros and partly as a result of the general population growth in Norway. Here, as elsewhere, population growth led to increased use of the commons in the form of summer farming, harvesting of resources from the commons, and bringing back moss and leaves as animal fodder. The Sami who resided here had their spring and summer pastures at the northern end of Riasten, and it is precisely in this area that the conflicts with the farmers were initially intensified.

The conflicts revolved around pasture, and damage to grass and grazing land associated with the summer farms that had been built in the mountain valley west of Riasten. Over time, these conflicts escalated sharply, first in 1794, and later in 1801 when some farmers together with the sheriff in Ålen, Didrik Lien, came into physical confrontation with the Sami who had their reindeer here. The Sami were chased away, copper kettles and other equipment were stolen, and their huts were burned down. The Sami complained about the treatment they received, and the events are well documented in the court records of the Gauldal district court. The burning of the huts was a heavy loss for the Sami and may have been the reason why four families in 1810 loaded up all their belongings in sleds and set course westward towards what is often referred to as the Forollhogna wild reindeer area and national park today. These four families were made up of 11 people and approximately 500 reindeer. We must believe that they had hopes of better times in the west, but it would turn out that worse was to come, and we have now come to one of the absolutely ugliest incidents between the South Sami culture and the local population.

From New Year onwards into the winter, the families resided near Elgsjøen, but moved southwards during the spring and built huts not far from Dalbusjøen. In early August, about 30 animals disappeared from the main herd; these animals were likely taken by villagers and slaughtered. After this, things escalated quickly, and on August 25, 1811, the sheriff Ole Skogstad used a church service in Os church to gather the villagers to chase the Sami at Dalbusjøen. On August 27, a group of 40–50 men set off into the mountains, most armed with rifles. Upon encountering the Sami, a man named Bersvend Engen pretended to be the sheriff and immediately ordered the Sami to leave the area. The Sami were given some few days to gather their herd, but already early the next day, the villagers returned and drove the entire reindeer herd southward. During the day, Zakarias managed to separate 100 animals, which he took back to Dalbusjøen. Upon arrival, he persuaded the two Sami women Lucia and Kari to join him and they went back to the valley settlers to save more animals. They succeeded in saving a few more, but witnessed the valley settlers slaughter approximately 400 animals.

The incident at Dalbusjøen was a great tragedy for all involved. Jon Mortensen, who was a large reindeer owner and considered a wealthy man, lost everything. Jon is found in a witness description recorded in connection with the Lapland Commission, and he is described as a poor beggar in Leinstrand. Jon died at the poorhouse in Røros. Zakarias Nilsen and his wife Sophia wandered around for a long time with their son Nils, who was born in 1810. After a long stay, they returned to the Røros area; Sophia had become 'very addicted to drink'. Zakarias received poor relief at Krogstad. They were deprived of their livelihood and did not recover after the incident at Dalbusjøen.

In the reindeer herd slaughtered by the valley settlers, there were also many so-called 'sytings reindeer'. These were reindeer owned by others but cared for by the Sami. In total, there were 84 such reindeer in the herd, owned by 13 different owners, several of whom were men with positions in society. From the court documents of that time, it is evident that both Prost Aschenberg in Røros, Priest Schnitler in Trondheim, Quartermaster Finne, also in Trondheim, and Chief Miller in Kongsberg were among the owners of these animals. The trial that followed, therefore, was no pleasant affair for those involved. In total, those who participated in the slaughter were sentenced to pay a fine of 18,000 riksdaler. A farm in this district was worth approximately 1,000 riksdaler at that time. The fine corresponded to the value of 18 farms. It is easy to think that the size of the fine had much to do with the sytings reindeer and who owned them. But the verdict and settlement also meant that the Sami committed themselves to staying away from Dalsbygda and adjacent villages for all time, an obligation that would later have significant consequences for both the Sami and the reindeer in this area.

But it was not only in Southern Norway that conflicts arose around reindeer husbandry. In many ways, we find something of the same situation in Northern Norway where a reduced population of wild reindeer is compensated for with increased use of efficient mass trapping systems. In the mid-1600s, the use of all trapping systems stopped, and in 1690 it is claimed that the trapping pits lay overgrown, deserted and abandoned. But there were still some wild reindeer, and with firearms now available reindeer hunting continued well into the 1700s. In 1702, the county governor introduced hunting seasons. In Vadsø, Vardø and Kiberg, the reindeer were protected from Candlemas (February 2) to St. Bartholomew's Day (August 24), although there were complaints from the coastal Sami that hunting had been too intense. On the south side of the Varangerfjord, snare trapping of reindeer is said to have continued well into the 1800s. By that time, the management of domestic reindeer had begun, albeit on a small scale among the coastal Sami, but extremely important for what is referred to as the mountain Sami.

In Varanger, sources from 1694 describe three categories of reindeer owners. There are Varanger Sami (coastal Sami) who have domestic reindeer as a supplementary livelihood, there are Norwegians, typically priests and merchants, who have their own herds managed by Sami, and there are mountain Sami. And it is the mountain Sami's use of the coastal Sami's areas that gives rise to disputes in the years to come, and the court records from Finnmark for the period 1620-1770 firmly establish this.

From the Varanger ting (court) we see that the coastal Sami in Varanger complained already in 1649 that mountain Sami from Enare and Arrisby 'both with fishing and in other ways seek their downfall and use' on Varangersiidaen. Three years later, the Varanger Sami claim that 'a lot of Mountain Finns do them great harm and damage to their rightful belonging Reindeerplaces, by bringing in a whole crowd of their Reindeer, which they lead there, eating up the Reindeer fodder for them, which they annually should have to raise their Reindeer with.' The Varanger Sami are upheld in court, and it is determined that the mountain Sami must leave the coastal Sami's areas, and, if they do not, the sub-deputy, at the head of the Varanger Sami, should take the mountain Sami's reindeer and bring them to Vardøhus fortress.

Around the mid-1700s, Governor Collett more or less advocated for the summer migration of reindeer herders to the coast to be abolished because the reindeer were destroying the locals' meadows. Collett attempted to enforce a ban on reindeer grazing closer to the sea than half a mile, but to no avail: 'despite all threats, they continue their old ways'. Cases of this conflict type can be found throughout Finnmark from the mid-1600s onwards, and in all of these cases the judgements favour the coastal population. In 1682 the Kjøllefjord ting (court), determine that mountain Sami Niels Rasmussen must remain on the mountain with his reindeer where he should be according to the coastal Sami. At the Talvik ting, it is decided that mountain Sami are not allowed to have reindeer in the mountains near the coast, and at the Hammerfest ting (court), it is determined in 1694 that Sami must keep their reindeer away from places where there are meadows. The same type of cases are handled at the Kjøllefjord ting and, in Alta, mountain Sami Michel Aslachsøn is told to stay away from the meadows with his reindeer.

While the coastal Sami have their rights to land and water respected, the judgements do not favour the reindeer herders. However, in 1763 three mountain Sami were allowed to keep reindeer on Sørøya, provided they did not come over to the northern side of the island where the merchant Buck had his reindeer – perhaps they met the judge on a good day.

A POPULAR THEORY THAT
CAUSED GREAT HARM

Tragedien at Dalbusjøen was in many ways just the beginning of a difficult period for the South Sami people, which also came to have significant effects on the wild reindeer populations. To understand the context of the story and gain a better understanding of what happened afterward, we must go back to Sumtangen and the discussions about who the first hunters were. Initially, the theory was that these people were indigenous, with ancestors from the Fosna culture, and, according to Wilhelm Frimann Koren Christie and Christian Magnus Falsen, they were Sami. As we have already touched upon, this theory was emphatically refuted by Anton Brøgger and Yngvar Nilsen, who were two heavyweights in their time. Brøgger was an archaeologist and curator at the University's collection of antiquities and a professor of Nordic archaeology, while Nilsen was a professor of geography and director of the Ethnographic Museum. He was also a pioneer of tourism in Norway, chairman of the Norwegian Tourist Association, and an advocate for the establishment of national parks. In other words, he was a well-positioned and active man, and additionally a friend and advisor to King Oscar II, teaching his sons. In short, they were no small-time players, and the conclusions they reached were crystal clear: the hunters at Sumtangen had been Norse since time immemorial.

When Yngvar Nilsen received a grant from the Lapland Commission in 1889 to investigate the historical presence of the South Sami in the Røros area, it was likely due to all the conflicts between reindeer husbandry and other groups in society that such work was initiated. Nilsen's work has since been described as the 'advance theory', a theory that is now undeniably refuted but was and still is detrimental to the people the theory concerns – the South Sami.

The basis for Nilsen's theory was a journey he made in the area between Femund and Namsskogan in 1889. Later, he referred to this as 'ethnographic and geographic studies of the Lapps', and presented his findings in a lecture at the Norwegian Geographic Society. The work was summarised in an article in the society's yearbook in 1891 titled 'The Advancement of the Lapps southwards in the Diocese of Trondheim and the County of Hedemark'. In short, he based his conclusions on the observation that, according to him, there were very few Sami place names south of Verdal, and he had not found Sami burial grounds or sacrificial sites in these areas. At about the same time, a Swedish professor, Gustav Storm, presented a similar theory in Sweden. The main point for both was that the Sami had first come to Tydalen in Trøndelag around 1700 and to the Røros area around 1750. Nielsen and Storm's theories were given great weight by the Lapland Commission, established in 1889, which determined the boundaries of the new reindeer grazing districts. The advance theory was also used as a basis in several Supreme Court judgments and in various compensation lawsuits brought against the Sami, and in 1897 a ban on reindeer grazing outside the reindeer grazing districts was imposed, a prohibition that would have particular effects on the Sami who at that time resided on the Gauldal plateau.

In the 1890s, there were three such groups in this area: Jon Thomassen and his family, Jakob Johnsen and his family, and Nils Thomassen Bull and his family. All of these were, after 1897, in an area where it was no longer allowed to engage in reindeer husbandry. Jon Thomassen, who had already been fined heavily at that time, therefore moved on with his family and eventually ended up in Setesdal, laying the foundation for reindeer husbandry there. Jakob Johnsen and his sons, also called the Jakobsson brothers, stayed in Kvikne for a few years but were eventually directed to the Essand reindeer grazing district. They lost many of their animals in the process, and a larger part of the original herd, despite several attempts to gather them, started wandering again in the Kvikne mountains. After barely ten years, this family was destitute and in 1901, described as 'Lapps without reindeer', receiving support from poor relief. Things did not go much better for Nils Thomassen Bull and his family. They had eventually settled near Øyungen, furthest east on the Gauldal plateau, and, according to the Lapland Commission in 1889, they had about 600 reindeer, of which 200 were animals they herded for others. But the discussions about possible reindeer husbandry on the Gauldal plateau were not over with this. The end of that story takes place in the 1950s.

THE NEW REINDEER
POPULATIONS

On the farm Søndre Høye in upper Rendalen, a crisis meeting was held in February 1726. Landowners from the eastern parts of Østerdalen had observed the poor condition of the moose and reindeer in the area and formulated a document with clear rules for how hunting should proceed. It was forbidden to kill animals between December 10 and May 15, with a penalty set at 21 riksdalers. Seven of these were to go to the king, seven to the church in the area where the animal was killed, and the remaining riksdalers were to go to the person who reported the illegal hunting.

A few years later, Norwegian authorities followed up by introducing a hunting season for all cervids in Norway. However, this did not yield the desired results. It wasn't until 130 years later that a general ban on the use of animal traps was introduced. By then, the wild reindeer in the northern parts of the country had long disappeared, and, in the south, perhaps only one to two thousand animals remained of the original wild reindeer population. However, the exploitation of the wild reindeer populations continued to be significant, and the wild reindeer was protected between 1902 and 1907. This marks a turning point in our relationship with the reindeer. For the first time in history, it became necessary to protect the last remnants of the European wild reindeer.

Through royal resolution, the principle of minimum area for allocation of hunting was established in 1930, which demonstrably had a positive effect, leading to significant growth in several of the wild reindeer populations. The growth in the populations also clearly showed that the development of Norway with roads and other infrastructure had its price; the previously contiguous large mountain areas became fragmented into smaller units. By the 1950s and 1960s, the populations in Hardangervidda and Snøhetta had become much larger than what the pastures in the isolated areas could sustain. In retrospect, management has paid significant attention to preventing overgrazing, and the consideration for pasture areas and their preservation has received increasing attention.

But before we delve further, let's take a look at the background of today's wild reindeer populations. To do that, we need to travel to the Sami people who moved away from Gauldalsvidda and the Røros area.

Jon Thomassen and his family were one of three families residing on Gauldalsvidda in the 1880s. Several lawsuits were brought against the Sami people during these years, and Jon was fined heavily for illegal grazing and had to leave the area. Jon then moved south with his family and ended up in the Setesdal mountains in 1882, bringing with him a herd of about 4,000 animals. This was by no means the first time domestic reindeer had been introduced to this area. For a long time, there had been various attempts to start reindeer husbandry, both in Setesdal and in other mountain areas where there were wild reindeer. The reason probably lay largely in the fact that the wild reindeer populations had become very small, so domestic reindeer were introduced to compensate for the decline in wild reindeer populations. In Hardangervidda, which today hosts Norway's largest wild reindeer population, the first timid attempts to start reindeer husbandry were made in the late 1700s when Hallstein and Lars Garden from Eidfjord travelled to the Røros area to buy 100 reindeer.

There is something to the idea that history seems to repeat itself. The situation in southern Norway in the late 1800s is in many ways like what we saw earlier in northern Norway. The wild reindeer became scarce, and therefore, attempts were made to control the reindeer populations by keeping domestic reindeer. But there is one major difference: the Sami people who developed reindeer husbandry had extensive knowledge of hunting wild reindeer in large herds, and they had an ancient living culture of keeping tame animals in smaller herds. The farmers who attempted reindeer husbandry during the 1800s did not have such knowledge and therefore had significant problems herding the flocks and keeping them tame. The newly started reindeer husbandries therefore had a short history. The domestic reindeer mixed with what remained of the wild reindeer and were mostly lost over time. Wolves were also occasionally a nuisance for the newly started reindeer husbandries. It was only when Sami herders were introduced into the newly started reindeer husbandries that they succeeded in keeping tame herds for a longer period. Over time, many such reindeer husbandries were started in areas where wild reindeer still existed. The last of these operations (Hol tamreinlag) was terminated in 1982. In other areas such as Jotunheimen, the wild reindeer never returned; there is still reindeer husbandry there today.

Before we conclude this part of the story, we need to go back to Sumtangen and Gauldalsvidda. Knut Røed and his research group have also studied the genetics of the wild reindeer living on Hardangervidda today and compared it with bone material from Sumtangen. The comparison shows that there is a significant genetic difference between the original reindeer that lived here and today's wild reindeer population. The reindeer on Hardangervidda today are more similar to domestic reindeer from the Røros district. The reindeer husbandries that existed in the 1800s and the early 1900s have therefore left genetic traces. The same is true for several of today's wild reindeer populations, which to a greater or lesser extent are found to have a kinship with domestic reindeer.

On Gauldalsvidda, the grazing ban introduced in 1887 put an end to reindeer husbandry. The last ones to leave the area were the Jakobsønne brothers, who had about 400 animals in 1897. As mentioned earlier, they were directed to Essand, but had problems gathering the animals and only partly succeeded in moving the flock there. A large part of the flock they moved with also reportedly escaped back. However, conflicts over domestic reindeer were not entirely over.

Those who engaged in reindeer husbandry in the Riast Hyllingen area eventually encountered significant problems in maintaining the flock. Constant lawsuits, poor economy and the problems it brought led to the animals spreading and getting out of control. In the end, there was a stray flock with many unmarked animals. Therefore, a campaign was launched to shoot down these animals and thus gain control of the flock. One of the challenges they faced was that animals easily crossed the Gaula River and thus entered forbidden areas on Gauldalsvidda. Here, too, a campaign was launched, in agreement with local landowners, to shoot such animals. However, the hope of resuming reindeer husbandry on Gauldalsvidda was not entirely forgotten, and in 1955 a concrete effort was made to buy domestic animals with the aim of resuming reindeer husbandry. Those behind this initiative had, according to Sverre Fjellheim, entered into an agreement with some of the landowners in Holtålen to lease grazing rights.

However, other rights holders in the area believed that Gauldalsvidda should rather be maintained as a wild reindeer area and worked towards such a solution. Ultimately, it was the wild reindeer solution that prevailed. The Directorate for Nature Management confirmed in 1955 that Gauldalsvidda, or Forollhogna as the area would later be known, was a wild reindeer area. And it has been ever since. This is how it happened that domestic reindeer, which did not originate from the original wild reindeer in Norway, nevertheless became wild reindeer.

THE LAST OUTPOST OF THE WILD REINDEER

Dovrefjell avoided the tragedy of the commons

While the intensive hunting of reindeer continued in the east and north of the country until the 18th century, leading to the extinction of the wild reindeer populations, the situation was different in the Dovre and Rondane areas. Norway's original wild mountain reindeer survived in an area where it had been subjected to extremely intensive exploitation for several centuries. Nowhere else in the country were trapping pits more densely packed, and perhaps nowhere else was the mass hunting of reindeer through the Viking Age and well into the Middle Ages more intensive. Reindeer trapping in the Dovrefjell area greatly con-tributed to the emergence of a market economy where the power structures of the time, along with kings and archbishops, ensured the establishment of clear rights related to their properties. And perhaps here lies the answer to why the wild mountain reindeer survived in this area. Clear rights and rules for the exploitation of resources in the mountains, tied to settlement and property relations, may have prevented the tragedy of the commons.

It was biologist Garrett Hardin who, in 1968, introduced the concept of the 'tragedy of the commons'. It describes a situation where all involved would collectively benefit if they cooperated, rather than if everyone freeloaded. Yet, each individual involved benefits by freeloading on others, regardless of whether the others cooperate or freeload. If everyone else follows the rules, the freeloader not only gains access to a well-functioning commons but also gains a large profit by overexploiting the commons. If everyone freeloads, the common resource will eventually disappear, but the cost of this is shared among everyone, and, in a transitional period, it can be offset by overexploitation of the commons. The individual actor cannot stop overexploitation alone, greatly affecting their willingness to consider other actors.

The metaphor gained traction and was quickly used to explain everything from situations of overfishing of herring stocks to overgrazing of reindeer pastures in Finnmark. While biologists quickly embraced Hardin's model, historians and social anthropologists eventually produced studies showing that people in many situations did not behave as the model predicted, but actually managed to develop sustainable ways of managing common resources. However, examples to the contrary were still predominant. It was ultimately the Swedish economist and Nobel laureate Elinor Ostrom who arrived at a set of criteria that must be in place to avoid the tragedy of the commons.

What must be in place is a clear understanding of who has legitimate rights to the resource and how it should be utilised, as well as a certain correspondence between rights and duties. Furthermore, it is important that those affected by the regulations are involved in their formulation. Any sanctions must be graded, depending on the situation and type of rule violation, and conflicts must be resolved by those with rights to the resource. There should be a hierarchically structured management system built around a coalition of local organisations, and the power exercised must be limited to a specific area and legitimised by the state.

An example of common lands being managed sustainably over centuries comes from the Alps. There, mountain pastures were typically communal, with all farmers from a specific area owning a pasture collectively. The pastures are theoretically subject to the tragedy of the commons, but this has been avoided because rights on the pastures have been regulated through strict agreements since the Middle Ages. Violations of the rules were punished with hefty fines or expulsion. The rules included a limit on the number of animals allowed on a pasture, a key for how this number was distributed among farmers in relation to the size of their farms, and the communal work expected in return.

We can see clear parallels to the conditions related to the trapping of reindeer in the Dovrefjell area. According to Egil Mikkelsen's extensive studies on reindeer trapping in these areas, the organisation of trapping was closely related to settlement and property relations tied to the farms in Dovre. And with both royal and ecclesiastical power in place, it can be safely assumed that there is a clear understanding of who has legitimate rights to the resource and how it should be exploited. The fact that this functioned as a hierarchically structured management system built around a coalition of local organisations also seems to be in place. Dovre was divided into two districts, the northern one engaged in reindeer trapping and other resource exploitation in the area between Dombås and Hjerkinn, and the southern district exploiting the outlying resources eastwards from Grimsdalen towards Rondane. It is not unlikely that the two districts operated different mass trapping facilities during the 300-year period they were in operation. From the royal farm at Tofte, the king could operate the mass trapping facility at Einsethø, perhaps using Sami expertise, while the archbishop and bishop in Hamar had significant ownership interests in the Bergsgårdene, which are closer to the mass trapping facility at Gravhø.

While the use of mass trapping facilities ceased by the end of the 13th century, the trapping pit systems were still maintained. Many of them can likely be linked to some of the large farms that organised the mass trapping facilities. Farthest north in Dovre were farms that were part of the northern district but where neither the king nor the clergy had ownership interests. It is assumed that these farms operated various parts of the long row of trapping pits stretching from Dombås to Hjerkinn.

Both east and north of the Dovre area, the Sami population developed a livelihood during the 17th century where herds of domestic reindeer were built up. To prevent domestic reindeer from mingling with wild reindeer herds, hunting of wild reindeer continued in parallel with the development of domestic reindeer herds. Therefore, hunting of the wild reindeer populations in the area continued well into the 18th century, and even further north there are reports of snare trapping of wild reindeer into the 19th century. These areas therefore lack the management systems and clarifications of the legitimate rights associated with the wild reindeer populations that are in place in the Dovre area. Perhaps it is therefore the former kings and archbishops who should be thanked for Norway, as the only European country, still having populations of original wild reindeer in some mountain areas.

FIG 5. The twentieth century was a century of great change. During this century much infrastructure was developed and reindeer habitats became fragmented.

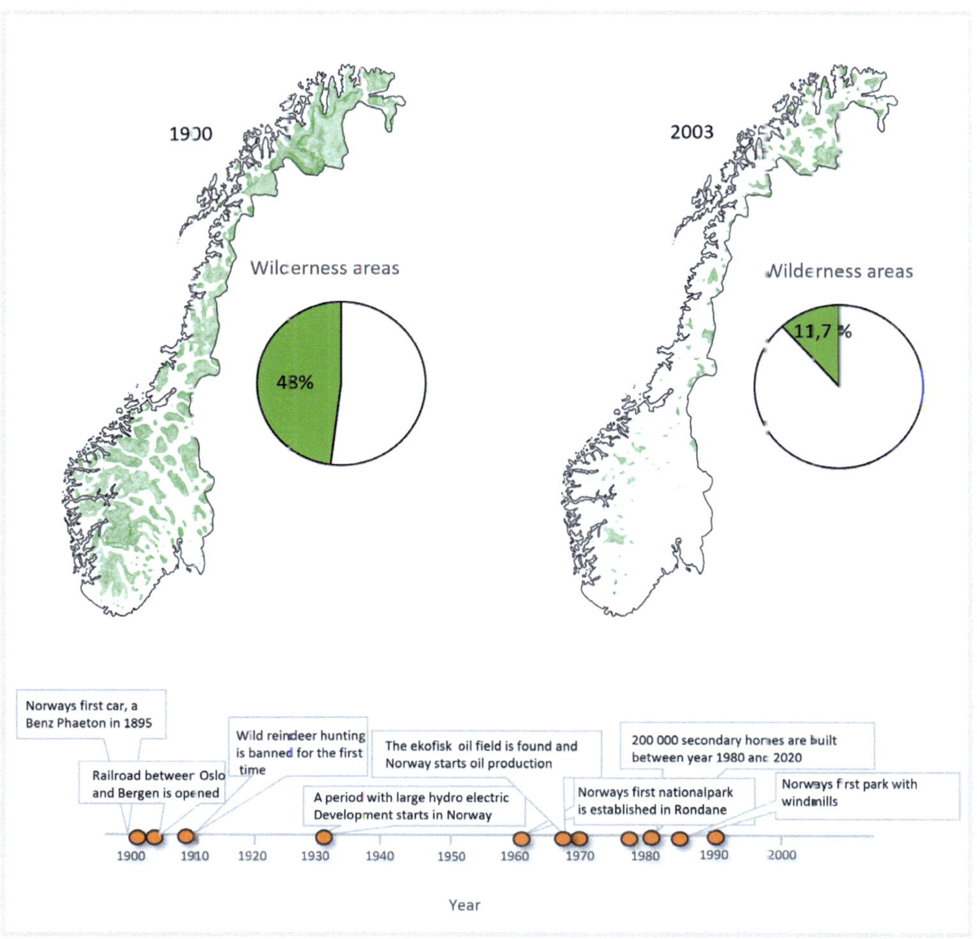

A NEW ERA

In 1911, the construction of the Bergen Line was completed, while the work on the Dovre Line and a continuous railway connection between the capital and Trondheim concluded after 70 years of effort in 1921. These giant projects can serve as markers for the beginning of what would become the industrialisation and modernisation of Norway. At this time, Norway, like the rest of the Western world, was characterised by hopes of innovation and progress. The beginning of the 20th century marked the start of a century that would change almost everything. It is telling that the word 'automobile' was first used in January 1889 (in the New York Times), and that the term 'Anthropocene' (the age of humans) was coined by atmospheric chemist Paul J. Crutzen in the year 2000. This term implies that human influence on the planet is now greater than all the natural influences combined. In the span of just one century, we have transformed the planet beyond recognition, and in the process much of the wilderness and indigenous cultures that were tied to the wild nature have been engulfed by modern civilisation. In our history spanning over 5,000 centuries , this is a concerningly short period of time. The loss of nature and the challenges it entails in reversing the negative trends we are facing is a global problem, as exemplified by the reindeer in our regions. In the next part, we will take a closer look at the relationship between reindeer and humans outside Scandinavia, and despite many differences we will also discover many similarities in the challenges that both reindeer and humans face.

PART VII

After over half a million years of utilising reindeer in Eurasia, the melting glaciers in Beringia, in the eastern parts of Russia and Alaska, provide hunters with opportunities to cross over to the American continent, where the strong connection between reindeer and humans continues. For millennia, on nearly one-tenth of the Earth's land area, reindeer have been the primary resource for dozens of different cultures in Eurasia and America. Although there are now nearly 5 million domestic and wild reindeer in this land area, the development of the populations is moving in the wrong direction. Warning signals are flashing on both sides of the Bering Strait.

HUNTERS ENTER AMERICA

As so many times before, it is the increasingly sophisticated methods of geneticists that shed light on the history of America's first inhabitants. They exploit the fact that even though the genetic material of two unrelated individuals is on average 99.9 per cent identical, there will be differences consisting of a single building block in the DNA being replaced by another, while the building blocks on each side of it do not vary between individuals. By comparing over 300,000 such specific variations among nearly 70 indigenous groups in North America and Siberia, geneticists can determine that there have been four different migrations to America across what is now the Bering Strait.

The first, and definitely the most extensive migration, occurred about 15,000 years ago, into what is now Alaska and further south along the west coast of Canada, and finally down into South America. Subsequently, two less extensive migrations bring new genetic material into the people who remained on the West Coast of Alaska and the islanders in the Aleutians, and to a lesser extent to the hunters who for the next 8,000 years would hunt reindeer in the northern parts of Canada – the Dene people. The fourth migration to America occurred about 4,500 years ago. It is the Dorset people who come and establish themselves in the Arctic areas on the east coast of Alaska, Canada and Greenland. According to the world-renowned biologist and geneticist Eske Willerslev from Denmark, this people brings with it a minimum of genetic variation. The whole people seem to stem from a single 'ancestral mother'. Whether this is the reason why the Dorset people on the mainland never number more than 2,000 individuals is unclear. What is clear, however, is that their culture disappears about 1,000 years ago, and the small hunter-gatherer societies along the coast and north of the tree line on both sides of Hudson Bay are replaced by a new culture – the Thule people, the origin of those formerly called Eskimos. Both the terms 'Indian' and 'Eskimo' are long outdated. Descendants of the first immigrants to America are now referred to as First Nations, while the various cultures stemming from the fourth migration are called Inuit. In addition, Métis – descendants of First Nations and the first European immigrants – are included in what is commonly referred to as Indigenous peoples.

Common to the Indigenous people who settle in the vast tundra areas and adjacent boreal forest areas from Alaska eastward to the coastal areas of Canada is that the vast majority are inseparably linked to reindeer. Extensive archaeological investigations reveal a surprisingly clear pattern. Over 8,000 years, there are four different hunter-gatherer cultures following four different herds of reindeer, and there is so little contact between them that the cultures develop their distinctive, easily recognisable ways of making weapons and tools, and they develop dialects still used today. Thus, we can trace the long history to our time. The reindeer that had their habitat furthest east, from the west side of Hudson Bay, with winter areas in the forest areas and calving areas on the tundra, are now called the Kaminuriak herd and are hunted by Eastern Chipewyan hunters. Further west, the Beverly herd is hunted by Western Chipewyan hunters, the Bathurst herd by Yellowknife hunters, and furthest west, the Bluenose herd by Dogrib or Tłı̨chǫ people.

Many in Norway are probably familiar with the book *Pelsjegerliv* (*Trapper Life*) by the Norwegian author, jurist, archaeologist, and adventurer Helge Ingstad. He lived for long periods with the Caribou Eaters, as the Western Chipewyan hunters were called, and convincingly writes about how dependent these hunter-gatherers are on access to reindeer from the Beverly herd. Although they hunted musk ox, moose, black bears, grizzlies and beavers, fished in the waters, and gathered eggs and berries, it was the hunting of the migrating reindeer herds that took up most of their time. In the hunting camps established at the places where the reindeer had to cross the large rivers on their journey to and from the calving areas and summer ranges on the tundra, among thousands of reindeer bones, only one musk ox bone has been found.

Archaeologists reveal that the hunting camps established in spring and late summer at the river crossing sites of the reindeer would number between 20 and 40 tents, each accommodating two families. Although parts of the group followed the reindeer onto the tundra in summer, it was crucial that the mass hunting at the rivers in spring provided enough food for them to survive until the autumn migration started. The fact that hunting could be effective is shown by the fact that wildlife biologists, at the same locations used by the hunter-gatherers, captured and radio-tagged nearly 7,000 reindeer over a six-year period not long ago. If one needs convincing of the effectiveness of the hunt, one can also go to where the reindeer cross the Burnside River.

From a long distance, one can still see the gleam of 3,500 antlers, which were used as underlying roof structures for four hunting lodges.

The late summer and autumn migration back to the winter areas in the forest areas in the south has evidently also been successful, providing the hunters with a fat-rich diet. There are many indications that this has affected the timing of childbirth. The amount of body fat affects pregnant women's chances of completing a pregnancy, and archaeologists suggest that this is why the Catholic Church's records after 1846 for the timing of baptisms show that four out of five children in the hunter groups are born in March and April, nine months after the reindeer's autumn migration.

In winter, the hunting camps move with the reindeer down into the forest areas, and they increase in size. Up to between 80 to 100 tents are recorded, which suggests that between 800 to 1,000 hunters were gathered. Freezing of waterways requires changes in hunting methods, and often traces of great activity are found in connection with open areas within the forest. Traces of fences suggest that the open areas were used as a form of enclosure to try to drive the reindeer into.

The total dependence on reindeer also exists in the areas east of Hudson Bay, in the northern parts of Quebec and Labrador. Here, both the Innu people and Inuit further north hunted the once so large George River herd. Like the Dene people further west, the Chukchi in Siberia, and the reindeer hunters in Ice Age Europe, reindeer are also the source of food, clothing and shelter for these hunter-gatherers. It influences their seasonal migrations, causes variations in body condition, and perhaps also the timing of when they should give birth to their children. It is therefore not so surprising that reindeer and their essence also permeate their mythology and supernatural beliefs.

BEHIND NATURE AND CULTURE – THE HUNTERS' COMMUNION WITH THE SPIRITS

One of the central areas of study in philosophy is the doctrine of being – ontology. It deals with how humans perceive themselves and human nature in relation to the environments they live in. According to the French philosopher Philippe Descola, there are four ontologies with a common starting point, as they all relate to how humans perceive the phenomena they encounter in the external world. The differences lie in how we expect other elements, such as animals, plants and places in the landscape, to be put together.

Today, much of the world relates to what is called naturalistic ontology, where essentially only natural phenomena exist, where everything in the universe can be reduced to the phenomena and objects that the natural sciences deal with, and where therefore the methods of the natural sciences are the only standard for the study of nature. The diametrical opposite of naturalistic ontology is animism, where animals, trees, plants, places and objects have different properties and external characteristics, but in return possess a common human inner nature – they have a soul! The idea that natural phenomena are animated has likely emerged through close contact with nature, and we find elements of this in earlier Sami religion, among American and Russian indigenous peoples, and among Aboriginal peoples.

What characterises ice age hunters and those who survive furthest north on the northern hemisphere after the ice age is that they are hunters. They live by killing animals and are themselves part of the environment consisting of large mammals. The hunters perceive themselves as one with nature; the community of animals and the community of humans are the same, the hunters must take a life, but there is an exchange of life. Although one should be careful about drawing parallels between the myths and beliefs that can be documented in today's hunting cultures on both sides of the Bering Strait, with those that existed among ice age hunters tens of thousands of years ago, it is highly likely that animism has been a common feature.

The Innu people on the Labrador Peninsula in Canada were traditionally a nomadic people, who in the northern and western areas had the caribou as their main prey animal. Although they tried to follow the caribou throughout the year, like the caribou eaters west of Hudson Bay, they had to be in the right place at the right time when the animals gathered and started their seasonal migrations between summer and winter grazing areas. The Montagnais people, who make up the majority of the Innu group, believed that these migrations were controlled by a master, a spirit who acted as the shepherd of the herd. This spirit was called the Caribou Man. He has a human appearance, white skin and a beard. He resides inside a huge cave, which can only be reached through a narrow passage. Inside the cave, he gathers his herd, and from there he sends out his animals on migration, after first deciding how many and which animals can be killed, and determining which hunters will be allowed to kill the different animals. However, the souls of the slaughtered caribou return to the cave, where they are incorporated into new animals to be sent out on the next occasion.

Although the individual hunter never approaches the cave or the area where the Caribou Man resides, a shaman from the Montagnais people can intercede with the Caribou Man and ask him to provide some more animals when times are especially lean for the Innu group. This is described by the philosopher Descola as a typical case of 'gift-giving' animism. The world is inhabited by spirits with a benevolent attitude towards humans. The Caribou Man and all the spirits that control the fate of other wild animals sacrifice their animals out of 'the goodness of their hearts', without expecting compensation, provided that hunting ethics are respected. The Caribou Man is the absolute master of the animals' destinies. He watches over them every day, pays attention to their well-being, controls their reproduction, and is the only judge when they must die. He is like a livestock breeder, which gives him the right and opportunity to dispose of the animals he controls as he wishes. As for the caribou itself, they present themselves to the hunters as a love-struck woman.

Mistassini Cree hunters in Quebec, who belong to the Innu people, say that the caribou is feminine by nature and can seduce the hunters. It takes the form of a beautiful girl who sometimes visits the hunters in their dreams. The killing of the caribou itself is considered a sexual act. This erotic symbolism associated with hunting is found in many regions of the world, but for Cree hunters, it is especially relevant, as it is only by a reindeer being killed by a man that a new animal can be brought forth.

On the other side of the Bering Strait, in north-eastern Siberia along the coast of the Arctic Ocean and the Bering Sea, the Chukchi also hunt wild reindeer, although the husbandry of domestic reindeer is the dominant activity today. As in North America, the fate of the reindeer here is also governed by spirits. The Chukchi call the lord of the wild reindeer Pičvu'čin. He is described as a tiny man, with a sled made of grass straws, and with mice as draught animals. Just like humans, he spends much of his time hunting, and his favourite game is lemming, which to him resembles a bear. Pičvu'čin lives with his reindeer in an underground den that can be reached through a deep cleft, and from there he sends out his herds to the hunters, except when the hunters fail to show him respect.

Unlike in North America, where the various hunting peoples have never tamed the reindeer, most Siberian ethnic groups have dealt with more or less domesticated reindeer. For the small and highly mobile hunting groups, access to a smaller number of domesticated reindeer was necessary to increase the efficiency of hunting their wild counterparts. The tamed reindeer were not only a secure source of milk and meat, but in some cases they were saddled and ridden, or harnessed in front of light sleds. Often, domestic animals were also used to attract wild counterparts. But the way they kept domestic reindeer varied. In the tundra regions, the Nenets, Yakuts and Dolgan people traditionally had large herds of domestic reindeer that they followed year-round. In the taiga regions, the reindeer herds were smaller and left to themselves for parts of the year. To the west, among the Selkup people, the domestic reindeer were also left to themselves in the summer and were not rounded up again until the first snowfall, when the hunting season for wild reindeer began. In the east, the Evenk people milk the female reindeer and therefore keep the herd near their camps in the summer. In the winter, they let them roam in the forest. So, when the snow begins to melt, they capture them again.

The Chukchi lord of the wild reindeer, Pičvu'čin, belongs to a class of spirits known as ke'let. These spirits have in common that they also have herds of domestic reindeer, which they use to pull sleds with. Some of the spirits also use tamed mammoths. In mythology, it is therefore not only the wild reindeer that is domesticated. According to the Evenki, who are found in Siberia in Russia, China and Mongolia, all wild species of animals and fish that we humans live on live in herds controlled by their masters.

Among the Yukaghirs, furthest east in Russia, they see the lords of the wild as happy guys who spend their time drinking and playing cards, and use the animals they are lord of as stakes. A species of animal can thus change hands depending on the luck of the game, a factor they believe can explain unexpected migrations of animal herds. Although the lords of the animals, like humans, primarily live by hunting, the relationships that humans establish with the lords of the animals are almost like an exchange relationship between livestock breeders. As compensation for the reindeer Pičvu'čin sends them, the Chukchi give him tobacco, sugar, flour and decorative items they have obtained from Russians.

There is a clear idea that the lord of the reindeer must, even if only symbolically, be compensated for the losses his herds incur as a result of human hunting. Furthermore, the wild reindeer bucks from Pičvu'čin are highly appreciated during the rutting season when they are attracted to the does in human herds and venture into the Chukchi camps. It is then easy to shoot them down, provided they have first mated with the does. Offspring from such pairings are considered very robust and valuable animals. When the bucks are finally killed, they are thanked with food offerings, and their heads are brought into the tents, where they are entertained with music. Perhaps these are traditions from far back in time. Do we sense here why ice age hunters made flutes from bird bones tens of thousands of years ago?

As in North America, the hunting of wild reindeer in Siberia has a sexual connection. The wild reindeer appears to the men in their dreams, in the form of beautiful young women who are daughters of the lord of the reindeer, and the men make love to them. Thus, there is an equivalence in gift-giving. The wild bucks provide the same sexual services to the Chukchi's domestic reindeer as the Chukchi provide to the daughters of the lord of the reindeer. The result on both sides is pregnancies that help increase livestock holdings. Like the wild reindeer, the Chukchi's domestic reindeer also depend on a non-human protector. The reindeer being, a spirit with somewhat vague properties, is totally different from Pičvu'čin, the lord of the wild reindeer, and belongs to a class of forces, va'IrgIt, that give soul to the whole world, including humans. While Pičvu'čin, and other types of benevolent spirits (ke'let, often have a relationship with humans, va'IrgIt are impersonal spirits with whom it is not possible to have any form of interaction.

Although the Chukchi in many ways try to identify with the reindeer being and work together with him to ensure the good health and protection of the domestic reindeer herd, no gifts are exchanged with the lord of the reindeer. So, there are slight changes in the relationships between humans and the spirit world as we move from the hunters in North America to the reindeer people in Siberia. It is therefore not a radical shift in people's relationship to the reindeer when going from being reindeer hunters to becoming reindeer herders. Nor is it the case that the availability of reindeer necessarily leads to the domestication of it. The hunting groups in North America refrained from following the same path as their Siberian neighbours.

At the end of the 19th century, the hunting people experienced a significant decline in wild reindeer populations on the Seward Peninsula in Alaska. Some then got the idea of importing domestic reindeer from north-eastern Siberia together with their Chukchi reindeer herders, to teach the Yup'ik people the techniques associated with reindeer husbandry. The idea for the whole experiment came from a missionary.

MISSIONARY IDEA HAS
MAJOR CONSEQUENCES

At the end of the 19th century, a missionary had an idea that would directly influence both the nature and culture of many indigenous peoples in Alaska and Canada until the beginning of World War II. The idea would also contribute to the presence of both caribou – wild reindeer, and reindeer – domesticated reindeer, in North America today, and indirectly lead to the fact that the first Santa Claus in America is Sami, that the world's first statue of a dog, with a well-known Sami name, is erected in Central Park in New York, and that a Sami person is nicknamed The Arctic Moses.

The missionary was Sheldon Jackson. Originally, he himself wished to do missionary work abroad, but the group of senior leaders in the Presbyterian Church believed that the short-statured, visually impaired, and disease-ridden missionary would be best suited for work in his homeland. He was therefore ordered to the western states of the USA before starting his work in Alaska in 1877.

In Alaska, both the inhabitants and the biological resources were in very poor condition. Russian Alaska had been heavily commercially exploited by fur trappers, seal hunters and whalers throughout the 18th and 19th centuries. The American fur and skin market seemed insatiable. Every American had to have a beaver hat, and dried whale baleen made its way south to be turned into corsets and frames for the American women's hoop skirts.

Conditions did not improve after Russia sold Alaska to the USA in 1867 for the friendly sum of 7.2 million dollars, equivalent to about 120 million dollars today. Rather the opposite. As if the smallpox epidemic that started in 1830 was not deadly enough on its own, migrating hunters brought influenza and measles, resulting in high mortality among the indigenous tribes in the area. By the time Sheldon Jackson arrived in Alaska, it was estimated that two-thirds of the Inuits, who can be divided into Yup'ik, Inupiat, and Inupiaq peoples, had died as a result of what was called 'The Great Death'. Those who survived were severely weakened by hunger.

Wildlife populations were greatly reduced, and hunting did not provide enough food for the indigenous tribes. Jackson, who at that time had made several trips across the Bering Strait to the Chukchi people on the Russian side, had seen how they had taken control of the reindeer. This not only provided them with a stable food supply, but they also used the reindeer for transportation and as draft animals. Jackson believed this should be tried in Alaska, and he had a long-term plan, which he now shared with his superiors.

Establishing Reindeer Stations adjacent to the missionary stations that were now emerging, he argued, would have several positive effects. Not only would domesticated reindeer husbandry elevate the indigenous people to self-sufficiency, they would also become friends and good helpers to the white man. In other words, the move would make the indigenous people dependent on their colonisers.

At the mission stations, they could also have the opportunity to convince the indigenous people to abandon their animistic worldview and instead embrace Christianity. The plan was well received by the authorities, who eventually appointed Jackson as General Agent for Education in Alaska. This would later give Jackson the opportunity to instruct all teachers to prohibit all teaching in the indigenous languages, a regulation that did not cease in Alaska until 1968! Jackson started cautiously.

The first 16 reindeer were brought from the Chukchi people in Russia in 1891, and released on Amaknak Island, which is part of the chain of islands stretching south-west from the Seward Peninsula in Alaska. The purpose was to see if they could survive in Alaska. The result was very satisfactory, so another 171 reindeer were brought the following year and released near the newly established Teller Reindeer Station on the Seward Peninsula. At the same time, Chukchi were hired as reindeer herders. However, these had long been trade rivals with the local Inupiaq people, and the cooperation between the two peoples was very poor – so poor that the Russians went home, and Jackson had to change his strategy.

Norwegian Sami from Finnmark came to the rescue. The Norwegian Kven William Kjellmann was employed as the chief at Teller Reindeer Station and sent to Finnmark to hire reindeer herders on three-year contracts. He succeeded well, and on April 10, 1894, the steamship Island departed from Norway with 13 Sami couples, 2 children, and a teenager on board. Just over a month later, they arrived in New York, where the Sami 'delegation' attracted considerable attention, dressed as they were in their traditional reindeer-skin jackets, tight trousers, and shoes or boots made from reindeer hides. The *New*

York Times reported that many had strangely shaped hats in garish colours, light blue eyes, and high cheekbones. It was also noted that the women were probably not going to participate in a beauty contest.

After transport by train across the continent and by boat from San Francisco, they arrived in Alaska at the end of July, over 3 ½ months after departing from Finnmark. Cooperation with the local hunting people went excellently. A multitude of youths who had lost their parents in The Great Death now received training in lassoing, fitting a halter on a reindeer, milking reindeer, making cheese, sewing skull caps from reindeer hide and making glue from the animal's hooves. The entire project was considered a success story. The reindeer herds increased in number, meat became available, and stories spread about the reindeer's formidable abilities as draft animals for transporting various goods.

The reindeer herders also seemed to thrive because when the contract expired in 1897, only three families returned to Norway. The entire project was scaled up in 1898. Early in February 1898, the old freighter Manitoban departed from Bossekop loaded with 539 reindeer, 418 sleds, 511 halters, and 250 tons of lichen, in addition to 113 Sami passengers. The reindeer were purchased by the US Army and were to be transported to Klondike in Canada to alleviate what the authorities feared could develop into a potential famine, as there was expected to be an influx of tens of thousands of American gold prospectors. It didn't go entirely according to plan. Both reindeer and people were delayed in Seattle. The lichen brought along was eaten up, and the animals were unable to utilise the grass offered to them in an area called Woodland Park outside the city. The animals weakened, about a dozen died, and when the survivors arrived in the port city of Haines, Alaska, to start the journey over the infamous Chilkoot Pass, the animals were too starved to begin the journey. The reindeer herders themselves went out to gather lichen for the starving herd, but with poor results. 387 animals died, and only 140 reindeer and 15 men made the journey over the pass. When they arrived at the settlement on the other side of the pass, the reindeer herders themselves were severely affected by scurvy, but access to large quantities of salmon made the herders healthy again, and they returned to the rest of the group after delivering the surviving reindeer.

The real work could now begin. Based on Teller Reindeer Station, the Sami passengers from Manitoba would play a leading role in the story of community development in the northernmost part of America. Over the years, they took in 600 apprentices from the Yup'ik and Inupiaq peoples, and trained them to become fully-fledged reindeer herders. The reindeer herds grew in size from a few hundred to over 27,000 animals by 1910. During this period, the most industrious Sami people themselves built up large herds of reindeer and hired both local and Sami reindeer herders.

At the same time, about 20 Reindeer Stations were established from Point Barrow in the north-east to Lake Charles in the south. Small post offices emerged in places where gold prospectors and fur trappers gathered, and on the several-mile-long mail routes, reindeer herders with sled-pulling reindeer took care of delivering mail and goods. They performed this task far faster and more efficiently than the previous dog sled teams could manage. The success was formidable. The reindeer provided both food and clothing for the local population, and especially food for the hordes of gold prospectors who had now arrived in Alaska after gold was found in Nome. Once again, it was the passengers from Manitoba who would play a crucial role, both directly and indirectly.

On the ship were both Samuel Balto and Jafet Lindeberg. Samuel Balto from Karasjok was widely famous at the time for his participation in Fridtjof Nansen's expedition across the Greenland ice sheet in 1888. The two had kept in good contact, and already in 1899, the year after he arrived in Alaska, Balto wrote a letter to Nansen. He told him that he and the other Sami people hired by Sheldon Jackson to operate one of the Reindeer stations had broken their contracts. The reason for the breach was that William Kjellmann, the Kven who was their immediate superior, had started selling off the provisions they were supposed to have, and then pocketed the money for himself. This resulted in poor nutrition and the development of scurvy. They had therefore headed west to Nome, where one of the other passengers had found gold.

Jafet Lindeberg from Kvænangen was originally supposed to be sent to Russia to buy more reindeer from the Chukchi people, which he refused. Sheldon Jackson became furious, and Lindeberg was dismissed, after which he took the steamboat up to Nome (then Anvil), where he met two enterprising Swedes. They quickly found large gold deposits and started The Pioneer Mining Company. The small Inuit village with a few hundred inhabitants saw an influx of tens of thousands of eager gold prospectors the following year, in 1899. Lindeberg, who would later be considered America's richest Norwegian, invited several of his friends from Norway to Alaska, one of whom was the Kven Leonard Seppala from Skjervøy. He quickly established himself as an outstanding dogsled musher and would soon be given an important task.

The gold mining activity in Nome lasted for several decades, and access to reindeer meat from domestic reindeer husbandry was crucial to sustain this activity. However, in January 1925, a disease epidemic began to spread among the gold miners. The cause of the infections in the nose and throat turned out to be caused by the diphtheria bacterium. A few managed to leave the city by boat transport, while the others depended on the antidote, diphtheria serum, which was located in Anchorage. Due to extreme cold, a plane in the city refused to start, and the serum was transported by train to Nenana, and loaded onto Leonard Seppala's dogsled. Together with lead dog Togo, he completed the longest leg of the 1,200 kilometre journey to Nome and handed over the 'charm leg' to the Kven Gunnar Kaasen, who chose Balto, named after Samuel, as his lead dog. Just five days after starting in Nenana, the serum arrived in Nome, averting the feared epidemic. Balto became, somewhat undeservedly, the great hero, and the same year a statue of him was erected in Central Park in New York City.

At the same time, domestic reindeer husbandry was growing. In 1920, there were over 600,000 domestic reindeer in Alaska, divided into 98 herds, and two Norwegian-American brothers, Carl and Alfred Lomen, saw the opportunities to create a small industrial adventure. In 1914, they established Lomen & Company and began purchasing reindeer, while also hiring Sami reindeer herders. In Alaska, they established large slaughterhouses and associated freezing facilities, and boats with freezing capacity transported large quantities of reindeer meat to Seattle. Eventually, they controlled the entire value chain, and both reindeer meat and Sami products were sold in their own warehouses across the United States.

In 1923, they ensured that Santa Claus and reindeer became an integral part of American Christmas history. The Sami Mathis Ivar Klementsen Nillika dressed up as Santa Claus and was sent with some domestic reindeer and sleds to cities in Alaska. This attracted national attention. So did the number of letters that Santa, oddly enough, had received from children across the United States. The letters, written by the Lomen brothers themselves, had detailed lists of gift wishes; presumably some of Lomen & Company's products were also on the lists. Sales of products from domestic reindeer husbandry increased dramatically.

Canadian authorities decided to participate in the reindeer adventure unfolding in the neighbouring country. In 1929, they purchased 3,442 reindeer from the Lomen brothers. The reindeer were located in the Kotzebue area far north on the Seward Peninsula and were to be delivered to Kittigazuit near the Mackenzie River in the Northwest Territories. Experienced reindeer herders estimated that moving such a large herd would take about 18 months. Canadian authorities began the hunt for individuals with the necessary expertise and hired the then 60-year-old Sami Anders Bær as the head of the entire operation. Together with a dozen other reindeer herders, they set out from Kotzebue on December 14, 1929. The journey would be far from easy. They encountered swollen rivers that couldn't be crossed, feed supplies were often at critical levels, and the herd had to be taken to other grazing areas than those planned. The relocation of the large reindeer herd received considerable attention both in the USA and Canada, and many eagerly followed the news. When Anders Bær arrived at the delivery location with 2,382 reindeer on February 25, 1935, after five years on the road, he had long been dubbed 'The Arctic Moses', and in Seattle and other cities 'The Andy Baer Day' on February 25 was celebrated for many years.

Long before the Arctic Moses arrived in Canada, American cattle producers had begun to react to the large-scale production of reindeer meat. The Sami and local reindeer herders also reacted. The reindeer herds of the Lomen brothers were growing, and the need for new grazing lands increased accordingly. The Inuit who had built up their own herds lost out in the competition with the Lomen brothers, and several Sami reindeer herders employed by Lomen Company resigned in protest. It all came to a head in 1929. Over half a million reindeer were using the same grazing areas, herds mixed, and in the chaos that ensued many domestic reindeer disappeared into the wild reindeer herds. Cattle producers, who had been actively lobbying central politicians, succeeded in establishing a Reindeer Council consisting of state representatives and Inuit, excluding the Sami. The goal of the Reindeer Council was to organise and regulate reindeer grazing areas in western parts of Alaska.

The work continued until September 1937. Then, Congress passed The Reindeer Act, which fell under the Bureau of Indian Affairs. They could then, with the law in hand, transfer ownership of all domestic reindeer to Native Alaskan citizens. This meant that all 'non-natives' must sell their reindeer herds. Sami reindeer herders were given 14 days to dispose of their herds and were offered $3-4 for each reindeer. The same applied to the Lomen brothers, who in 1939 sold all their reindeer to the state for $720,000.

Many of the Inuit quickly lost interest in domestic reindeer husbandry, as it came at the expense of time they preferred to spend hunting, fishing and trapping fur game in the winter. Consuming meat that they had 'produced' instead of acquiring meat by continuing to collaborate with the lord of the wild reindeer, as they had done for millennia, was also unpopular. Therefore, the reindeer husbandry industry was in freefall.

But after World War II, domestic reindeer husbandry was re-established with about 25,000 domestic reindeer on the Seward Peninsula. In 1997, the ban on 'non-natives' owning reindeer was lifted, and today there are about 18,000 domestic reindeer in Alaska, managed in about 20 herds, most of them on the Seward Peninsula. When parts of what is called the Teller Kakaruk Lee herd are gathered for slaughter, Donald Olson is often present. He is best known as a practising physician and senator for District T in Alaska, and he is the grandson of one of the Sami who enlisted on the Manitoban in Bossekop in 1898. So, once again, people with Sami blood are actively involved in American domestic reindeer husbandry, all thanks to a missionary from the Presbyterian Church.

NOW WARNING LIGHTS ARE FLASHING IN THE CIRCUMPOLAR NORTHERN REGIONS

On one-tenth of the Earth's surface, there is still a strong interdependence between humans, and wild and domestic reindeer. In the circumpolar tundra, mountain and forest areas, the adaptable reindeer has developed various strategies to survive. Some mountain reindeer undertake seasonal migrations between alpine meadows and lush forest valleys, others reside in forested areas year-round; many migrate between winter areas in forests to summer areas on the tundra, while a few travel on sea ice between Arctic islands. What they all have in common, whether partially domesticated or wild, is that they constitute a very important part of the lives of the people who live in the same areas. In most cases, it is correct to say that people could not have utilised these areas if it were not for the reindeer.

Roughly speaking, there are as many wild reindeer as there are domestic reindeer in the world today, about 2.5 million of each. With 5 million cold-adapted and resilient animals spread over a vast area, one would therefore assume that the situation is good, and that the relationship between Rangifer and *Homo*, which has lasted for over half a million years, can be continued far into the future. Unfortunately, that is not the case. Warning lights are now flashing on both sides of the Bering Strait.

In the 1960s, Salt Spring Island in the strait between mainland British Columbia and Vancouver Island was a sanctuary for American boys and men who wanted to avoid being sent to Vietnam to fight. Today, it is a secluded residence for the experienced caribou researcher Anne Gunn. This petite, now gray-haired woman, is characterised by her younger colleagues as a symbol, almost an icon, and everyone listens when she presents her findings in her quiet manner. For over three decades, she worked in the Northwest Territory in Canada, where she monitored the development of the Bathurst herd, which the Tłįcho people hunted. When she started her work in 1986, the herd counted 500,000 individuals, and the Tłįcho people could harvest about 14,000 animals annually. This was enough to feed the members of the hunting group, while some animals could be exchanged for goods and services the group needed, and, most importantly, enough for their ancient traditions related to hunting and the use of resources to be passed on to the young members of the group.

When Anne stepped up to the podium at the Hotel Captain Cook during a North American caribou conference in May 2023, she could report that the Bathurst herd was now down to 6,240 individuals. Calmly, with slightly teary eyes, she exclaimed, 'I'm glad I'm not a biologist up there now. It would have been heartbreaking to see an empty landscape.' Unfortunately, that's not the only empty landscape.

Doctoral student Melanie Dickie from Okanagan University in British Columbia is one of those following in Anne Gunn's footsteps. In collaboration with the Alberta Biodiversity Monitoring Institute, she monitors the development of the many small and fragmented populations of woodland caribou in Alberta and British Columbia, and her message in 2023 reached all national media in Canada; 'We have lost seven caribou herds since 2003. Banff, Purcell Centre, Burnt Pine, South Selkirk, George Mountain, South Purcell, and Maligne are all completely extinct.'

The beaver is indeed the country's national animal, but it is the caribou – reindeer – that is imprinted on Canada's quarter, and most Canadians have a relationship with the animal. So while the extinction of the Maligne herd from Jasper National Park in 2020 only elicited a small, inconspicuous note on the homepage of Parks Canada, others were more vocal. They believed this was a tragic, but definitely predictable event, resulting from decades of failed management.

The authorities, with strong support from Parks Canada, had rejected the demand to close the roads into the park in winter because this would have too negative an effect on the tourism industry. The roads not only gave ski tourists opportunities to enjoy themselves for four winter months, they also provided easier access for wolves to the areas. The reindeer's avoidance of good winter pastures and intense predation from wolves are considered the main reasons for the extinction of the Maligne herd, while two other herds in the national park, the Tonquin and Brazeau herds, seem to be suffering the same fate.

Anne Gunn is not surprised. Together with her good colleague Don Russell, she has documented the situation for wild reindeer in all seven countries where the animal is still present, and has contributed to the fact that wild reindeer are now characterised as vulnerable on the international red list, after a general decline of 40% over the past 20 years. In the vast areas where wild reindeer live, the population figures they have access to show that there are various factors affecting the condition of the reindeer herds. The southernmost herds of reindeer on both sides of the Bering Strait are mainly affected by various forms of human activity, while the dramatic fluctuations occasionally recorded in the many small populations on the barren Arctic islands in both Canada and Russia are probably caused by extreme weather conditions. For the vast majority of the world's wild reindeer – the far-ranging reindeer that spend much of the summer months on the tundra – the picture is more complex, but where climate change now plays an increasingly significant role.

In the confined mountain and forest areas in Canada, there are now nearly 40 herds of reindeer with fewer than 100 individuals. Common to all of these is that they live in areas with significant human activity, and they now use less than half of their original grazing areas. Fully 70 per cent of the original winter pastures for these reindeer herds are affected by some form of human activity. Winter tourism is increasing, cabins and roads are being built, lichens that cling to trunks and branches in old coniferous forests disappear when the forests are replaced by rapidly growing deciduous trees for biofuel production. All of this leads to changes in the reindeer's habitat use. The traditional migrations from summer to winter areas cease, and survival decreases. Of Canada's three so-called ecotypes of mountain reindeer, all are on the environmental authorities' lists of species that are either highly threatened or require special attention. In total, the various herds amount to no more than 45,000 animals, and the decline has been between 30 – 65 per cent over a 20-year period. The situation is not better for the Canadian woodland caribou, of which there are now only about 25,000 individuals left.

Unfortunately, the situation in Canada is recognisable wherever reindeer inhabit confined mountain areas and forests. Also, in Russia and Alaska, the mountain and forest reindeer are in a vulnerable position. In Russia, the decline in the number of reindeer in mountain areas is about 40 per cent, and in Alaska, the 23 different herds of mountain reindeer have been halved in size since the mid-1990s, now totalling 150,000 individuals. Common to small reindeer herds located in confined mountain and forest areas is that random events can have major consequences. Dry hot summers, harsh winters, and outbreaks of disease can lead to collapses in the herds, and the hunting of animals must be quickly adapted to such conditions to avoid the herds disappearing completely. Even in the sparsely populated border areas between Russia, China and Mongolia in the Altai-Sayan region, the long-legged woodland reindeer with the lovely first name valentinae have had their winter areas fragmented thanks to roads and railways built as a result of extensive mining, while winter tourism has increased in activity.

However, it is the large variations in the herds of far-ranging tundra reindeer on both sides of the Bering Strait that receive the most media attention. These once enormous herds have been greatly reduced. When gold miners came to Yukon in the late 1800s, the then 600,000-strong 40-mile herd took several days to cross the Yukon River. By the 1970s, the herd was reduced to 4,000 animals, and the migration between Alaska and Yukon ceased completely. In Canada, in 2020, there were still 730,000 far-ranging tundra reindeer, but the decline in some of the herds had been extreme. The George River herd in Labrador has been reduced by 99 per cent over the past three decades, from 823,000 in 1993 to 5,500 in 2018, before a small increase to 7,200 animals in 2022.

The decline in the number of wild tundra reindeer is also being observed in Russia. On the Taimyr Peninsula, the northernmost part of Russia, the world's largest herd of migrating tundra reindeer still exists. The herd is believed to have once been as large as 1.3 million animals, providing the Dolgan, Nenets, Nganasan and Evenki people with the resources they needed to survive in these climatically harsh areas. By the 1970s, the herd had been reduced to 400,000 animals, but that did not stop the Russian state from initiating commercial exploitation of the herd to bolster the local economy. However, after the dissolution of the Soviet Union in 1991, the subsidised hunting of reindeer was stopped, and the herd increased to 1 million animals by 2000. Since then, there has been a significant decline due to increased human activity and warmer climate.

Construction of roads, railways and gas pipelines now prevents the reindeer from reaching their old winter pastures in the south-west, while high summer temperatures have increased insect infestation, causing the herd to exploit higher-altitude areas where food availability is poorer. In winter, periods of rain occur more frequently. This often freezes on the ground, and the winter pastures are covered with an impenetrable layer of ice. This is, of course, also a challenge for domestic reindeer herds. Today, approximately 2.5 million domestic reindeer graze over 4 million km² of the northern land areas of

Eurasia, and the over 100,000 herds of domestic reindeer are central elements in the social, cultural, spiritual and economic life of more than 20 different indigenous groups. A circumpolar cultural and ecological mourning is spreading on both sides of the Bering Strait.

PART VIII

A cultural and ecological sorrow is spreading. It is the same thing happening on both sides of the Bering Strait, regardless of whether the reindeer are wild or domesticated, regardless of whether people speak Inuktitut, Nenets, Southern Sami, Northern Sami, or a dialect from Harding; the reindeer's former grazing areas are being fragmented due to various forms of human activity, warmer climates pose significant challenges to the cold-adapted reindeer, and it is increasingly difficult to pass on traditional knowledge, language and ways of life.

CIRCUMPOLAR CULTURAL AND ECOLOGICAL SORROW

Various forms of reindeer husbandry occur in 9 countries, 10 if we also include the management of the 150 animals in the Cairngorm Mountains in Scotland, descendants of the animals brought over by Mikel Utsi from Sweden in the 1950s. He was on his honeymoon in the area with his wife Ethel Lindgren in 1949, but still had enough time and energy to ponder why he hadn't seen any reindeer in the mountains. When he was told that the last reindeer disappeared from the country over 1,000 years ago, he decided to do something about it. And the rest is history. We already know the stories of reindeer husbandry in Alaska and Canada. The descendants of the reindeer brought by the Arctic Moses, Anders Bær, from Alaska to the Mackenzie Delta in 1935, are now managed by the private company Canadian Reindeer, which in collaboration with the local Inuvialuit community organises the Crossing the River Event every year in early April when the reindeer herd crosses the river on their way to the calving areas.

Reindeer are found at the southern tip of Greenland, where the privately owned Isortoq Reindeer Station manages the approximately 2,000 animals descended from reindeer brought in from Karasjok in 1952. Reindeer husbandry also exists in the northernmost parts of Mongolia and in the north-eastern parts of China, but it is in Fennoscandia and Russia that we find the large-scale management of domestic reindeer.

THE SITUATION IN EURASIA

The northern regions of Russia have been home to a large number of indigenous groups with one commonality – for thousands of years, they have been entirely dependent on reindeer. Farthest north, long migrations after the reindeer, which utilised the tundra areas in the summer season, were the most important element in the livelihoods of both reindeer herders and hunters. In the taiga areas further south, the seasonal movements of reindeer were not as long, but the people still had to be mobile. In the 16th century, people engaged in agriculture with the breeding of horses and cattle began to enter the southern parts of Siberia. Former hunting grounds were gradually converted into pastureland through the burning of forests, and by the 17th century some indigenous peoples were assimilated into settled communities, abandoning their way of life, language and culture. And it would get worse. With the October Revolution in 1917 and the establishment of the U.S.S.R., Russia almost overnight became a socialist state. The lifestyle of indigenous peoples was radically changed, with forced relocations of entire ethnic groups and the influx of new ones.

The nomadic movements of domestic reindeer herders and hunter-gatherer communities over vast territories and decentralised food production did not fit into the state's five-year plans for the collectivisation and industrialisation of both rural and urban areas. Previously nomadic reindeer herding and hunting communities were forced to settle and were relocated to increasingly compact production centres. In order to plan relocation and at the same time gain an overview of the production the people could be assigned to, an inventory of the various indigenous groups in the north was needed. In the 1920s, lists of 'small-numbered peoples' and 'large-numbered peoples' of non-Slavic origin were created. KMNS was the abbreviation Russian authorities used for a list of 'numerically small indigenous groups in the north, the Far East, and Siberia in the Russian Federation'. Forty different groups were named, thus meeting the criteria that there are fewer than 50,000 individuals, localised and living in their original territory, maintaining their traditional culture and way of life, and considering themselves as a distinct ethnic group. For nearly half of these ethnic groups in Russia, the reindeer defined their way of life and culture.

Now 73 years old, Maria Pagodaeva belongs to one of these groups. She belongs to the Eveny people who, for millennia, have engaged in small-scale domestic reindeer herding in the forest. She is dismayed that what she calls 'reindeer nations' have never been considered equal partners. It's always other nations making decisions that change the traditional way of life of reindeer people, forcing them to become settled, separating children from parents, stopping private ownership of reindeer, and ensuring that traditional knowledge, language and culture are lost. And she is dismayed to hear that even though the transfer of reindeer herds to the state was a painful process, people accepted it. This is not correct, she asserts. People did not accept it, and collectivisation caused enormous moral damage that has not yet healed. Maria believes that the Nenets fared the best, thanks to their ability to maintain some reindeer herds in private hands.

The Nenets, people who refer to themselves as Nenèj nenec – the real people, were previously called Samoyeds and are located on both sides of the Ural Mountains, making them both Europeans and Asians. With just over 40,000 people, the group is the largest among the few, and most of them are involved in large-scale nomadic reindeer herding on the tundra. The journey from the winter pastures in the south to the summer pastures in the north of the tundra is long, for some over 700 kilometres. It is not difficult to understand that to manage the task of herding a herd of thousands of reindeer through an entire year in Arctic conditions, a significant amount of knowledge about various aspects is required, knowledge that can only be acquired and learned through active participation under the guidance of experienced elders.

The Nenets' domestic reindeer herding is characterised by close contact with the animals throughout the year and, previously, the entire family participated in the migrations between the seasonal grazing areas. The role of women in maintaining traditional knowledge was particularly important. The younger generation were taught skills such as making and maintaining tents on the Arctic tundra, producing clothes and shoes from reindeer skins, caring for children during and after childbirth under nomadic and extreme Arctic conditions, and general child-rearing knowledge on the tundra. But this transfer of traditional knowledge is now breaking down, even for the Nenets. The state education system, while aspiring for ethnic groups to receive education in their own culture and language, is undermining the opportunities for the traditional and unique nomadic Arctic culture to be passed on. School education does not cover any of the knowledge required to return to a nomadic life, and most girls and women choose to permanently settle in villages after completing their education. This puts the culture of several of the small indigenous groups, not just the Nenets, at risk. For they are not many. Scattered throughout the vast northern Russian territories, which make up more than half of the country's area and span over 11 time zones, it is estimated today that the indigenous groups that before the 17th century almost ruled over this area alone, number around 250,000 people. This constitutes 0.2 per cent of the total population in the area, as until the collapse of the Soviet Union in 1991 many residents in Northern Russia were attracted northward mostly from western areas of the Soviet Union by a combination of Soviet-planned economic incentives and state-regulated immigration.

Many places in northern Russia are now fighting for their existence, while some have already lost. The tragic story of the reindeer herders living along the Viliui River, far west in the Sakha Republic (formerly known as Yakutia), contains all the elements that today also pose a threat to the existence of various indigenous cultures in Russia: assimilation into a larger dominant culture, loss of control and access to former grazing areas and natural resources, and forced relocation to make way for industrial development.

Before the immigration of agricultural groups in the 16th century, reindeer husbandry and hunting were the main activities of the Evenki people in the area. The people who now entered the area engaged primarily in horse and cattle breeding, quickly starting to create new pasturelands by burning down forest areas. This not only destroyed the reindeer lichen, but also resulted in a depletion of the wild resources that the reindeer herders had relied on. Gradually, the reindeer herders were forced to move to more remote mountainous areas – areas unsuitable for animal husbandry and agriculture. Written sources from the late 19th century, however, show that many of the former reindeer herders had been assimilated into the larger Sakha culture, adopting both the language and lifestyle of the agricultural people. There are believed to be two different reasons for this assimilation: an epidemic outbreak in the 1830s that caused high reindeer mortality, and a high demand for reindeer to serve as pack animals after a large gold mine was opened in the area. Many chose to sell their reindeer and instead engage in horse and cattle breeding. By the 20th century, there were only two reindeer herding communities left in the Viliui area. One group, the Shologinsky people – which literally meant 'inhabitants of the upper river areas', were forcibly relocated by the Soviet government to more northern areas two years before the first of two large diamond mines was opened in 1954. The other group, the Sadinsky people, were initially granted their own region – the Sadinsky national region – but in 1947 the Soviet government deemed the entire region lacking prospects and abolished it. The official reason was that hunting and reindeer herding communities would never develop agriculture, seen as their only hope for progress. The total population was also too small to become independent collectives, and the population was too scattered for effective administrative guidance.

The final blow to the last remnants of reindeer husbandry in the area came when it was realised that diamond mining required large amounts of energy. A large reservoir was therefore planned in the Chona Valley, which would flood both settlement areas and the best grazing lands for reindeer. Protests helped little, and the reindeer herders were now promised good conditions at the newly established agricultural collective that would supply meat and milk to the rapidly growing mining town in the area. When the valley was flooded in 1967, it marked the end of the reindeer herding culture in the area, and for the 270 people who moved, it also marked the beginning of a difficult time. Today's doctor at the agricultural collective was herself involved in the relocation as a little girl. The grief and stress over the loss of culture affected the elders and reduced their quality of life to the extent that it had medical consequences, she says. Not surprisingly, she says, because 'it was such a lush and wild place – moose and bears came up to our door – we lived off hunting and reindeer herding, and on Toy Khaya, the highest mountain in the area, the beautiful snowdrops bloomed in the spring, and we gathered there and danced the circle dance.'

That the former owner of the Chelsea Football Club, oligarch Roman Abramovich, has a small role in the story of man and reindeer may surprise many. But far north-east in Russia, in Chukotka, the area that formed the gateway for immigration to North America and where missionary Sheldon Jackson obtained his first reindeer, Roman is highly regarded. Chukotka is one of the world's most remote places. There are no roads leading into the region, and the only way to reach Chukotka is by the weekly flight from Moscow, nine time zones further west. Its remoteness is likely also the reason why the area was the last to come under communist control. A small coastal population that mainly subsisted on hunting marine mammals was now moved into state collectives together with the much larger group of Chukchi, most of whom herded large reindeer herds on the tundra. For a period, reindeer numbers increased. By the 1980s, there were over half a million reindeer in the area. But the collapse of the Soviet Union also caused a collapse in reindeer husbandry here. State subsidies disappeared, collective farms were shut down, and many had to give up reindeer husbandry, with reindeer numbers dropping to around 90,000 at the start of the new century.

Just a decade after the fall of the Soviet Union, Roman Abramovich had managed to amass great wealth from dividends and sales following the privatisation of former state enterprises, mainly steel and coal mines. In 2000, 33-year-old Roman was appointed governor of Chukotka by Vladimir Putin. He had more than hinted that Roman should use part of his fortune on infrastructure in the area, and over the next eight years, large sums were invested in modern slaughterhouses, schools, hospitals and roads. Reindeer husbandry increased again, and optimism returned to the population. When Roman politely declined a new term as governor in 2008, the leader of the Chukotka parliament, Vasily Nazarenko, stated that Governor Roman had saved the entire region's population from death, and he now saw the future in dark colours. Others, however, point out that even though reindeer husbandry is a difficult and challenging way of life, it can function almost disconnected from the outside world, so if our civilisation were to end, the Chukchi would continue to live as they do today. Not impossible, but to achieve that the northern reindeer husbandry's greatest challenge – global warming – must be controlled.

Russia is highly vulnerable to the effects of global climate change. Global warming in the Russian north will lead to the degradation of permafrost, increasing air temperatures, precipitation and the frequency of extreme events. The taiga, the boreal forest belt that stretches over large parts of the northern hemisphere, is the world's largest carbon reservoir by far. With rising temperatures, it is estimated that in Northern Russia, half of these forests will be replaced by more heat-demanding deciduous forests.

One of those who will notice the increasing temperatures the most is Jakov Japtik. For thousands of years, Jakov and his ancestors from the Nenets people have been migrating with the reindeer along the 70-mile-long Yamal Peninsula in Northern Russia. In the summer, they head north to the summer pastures, and in the winter, they travel the same way south. But even in this remote region in north-west Siberia, one can see the effects of global warming. Traditionally, Jakov and the reindeer crossed the frozen Ob River in November, but now the winter migration is delayed. It's not until the end of December that the ice is thick enough. The delay causes the reindeer herd to overgraze the pastures. 'Our reindeer were starving, there wasn't enough food, and in spring, the snow melts faster and faster, making it difficult for the reindeer to pull the sleds. They get tired,' says Jakov. The Nenets people clearly notice that the weather is becoming increasingly unpredictable. Snowstorms can occur when the reindeer give birth in May, while autumns are longer and milder. 'The changes are not good for the reindeer, and, ultimately, what's good for the reindeer is good for us,' Jakov claims.

One year, Jakov and his family arrived at their summer camp and discovered that half of their lake had disappeared. The permafrost had melted, and a landslide had changed the course of the water. Although avalanches can occur naturally, scientists say there is unmistakable evidence that the ancient permafrost of Yamal is melting. Jakov can also report other strange changes – there are fewer mosquitoes, but a drastic increase in both horseflies and blackflies. These are insects that the reindeer try to avoid by seeking out snowdrifts or higher-altitude areas and, in the worst-case scenario, attacks by horseflies and blackflies can weaken the animals and cause high mortality.

Both Russian and international researchers are now linking such changes to the ongoing process of global warming. Increasingly, it is claimed that the melting of Russia's permafrost will have catastrophic results for the world, as billions of tons of carbon dioxide and methane previously trapped in frozen soil are released. For Russia, which is already warming one and a half times faster than other parts of the world, the impact will be catastrophic. Much of Russia's northern region would become impassable swamp, and reindeer herding on the tundra would become impossible. Already, houses in several Arctic cities are beginning to sink into the ground, and more and more people are speculating about what will happen to the 8,000 kilometres of railway tracks built on permafrost.

For now, Jakov is still on the tundra. 'I've lived my whole life on the tundra. Reindeer for us are everything – food, transportation and shelter. All I hope is that we can continue with this life.' We can only hope.

THE SITUATION IN
NORTH AMERICA

In North America, on the other side of the Bering Strait, hunters first noticed the influx of new ethnic groups in the 1800s. Admittedly, Leif Erikson probably had contact with the Dorset people, the predecessors of the Inuit, both on Baffin Island (referred to as Helluland in the saga), Labrador (Markland), and Newfoundland (Vinland) over 1,000 years ago, but there probably wasn't much prolonged interaction between the Norse people from Greenland and the 'skrælings', as Leif called them. It's only three centuries after the Italian Columbus's navigational error and the opening up to European immigration that fur traders and gold diggers find their way to the northernmost parts of the continent, marking the start of a tragic period in North America's history.

The process of nation-building in Canada involved the exclusion and marginalisation of many indigenous groups. They were systematically deprived of any rights and denied the right to vote in local and federal elections. To become citizens, they had to give up their status and demonstrate literacy, debt-free status, and good moral character (in 1876, only one man was found to meet these criteria). Many indigenous people were placed in reserves, but they had no property rights, which limited their economic development because it was impossible to mortgage the land for credit. The Indian Act of 1876 required that chiefs of the various groups should attain their position through formal elections, but the government later gave itself the power to depose chiefs. Women who married men of European descent had to relinquish their indigenous status, which, of course, did not apply to men. Women who lost their status also lost the right to reside on indigenous lands and the right to be buried within a reserve. They could not regain their status and thus return to their homes if the marriage ended. This provision was not changed until 1985. Women were also not allowed to run for leadership positions, and widows had to prove they had 'good moral character' to inherit property.

In 1884, the federal government banned the potlatch, the traditional ceremony involving feasting and sharing of goods to promote reconciliation and cooperation among indigenous peoples. In the 1880s, there were also demands for indigenous children to attend schools. These residential schools, often run by Christian missionaries, had a clear goal of promoting the assimilation of indigenous peoples. Tens of thousands of children were deeply traumatised and alienated from their families and communities as a result of the treatment they received at these schools. Together, this policy functioned as a well-coordinated attempt to undermine indigenous cultures and ways of life. Indigenous groups that were not placed in newly established reserves were often subjected to forced relocation.

Inuk David Serkoak was just a child when his family and others from the Ahiarmiut people were repeatedly moved by the Canadian government to various locations in the Arctic, partly to free up land for government activities and partly to keep the Inuit population under government control and surveillance. For almost three decades, he has researched the history of his people, and together with the Canadian Museum for Human Rights, created an eye-opening exhibition. Unfortunately, the sad story that unfolds is not unique. Reindeer-hunting indigenous peoples have been forcibly relocated on several occasions in the Northern Canadian Arctic regions.

The Ahiarmiut people had their hunting grounds around Ennadai Lake, and their entire way of life was based on the exploitation of caribou. After World War II, the Canadian Army built a military radio station in the area, and reports from the station operators were the trigger for the first of many subsequent relocations. The operators had noticed food shortages in the hunting group and feared that the hunters would become dependent on assistance from the military base. For David and the others in the group, the situation was not unusual. They were well aware that the caribou migration routes could change, and that there could be periods of insufficient food. 'We accepted it because we know it's how it is,' says David. They were therefore completely unprepared for what was about to happen.

Without warning, heavily armed military personnel accompanied by a policeman arrived at the camp. Everyone was ordered out of the tents, a bulldozer was started, and the camp was quickly leveled and buried. They were then ordered into seaplanes that transported them to Nueltin Lake, hundreds of kilometres farther east. No tents were brought on the trip, and the group had to sleep outdoors. Some of the elders in the group froze to death. In late autumn, as the lake began to freeze over, the remaining group decided to return to their original settlement, and by Christmas most were back at Ennadai Lake.

The Canadian government did not give up easily, so, in 1957, still without the consent of the Ahiarmiut people, the group was transported to Henik Lake, 200 kilometres farther north-east. They had brought food rations with them, but the caribou herds expected to migrate through the area did not appear, and there was simply famine as winter approached. As David describes it, some starved to death, while others froze to death in the cold, both old and young. Some also suffered from severe mental health problems. And this is where David introduces Kikik – through her story we get a rare insight into how demanding life could be for a people entirely dependent on the migration of reindeer.

Kikik, her husband Hallauk, and their five children, her half-brother Ootuk and his disabled wife had their dwellings close to each other. Hunger had ravaged the two families for some time, and they had eventually eaten all their dogs except one, surviving on occasional fish that Hallauk managed to catch by ice fishing. Over time, Ootuk became increasingly mentally unstable and eventually unable to contribute anything to the little group's survival. When Hallauk revealed that he and his family wanted to leave the area, Ootuk realised that this could be a death sentence for himself and his disabled wife. In desperation, and in a fit of madness he shot Hallauk. Afterwards, he also tried to kill Kikik, but she managed to defend herself, forcing the emaciated and weakened Ootuk to admit that he killed her husband. Sitting over Ootuk, she ordered her only son Karlak to fetch a knife, which she then used to kill Ootuk. She then gathered her five children and set out on the over 70-mile journey to Padlei, the nearest settlement.

She and the children were already weakened by hunger, and after five days on foot through the ice-cold snow-covered landscape, she realised that not all of them could continue the journey. She was already carrying her youngest daughter Nurrahaq and most of the equipment they had with them, and when two of her other daughters clearly couldn't go on, she decided to leave them behind. She managed to make a small igloo using a frying pan to chop and carve out snow blocks, wrapped the two girls in reindeer skins, and continued the journey towards Padlei. How the Royal Canadian Mounted Police were informed that Kikik and the children were trekking towards Padlei is unknown, but a rescue plane was sent out and found Kikik and the children. She told them where she had left two of her daughters, and a dog patrol found the spot and could confirm that one of the daughters had frozen to death.

This is the background to how Kikik was charged with two murders and abuse of her children. There is a faded black and white photo from that day in 1958. The photo shows Kikik in the courtroom. She has a small smile on her face, but her eyes are distant. It is painfully clear that she was actually somewhere else. She belonged to another time, another world. She spoke only her own language, and everything that happened in court had to be translated. The translator, in turn, struggled to understand English well enough. In this situation, Kikik had no voice of her own; she was truly a stranger.

Kikik was acquitted of the murder charges, with the reasoning that everyone would probably have done the same, or at least tried to do the same as she did. When the verdict was delivered, it was translated to her with the words: 'the judge says you didn't do it'.

The trial of Kikik was reported in national media and revealed the tragic results of the government's failed relocations. The following year, the book *The Desperate People* by Farley Mowat, documenting the forced relocations of the Ahiarmiut people, was published, sparking a national debate and leading to the Canadian government changing its strategy from the 1960s, starting to forcibly relocate hunter-gatherer peoples to centralised communities. But before this happened, the Canadian government tried to 're-educate' the reindeer hunters to become seal hunters, and the Ahiarmiut people were forcibly relocated to Whale Cove twice. But as David describes it, '… for our parents, this was difficult. They had never experienced saltwater before, high tides and low tides. Never seen a seal or tasted one before. All of this was new to them.' They left the area, but were caught up and moved back to Whale Cove again.

Kikik eventually got a new husband and new children but refused to talk about this case for the rest of her life. Her children knew nothing of the trials she endured, and it was only when her youngest daughter Nurrahaq found Farley Mowat's book in adulthood that they became aware of their own mother's dramatic story. The silence had been total.

Nurrahaq contacted Mowat in 2001 to get closer to her own story, and together with the Norwegian-Canadian Ole Gjerstad they make a documentary about Kikik. At the end of the film, they, along with two elders who experienced the forced relocation in 1957, returned to their original homeland near Ennadai Lake. The radio station has long been abandoned, but among heather and shrubs, the elders manage to identify the place where they had their camp. There were still some reindeer bones and remnants of the tents they once had here. Through her daughter, Kikik had finally gained a kind of voice, but not her own.

Canadian human rights researcher Rhoda Howard-Hassmann sums it up like this: 'As a human rights researcher, I have long argued that Canada committed a cultural genocide against indigenous peoples. But recently, I have come to the conclusion, regarding the Ahiarmiut, that it is not cultural genocide – it is actually physical genocide.'

It was not only the Inuit who were subjected to forced relocation. In other parts of the Quebec-Labrador Peninsula, the Innu people received the same treatment. They were not Inuit but belonged to the First Nation group and originated from the people who first crossed the Bering Strait. What they had in common with the Inuit is that the reindeer was crucial to their way of life, and the same large herd, the George River herd, was their most important resource.

Just like for the Inuit, Europeans had little negative impact on the lives of the Innu people until the 1800s. Scattered around a large area on the peninsula, small tent camps could be found where hunting and the use of caribou were the main activities. The establishment of European trading posts in Labrador and northern Quebec in the 1800s heralded a new era. Many Innu hunters now became suppliers of fur game to the Hudson Bay Company, but by the turn of the century competition from newly established fur hunters was increasing, and when the collapse in fur prices came in 1930, at the same time as the reindeer herds were significantly reduced, this led to great suffering among the Innu people.

The influx of people to the mining towns that were established increased, and they brought with them diseases that the Indigenous people had poor conditions to resist, and the mortality rate was high. At the same time, the Indigenous people were forced to adhere to hunting regulations formulated by the provincial government. The Innu people at Davis Inlet truly felt the arrival of 'civilisation': first, a vast and good hunting ground was flooded during the establishment of the Smallwood Reservoir in 1970, later NATO expanded its military aircraft training area to cover large parts of the old hunting grounds. Cultural collapse and subsequent mental health problems began to emerge, but it was the collapse of the George River caribou herd that truly alarmed North America and made the term 'ecological grief' known to the population throughout North America.

The George River caribou herd was once the world's largest, and within its 100,000 km² habitat it had been the lifeline for Inuit, Innu and Cree peoples for thousands of years. Thirty years ago, there were 800,000 caribou that migrated hundreds of kilometres north from their winter areas in northern Quebec and Labrador's taiga regions to the tundra, where the females gave birth to their calves during a couple of hectic weeks. Reindeer herds in North

America and Europe have always varied in size. The large reindeer herds on the tundra in Russia are claimed to vary with 100- to 115-year cycles, while the herds in North America seem to have 60- to 70-year cycles. So when the George River herd, which for millennia had been the main food source for various indigenous groups, began to decrease in size, it took some time before the alarm bells rang.

Among many Indigenous peoples, there was widespread skepticism towards the scientific research community, which in the early 1960s had claimed that the large reindeer herds that annually migrated from the southern taiga areas to the northern tundra would be extinct by 1969. They had estimated that by the turn of the century there were 2.4 million reindeer, but that these had been reduced to 670,000 in 1943, and further to about 200,000 in 1957. The decline was attributed to excessive hunting. Pictorial material from a slaughter site belonging to the Dene people created great national attention in 1955. They had had one of their successful hunts at one of the river crossings of the reindeer herd, and the pictorial material documented large numbers of dead reindeer. The Indigenous people were promptly labelled as reindeer killers. This impression would permeate many scientific and ethnological reports in the coming years and was the background for the establishment of The Northwest Game Act in 1971. Overnight, Indigenous access to their most important resource was regulated.

Despite an ingrained skepticism towards national regulations, Indigenous peoples themselves took initiatives for regulations. When the George River herd was halved in 2001, and nine years later was down to about 70,000 animals, and in 2012 reduced to 27,000 animals, the Innu, Inuit and Cree peoples took action. They convened a roundtable conference, resulting in the following statement:

'The land is changing, and the effects of climate change, industrial development, and the growing human population and easier access to the herd cannot be ignored in the management measures to be promoted. With the exponential rate of development, the protection of caribou habitat is severely lacking and must be taken seriously.'

Ungava Peninsula Caribou Aboriginal Round Table

The local government in Nunatsiavut recommended that the calving areas of the George River herd should be protected, and established a 14,000 km² protection zone, which was included in the regional land use plan for the Labrador Inuit settlement area. The government of Newfoundland and Labrador went further and enacted a total ban on caribou hunting in 2013, a decision that still stands today. But the hunting ban did little. In 2022, the herd was down to 7,200 animals, a decline of 99 per cent in 30 years. In a press release the same year, the provincial government noted that 'the continued illegal harvesting of George River caribou by a relatively small number of people continues to delay and threaten the herd's recovery.'

Even though the majority of the old reindeer hunters adhered loyally to the hunting ban, it was difficult to control everyone who travelled within the large area. But for the vast majority of Indigenous people in the area who had tried to maintain their culture, language and way of life for a long time, a decade without reindeer hunting has had such significant consequences that national politicians, health professionals and various research communities have long been involved. In collaboration with the local population, a documentary has now been completed supporting earlier reports on the health and psychological effects of reindeer loss. In the documentary 'Herd', we meet many of the old reindeer hunters.

'We are going to lose who we are as a culture and as a people,' explains Ocean Lane from Makkovik, Nunatsiavut. And it seems clear that the loss of access to reindeer has affected both culture and identity, and has caused complex emotional reactions, including strong feelings of sadness, distress, anxiety, fear, frustration, pain, as well as a general moral decay. 'It just tears me down to think that we don't even know how long we have to wait before we can harvest a caribou,' says Woodrow Lethbridge from Cartwright. Others express sadness that cultural knowledge and practices are not being passed down to younger generations. 'We are losing the language. We are losing traditional ways of living; we are losing knowledge of how to make food from the reindeer, which is as important as language, crafts and art. Our children don't know the difference between moose and reindeer,' claims Judy Voisey from Happy Valley-Goose Bay. 'The best meat in the world,' believes Patrick Davis a sentiment shared by many throughout Labrador. But caribou is much more than just a food source: 'It's almost like caribou was the cause, and everything else happened afterward,' claims Joey Angnatok from Nain, Nunatsiavut. There is no doubt – reindeer connect people to their communities, to the land and to each other through collective experiences, where placed-based knowledge and ancient practices are learned and shared. This is being lost.

An overwhelming number of studies document both the short-term effects of not having access to wildlife resources and the long-term effects of the policies that have been pursued for more than a hundred years. For Indigenous peoples who have been completely dependent on reindeer for generations, the greatly reduced reindeer populations and hunting bans trigger a condition known as ecological grief. The loss of cultural practices and knowledge directly affects Indigenous people's perception of their own identity and has a range of socio-economic consequences. In many small communities, access to reindeer meat has been an important part of the household, and the lack of this resource forces households to acquire more expensive food from stores. The challenge to food security also creates anxiety about the future. All of this is exacerbated by the policies pursued over the past hundred years, with forced relocations, residential schools, forced assimilation and loss of language.

It's no surprise that the feeling of control and freedom over one's own destiny has positive well-being effects, and an increasingly strong involvement of Indigenous peoples in shaping regulations related to the utilisation of natural resources now appears to have positive health effects. Despite strong local involvement, disagreements persist regarding how intensively wildlife resources can be exploited, and the perception of what constitutes sustainable harvesting can vary significantly between local representatives and centrally positioned experts. Regarding the management of the George River herd, there have also been disputes among the various Indigenous groups. While the Cree and Inuit peoples have adopted a voluntary hunting ban, the Innu people did not accept this. However, in 2022, a joint solution was reached where the Innu people were granted permission to harvest a certain number of reindeer from the Leaf River herd, which resides in Cree territory. Perhaps this can contribute to the survival of the culture.

NORWAY –
THE RECOGNISABLE HISTORY

There are many similarities in the stories unfolding in the northernmost parts of North America and Russia. After the last ice age and the following 10,000 years, various indigenous peoples have utilised reindeer as the most important element of their way of life. Without reindeer, there would be no people in these areas. Common to most of them is that the reindeer imposes a nomadic way of life on them. The reindeer is the great wanderer of the animal kingdom, and those who want to exploit the reindeer must themselves be mobile. Consequently, large permanent concentrations of hunter-gatherers and reindeer herders do not form. There are no large societal structures that need to draw borders on a map, and there are no nation-states with written records of laws and regulations. Thousands of years after the reindeer people began to use the areas, people with completely different lifestyles enter. They establish territorial borders without considering the indigenous peoples in North America and Russia as equal partners, and on both continents the quality of the reindeer's former grazing areas is reduced due to various forms of industrial development and climate change.

The history of reindeer and humans in Norway closely resembles the stories unfolding in North America and Russia. The short version is that in the south-east of the country, a hunter-gatherer people are displaced from their original hunting areas in the forested areas and become first reindeer hunters, later reindeer herders. In both the north and south, groups of people with different societal organisation enter and dominate the land areas, establishing territorial borders, and influencing both the reindeer people's language and religious practices. The subsequent societal development requires more land, and former reindeer grazing areas both south and north in the country are fragmented due to industrial development and tourism. In the south, populations of wild reindeer are divided into small vulnerable populations, and across the country a steadily warmer climate poses major challenges to the cold-adapted reindeer.

The most significant difference between what is happening in Norway compared to North America and Russia is that Norway had been inhabited by hunters for several thousand years who have not been recognised as indigenous peoples. In Norway, the Sámi are considered indigenous or aboriginal peoples. This creates an immediate perception that the Sámi-speaking people came first to Norway or to parts of Norway, and this misconception is incorrectly depicted in many textbooks from primary school level up to master's level in law studies. New genetic research has now revealed a much more exciting history. Previously, there has been a significant focus in research communities on investigating 'patrilineages'. By examining recognisable mutations of genes on men's Y chromosomes, ancestors thousands of years back in time have been found. Based on this, it has been established that the men who came into the Baltic Sea area about 3,000 years ago are the ancestors of today's Estonians, Finns, Sámi and Kvens. Now, similar studies on the genetic material inherited through women's mitochondria, have revealed that Sámi women can trace their ancestors back to the first reindeer hunters who migrated into Scandinavia. A male-dominated group of migrating hunters, from an origin still unknown in the east, thus largely found their partners among women belonging to the pioneers who arrived shortly after the last ice age.

Perhaps the most exciting part of the story is how genetically similar we are. Tracing individual paternal or maternal lineages back in time says very little about the heritage we carry from all our ancestors. For example, today's Finns, Sámi, and Kvens have retained only between 3 and 6 per cent of the genetic material of the immigrants who came 3,000 years ago, and the Sámi have as much genetic material from the later incoming farmers as other Norwegians.

In the history of humans and reindeer, this is actually of secondary importance. You don't need to be good at throwing a lasso or speaking Northern Sámi or Southern Sámi to feel concern about what is happening in Norwegian mountains and plateaus. You don't need to speak a dialect from Hardanger or Gudbrandsdalen to feel dismayed that former reindeer grazing areas are being turned into cabin areas, and it is possible to be 'forcibly relocated' to a city and speak Trøndersk or Southern Norwegian, while still feeling sorrow that perhaps you won't experience the joy of seeing herds of reindeer wandering in mountains and plateaus. Because there are many who feel sorrow and concern that the reindeer, the animal that followed the retreating ice sheets northward, that uses as few resources as possible that nobody else wants, and that kept us alive through hundreds of thousands of years, is now in danger. And the concern applies to both wild and domesticated reindeer, and the different cultures associated with them.

That is why many can understand the feelings of wildlife manager John Krebs when he found the remains of the last reindeer in the South Purcell herd that previously grazed in the border areas between Alberta and British Columbia. Until 2023, this was one of 14 isolated herds that resided in the southern mountain areas of Canada, and the seventh to disappear since 2003. Now, radio telemetry equipment had led John to the dead animals. 'When the reindeer are gone, we are left with a pervasive ecological grief. I needed a quiet moment. I don't feel that we have betrayed the reindeer, but we have failed to recognise the interplay of the various threats,' he told Canadian Geographic, and continued, 'Is it climate disruptions that interfere with the many factors the caribou depend on in their delicate dance to survive? Is it too much hunting? Too many wolves? Is it all the roads, seismic lines, mines, oil and gas drilling? Clear-cutting? The general increase in human traffic? Our greed?' Are we approaching Canadian conditions here in Norway?

PART IX

The end of the long journey?
What is the status so far? Homo sapiens has cleared away
seven to eight possible competitors from its own genus and
established itself on all continents of the globe. The
descendants of the ancient hunters are soon to number eight
billion, and everywhere they have adapted the environment to
their own needs and desires. A surprisingly large, and tragic,
number of animals and plants have disappeared along the
road to world domination. The reindeer, the most sought-after
prey for hundreds of thousands of years, is still here. But for
how long?

THE RULERS OF THE GLOBE

When small groups of *Homo sapiens* ventured out of Africa less than 70,000 years ago, it was not the first time our species was on the move. But it was certainly the most significant in the history of this planet. When sapiens first realised they had the potential for world domination, we do not know, but the idea could have emerged while they were all still in Africa. For while groups of sapiens increased in number and size, relatives in South Africa (*H. naledi*) and Central Africa (*H. rhodesiensis*) disappeared. We obviously had some competitive advantages. The small groups of sapiens that ventured out of Africa and moved eastward into Asia encountered the Denisovans and exchanged genes with them. The same happened with the Neanderthals further west in Europe, but intimate relationships were not enough. After several thousand years of coexistence, both Neanderthals and Denisovans disappeared. The same fate befell 'the upright man' *H. erectus* and the small island dwellers *H. floresiensis* in Indonesia, *H. luzonensis* in the Philippines, and the mysterious Deer Cave people in China. Eight human species vanish from the surface of the planet, and only sapiens remains.

Among paleoanthropologists and others, discussions about why sapiens ended up in such a position have been many and intense. While some have argued that our enlarged and more complex brains gave us the necessary 'upper hand', others have pointed out that Neanderthals consistently had larger brains than us, and that even 'the upright man' had a brain volume within the normal range for modern humans. Still, others have argued that climate change weakened the other human species to the extent that it was easy for immigrants from Africa to take over the habitats and resources. The theory that Neanderthals and Denisovans, who had adapted to a colder and more variable climate than the immigrants over hundreds of thousands of years, suddenly became so weakened that they died out, has little support in the scientific community today.

Did we overpower the other human species by brute force? The savagery exhibited by our closest relatives among the great apes and chimpanzees, in battles between rivalling groups, is genetically determined behavioural traits that undoubtedly have been passed down in our own species. War is not a new phenomenon; war is an old phenomenon, and archaeologists believe they have found clear signs that there were war-like conditions between rivalling groups of Neanderthals at times. This could also mean that battle-hardened, strong Neanderthals with good night vision encountered the immigrants moving westward into Europe. How could comparatively frail immigrants match this? Archaeologists believe they have found the answer along the southern coasts of Africa.

Not many thousand years after modern humans emerged as a separate species about 200,000 years ago, Africa and the rest of the world were in a cool period. Small groups of nomadic hunters who had previously followed the tracks of plant-eating prey in their seasonal migrations between different grazing areas became territorial. Along the coastlines in the south of the continent, they found good living areas with abundant and, most importantly, predictable resources. Resources that needed to be defended! An effective defense required cooperation among many people, including people they were not closely related to. This had not happened before in the history of the *Homo* genus! Sapiens evolved into one of the world's most social creatures. Even though contributing to helping a larger group of people maintain access to vital resources could have significant and often deadly consequences for the individual, many believe that the conditions during the early history of sapiens contributed to such development.

Most in the scientific community believe such self-destructive behaviour, which biologists call altruism, can only arise when they are related to those they sacrifice for – so-called kin selection. But the groups that have such hyper-social individuals who can also show 'selfless' behaviour, even though they are not related to all individuals in the group, will increase in number. If the number of less selfish individuals increases in a group, those who exhibit this type of behaviour can expect to 'be repaid' at a later time, as some they are not related to 'sacrifice' themselves for them. A collection of such groups defending a common resource can eventually form a collaborating tribe. It is this type of behaviour that sapiens further perfects. We become hypersocial! Cooperation between larger groups of people also leads more easily to the spread and further development of innovative ideas, and in the case of sapiens this results in a continuous improvement of tools and weapon technology. Thus, it was social, well-coordinated hunters with effective weapons who ventured out of Africa.

We can try to imagine the situation of the Neanderthals in the Rhône Valley just over 40,000 years ago. They had not been out of the valley for tens of thousands of years, so they had not formed good cooperative relationships with surrounding hunter groups. The valley had provided them with access to what they needed, so they had not seen the need to enter into any form of cooperation with their fellow species. Now they saw the sky lit up over flaming fires in several places on the slopes around them. Neanderthals with the best hearing could also hear singing and flute playing faintly reaching them from the intruders' camp. From the wing feathers of the large vultures they were familiar with, the intruders had got the strange idea to create tools that produced soft but penetrating sounds. The flute sounds, combined with the sound of harmonious singing, were unsettling and made them realise that they were dealing with a formidable competitor. It might be best to leave the hunting grounds to the newcomers. Rumours had reached them that it was still possible to survive on the southern tip of the continent without interference from the dark-skinned intruders with their strange customs. It might certainly be possible to survive on resources other than reindeer meat too?

So, we do not know if all hunting grounds were left to sapiens without battles, but what we do know is that the rulers of the globe, *Homo sapiens*, would soon contribute to massive ecological changes on all continents except Antarctica. The first small groups of sapiens who crossed the 'Gate of Tears' – Bab el-Mandeb, the 30 kilometre narrow strait between Africa and the Arabian Peninsula, less than 70,000 years ago, headed eastward. Their distant relatives had taken the same route before, but they had not reached as far as Australia. To reach this large continent surrounded by sea, one had to master the ocean. And they did – more than 50,000 years ago, our species, and our kind, set foot on the Australian continent for the first time. They surely thought that the arduous sea journey was worth the effort, for they found the land areas full of potential prey. Most of them were very different from the large prey they had hunted before. They gave birth to tiny infants they placed in a pouch equipped with mammary glands; they were mammals, but also marsupials. A total of 24 genera of such marsupials lived in Australia when sapiens arrived, but after a few thousand years, only one genus of marsupials remained! In total, nearly 90 per cent of all animal species over 45 kg, what scientists call megafauna, disappeared.

Not less dramatic are the ecological changes in America 30,000 years later. Small hunting groups in the eastern parts of Eurasia, a great mix of European and Asian hunters, arrived in the vast ice-free but cold region of Beringia over 20,000 years ago. The area stretched from Kamchatka in Russia to Alaska, but massive glaciers initially prevented any intrusion further south. Only about 15,000 years ago did these hunter-gatherers manage to penetrate the areas south of the glaciers, probably by sea along the west coast of Alaska and Canada. Like those who first entered Australia – the Aboriginals – they must have been very pleased with the qualities of the hunting grounds. Large herds of horses and camels grazed in the productive grasslands alongside elephants, mammoths and huge mastodons. They were all hunted by cheetahs and sabre-toothed cats, while giant condors soared above them, and giant beavers inhabited the rivers. Within a relatively short period, perhaps only 1,000 years, almost all large mammals disappeared.

The same thing happened in South America. Giant sloths, giant armadillos, camels and entire orders of ungulates disappeared. The pattern is thus similar in Australia, North America and South America: humans enter new areas, and shortly thereafter the majority of large mammals disappear. Already at the end of the last ice age, just over 11,000 years ago, half of all large mammal species had disappeared. In Australia, 88 per cent of all genera of large mammals disappeared, in South America 83 per cent, and in North America 72 per cent.

If sapiens can cause such a cataclysm of extinctions on other continents, why do populations of reindeer, our species' most coveted prey, survive in Eurasia? There are likely several factors that can explain this apparent paradox. One reason is probably hidden in the long-standing relationship between the *Homo* genus and the reindeer. For more than half a million years, reindeer have had to deal with the two-legged hunters, and have therefore had the opportunity over time to develop behavioural traits that reduce the chance of fatal encounters. There is much evidence to suggest that the longer prey have to adapt to two-legged hunters, the better they are able to survive in areas with carnivorous hunters. In Africa, where our genus has resided for more than 1 million years, and where our own species has been present for more than 200,000 years, only about 20 per cent of large mammal species disappear. In the northern parts of Eurasia, where our genus has also been present for many hundreds of thousands of years, eight species of large mammals disappear. But unlike the rapid extinctions that characterise Australia and America, these species disappeared over a period of over 35,000 years. The straight-tusked elephant and hippopotamus were the first to disappear. The youngest fossil bones of these are about 45,000 years old. Twenty thousand years later, it's over for the rhinoceros. Common to these three species is that they were warm-loving species that during the warm period between 127,000–113,000 years ago had large contiguous habitats, but now could only survive in small confined areas farthest south in Europe. Only as we approached the end of the last ice age do the last five species disappear. The woolly mammoth disappeared in most areas between 14,000 and 10,000 years ago, but survived on the Wrangel Island off the north-eastern coast of Siberia until about 4,000 years ago. The woolly rhinoceros, the Irish giant deer, the cave bear, and the cave hyena disappeared simultaneously with the woolly mammoth. Another coveted prey species for our ancestors was the horse. If we assume that what many call the tarpan were the last wild horses in Eurasia, then these persisted until the end of the 19th century in Russia. The last one died during a failed capture attempt in 1879.

Other important factors that have contributed to the survival of reindeer over the many hundreds of thousands of years of pursuit are probably the species' outstanding ability to survive under extreme climatic conditions, and its formidable ability to migrate far to find the most favourable habitats. A frozen Europe, with glaciers extending far into England and Germany, could still offer favourable habitats for reindeer. On barren lichen mats, they could survive the winter, and south of the glaciers, grass-covered steppe tundra could provide good summer pastures, but favourable conditions for hunters were not there. All studies show that in the most climatically challenging periods, the number of hunters was very low. In the high mountains or far to the north, there has always been a climate that is too harsh to support large densities of two-legged hunters. The animals' herd behaviour has also meant that meat resources have had an unpredictable distribution in the hunting grounds. This is difficult to deal with for hunter-gatherer groups that require a steady supply of energy-rich meat resources.

We know the recent history well. For about twenty different cultures spread circum-polarly in Eurasia and America, the solution was to develop various forms of reindeer husbandry that provided greater predictability in resource access. In other areas, legislation was gradually developed to regulate the harvest of animals, while dependence on reindeer as a resource was reduced through the development of agriculture. Therefore, it is no longer the pursuit of hunters that poses the greatest threat to the reindeer species, but the descendants of hunters have drastically changed the reindeer's living conditions by causing a significant increase in global temperatures, while the reindeer's original habitats are used for activities far exceeding the effects of past hunting and trapping.

REINDEER DON'T BATHE
WITH HIPPOS!

For the past couple of million years, the planet we inhabit has been a rather cold and, at times, inhospitable place for most species. The norm has been that long periods of cold and the buildup of glaciers have been interrupted by short periods – interglacials – of warmer climate. The reindeer, which evolved on the North American continent, entered the steppe-like central parts of Europe via the ice-free Beringia area, just over 700,000 years ago. It was well adapted to the tough climatic conditions and has demonstrably been one of the most important resources for various human species that have inhabited Europe.

For the pattern, as we have seen, has remained the same for more than half a million years! Even though various human species have come and gone, they have had one thing in common: they hunted reindeer. Whether it was the Heidelberg man or the pioneering antecessor who inhabited the shores of the Mediterranean over half a million years ago, we do not know – but they hunted reindeer. The same was true for Neanderthals across much of their range, and in long periods when the climate was at its toughest, nine out of ten prey brought to the settlement were reindeer.

We modern humans have followed the same pattern. Studies of bone material from hundreds of settlements show that reindeer completely dominate in the coldest periods. The same goes for hunter-gatherers who, at the end of the last ice age, inhabited areas up to the ice sheet covering Scandinavia. Hunters' settlements in Denmark and the northern parts of Germany are filled with bone remains from reindeer.

While woolly mammoths and rhinoceroses, which often shared grazing areas with reindeer, are now gone for good; the reindeer is still here, but for how long? Everything indicates that the species, which is inextricably linked to the evolution of the *Homo* genus, will have even worse survival chances in the future, and there are mainly two factors working against the reindeer: global warming and our own relentless ability to fragment previously wilderness areas with roads, buildings and various types of infrastructure. A dilemma we face now is that in our quest to reduce greenhouse gas emissions, we must use larger areas to produce renewable energy – the 'green shift' is land-intensive.

Humanity is on a 'highway to climate hell', said UN Secretary-General António Guterres to delegates from 193 countries gathered at the climate summit in Sharm el-Sheikh in November 2022, 'and we still have our foot on the gas pedal'. He continued to argue that the fight for a liveable planet will be won or lost in the decade we are now in. 'We are actually fighting for our lives, and we seem to be losing. Our planet is rapidly approaching a tipping point that will result in a climate chaos that we will not be able to reverse.'

Most participants in the meeting had gathered at a similar meeting in Glasgow the year before, and they were reminded that they had agreed there that all countries would create new plans to reduce greenhouse gas emissions. Only 24 countries had kept this promise, and calculations made by UN expert groups showed that greenhouse gas emissions would increase by over 10% in 2030 compared to 2010 levels. Previous goals to limit warming to 1.5°C by the end of this century seem unrealistic – we are now heading towards a much warmer planet. According to the Secretary-General himself, a 2.7°C increase is a more realistic temperature rise if we do not implement stronger measures.

This is bad news for the reindeer. A warmer climate is not what this species is adapted to, and its habitats are constantly shrinking due to our own activity. Through excavations of our ancestors' settlements and kitchen middens after the last ice age, an American and a French archaeologist had found that increasing temperatures led to fewer reindeer, and the last reindeer left France 11,500 years ago. They concluded that further warming of this planet would eventually lead to there being no areas where reindeer could survive. International concern arose only when American media could report that if the warming of the Earth did not stop now, Rudolph with the red nose and the other reindeer of Santa would not be able to deliver the gifts to the children.

Those who are only interested in the survival of the myth could rightly claim that Santa could have acquired a more heat-tolerant draft animal. Well-trained fallow deer could have done the job, and they are nice to look at too. However, those who are also a bit concerned about how we are creating a planet where species are disappearing at a faster rate than ever before might think that it's more than just Santa who would have problems if the reindeer as a species disappeared from history.

There are still some who believe that the planet will sort itself out. Haven't we seen that warm periods are followed by long periods of cold climate? But unfortunately, there is no improvement in sight! There is much evidence to suggest that we have managed to break the nearly 2-million-year-old pattern where relatively short warm periods are followed by long periods of cold climate where glaciers are built up and larger parts of the sea are covered by ice. In an article in the highly respected journal *Nature*, a group of researchers has shown how the amount of CO2 in the atmosphere and variations in the Earth's orbit around the sun can predict the onset of ice ages far back in time. They also find that our planet narrowly avoided the onset of a new ice age just before the industrial revolution, and that without human influence, a new ice age would only occur in about 50,000 years. But because of our addition of CO2 to the atmosphere, the onset of an ice age will likely be postponed for an additional 100,000 years.

The IPCC has created five different scenarios. In the moderate one, which they call the 'middle of the road' scenario, it is assumed that we find more sustainable ways of living, but that greenhouse gas emissions remain at current levels and that we do not achieve the goal of net zero emissions during this century. This results in a 2.7°C temperature increase by the end of the century. So if we are heading towards a planet that is 2.7°C warmer than pre-industrial times, what does that actually mean now? And won't an increase from 1.5°C to 2.7°C be perceived as insignificant? Unfortunately not.

In earlier periods when our planet has undergone warming, it took nearly 5,000 years to increase the temperature by 5 degrees. The rate of temperature increase now seems to be 20 times faster! The goal of limiting temperature increase to 1.5°C will be exceeded early in the 2030s. However, there will be significant regional variations, with warming being higher over land than over the sea, and higher the further north we go. The reindeer's habitats will experience faster temperature increases than areas further south. Arctic areas have already experienced twice as rapid warming as other parts of the planet. The reason is that year by year there is less sea ice. While ice reflects much of the sunlight, open water and land areas will absorb more solar radiation. Therefore, less sea ice contributes to temperature increase.

Precipitation will increase, but again with significant regional differences. Most of the increase will occur in northern land areas and in already wet tropical areas, while it will decrease in already dry areas. Arctic sea ice will melt, and the mass of the Greenland ice sheet will decrease, resulting in a global rise in sea level, in addition to increased carbon absorption making the ocean more acidic. Together, this will result in a significant portion of the world's mammals, plants and insects losing large parts of their habitats.

We can get an insight into the effect a 2°C temperature increase could have on our surroundings by looking at the conditions during the second-to-last interglacial period (we are now in the last one) between 130,000 and 115,000 years ago. Experts call this period the Eemian, where the climate was slightly warmer than during the warmest periods after the last ice age. The amount of greenhouse gases in the atmosphere was at pre-industrial levels, but solar radiation was more than 50 watts higher than today, because the distance between the Earth and the sun was considerably shorter due to the Earth's orbit around the sun being different from today's. In addition, the Earth was closest to the sun in summer, not as today, where the Earth is closest to the sun in winter. In fact, we are almost 5 million kilometres closer to the sun in January than in July!

Like today's situation, warming in the northernmost areas was higher than further south in Europe, and is estimated to have been 4°C higher than today. Trees grew at Nordkapp, and oak trees grew as far north as Oulo in Finland, the northernmost part of the Gulf of Bothnia. More spectacularly, during this long warm period, hippopotamuses had made their way northward and bathed in the Rhine and Thames rivers. Few would believe that a similar temperature increase today would lead to hippopotamuses again finding their way northward in Europe; both physical changes to the landscape and regulations related to alien species would likely stop any bath-loving hippopotamuses before they could take their bath in the Rhine. There are probably not many who believe that reindeer bathed with the hippopotamuses at that time, as the preferred bathing temperature for the two species differs. What most can agree on is that climate change brings changes to the distribution areas of all species, including humans. The next time oak trees creep towards the northern end of the Gulf of Bothnia and Nordkapp is covered in trees, there may not be reindeer present to witness it.

We have already seen many examples of what happens to reindeer in the northern regions when temperatures rise and precipitation patterns change. When Tokcha Khude and his family crossed the Ob Bay with 600 domestic reindeer in March 2013 to start their journey north on the Yamal Peninsula, everything was normal. It seemed to be a good year for Tokcha and the other 6,000 Nenets people who have Yamal – the peninsula at the world's end – as their main grazing area. They moved quickly from one area to the next to avoid overgrazing, but throughout May, they stayed in the same area to allow the female reindeer to rest during the birth of a new generation of calves. Early in June, they were on the move again northward along the traditional migration routes. The tracks from previous years were easy to follow; even on satellite images, the old migration routes are visible. In mid-July, they established the fishing camp. Here, the elders stayed behind to fish throughout the summer. Dried fish was their main source of protein through the winter, and working in the fishing camp was considered very important. For the others, the journey was not over. With the reindeer herd, sleds loaded with chum – the traditional tents of the tundra people – and other equipment, they headed all the way up to 69°N. The Yamal Peninsula is a whopping 700 kilometres long, meaning that some domestic reindeer herders cover nearly 1,500 kilometres in one year.

Summer is short in the northern regions, and after a couple of months in the summer grazing area the first frosts arrive, and Tokcha and his family start the return journey to the fishing camp. Fishing had been good there; it truly seemed to be a good year. But the snow came earlier than usual. By late October, a layer of snow covered the entire area. Ten days later, on November 8th, a veritable rainstorm swept over parts of the Yamal Peninsula in just a few hours. The next day, the soaked snow froze, forming a 3 cm layer of ice over the low pastures. An area the size of Belgium – 27,000 km² – was inaccessible to the reindeer. The reindeer became restless, dividing into smaller groups and mingling with other small herds, all desperately searching for food. New snowfall, followed by more rain and subsequent frost, meant that there were now two layers of ice for the reindeer to navigate. Animals died in large numbers. Of the Yamal Peninsula's total summer reindeer population of about 275,000 animals, 60,000 died. Some families were left with only a few dozen animals. Tokcha's neighbour, who had one of the largest herds, now had only 100 animals in his flock. Tokcha himself was both lucky and skilled; he deviated from the traditional migration route, found small pockets of available pasture, and avoided the worst losses.

2013 was a serad po. All Nenets people who have dealt with reindeer have experienced a so-called serad po year, with the pastures freezing over in winter. The peculiar thing now is that this happens very frequently. In this tundra area where the lowest temperature has been measured at -57°C, winter supplementary feeding has now become a common activity. Gas companies that have established themselves in the area in recent years compensate for the inconvenience their installations pose to reindeer migration and now contribute by transporting feed to reindeer located in areas with frozen pastures. Such supplementary feeding has been common in the northern regions of Norway, Sweden and Finland, and now this is spreading to domestic reindeer areas furthest north-east in Russia. Even in Svalbard, the short-legged Svalbard reindeer cannot avoid frozen pastures.

Research communities in Svalbard have the entire archipelago as their laboratory and have discovered that winters are becoming milder, and rain freezing on the ground and covering the sparse vegetation occurs more frequently than before. Such frequent episodes of rain on snow help stabilise the reindeer population, so the previously annual large variations in the number of animals are dampened! This may sound somewhat strange. There is no doubt that extreme weather conditions often lead to dramatic fluctuations in populations, and even to species extinction. We have many examples of this, both among mammals, plants and insects. But what is happening in Svalbard is that when there is a large reindeer population, icing of the pastures leads to increased mortality among calves and older animals, while the strongest survive. A smaller population of strong animals will be less affected if a new episode of frozen pastures occurs the following year. This means that both the number of animals present in the area and the age of these animals will help mitigate the effects when previously rare weather conditions occur more frequently.

But there is little doubt that such weather conditions will reduce the number of animals and thus make a population more vulnerable to other conditions. But Svalbard is a relatively simple ecosystem. In addition to the Svalbard reindeer, during the winter, there are only the Svalbard ptarmigan and the east mark mouse – a stowaway that came with freighters from Russia – that depend on access to ice-free grazing areas. The Arctic fox, and an occasional wandering polar bear, are the only four-legged predators on the island. They feed on reindeer carcasses when available, while two-legged hunters only shoot a few hundred reindeer within limited areas. Therefore, reindeer are completely unaffected by factors other than climate over large parts of the island. Given that the climate scenarios of the Intergovernmental Panel on Climate Change are accurate, we must expect annual icing of the pastures and that the population of Svalbard reindeer will not increase in the future.

Mainland Norway has about 280,000 reindeer on winter pasture, just over 30,000 of these are wild reindeer. These are populations that we harvest in various ways. Harvesting is the basis for maintaining both a diverse Sami culture from the inland in the south to Finnmark in the north, and a hunting culture that has been a central part of our own species' last 50,000 years in Europe. It seems indisputable that changing climatic conditions will affect this activity.

'GREEN SHIFT' THREATENS UNTOUCHED NATURE

These are challenging times for Norwegian government politicians. They must be as flexible as a cat to navigate the tightrope they frequently find themselves on, yet stand tall and tough enough to weather the storm of criticism. First, they enthusiastically participate in UN climate summits and agree on measures to reduce greenhouse gas emissions, only to return home and issue new licences for oil exploration. After a few weeks' break, it's off to another UN summit, this time focusing on the preservation of nature. One of Norway's climate and environment ministers barely made it home in time for Christmas. In his luggage, he carried an agreement characterised as 'A Christmas gift to all the children of the world.' Quite the package! A few days later, politicians were calling for 'brave mayors' willing to allow the development of wind power on municipal land.

Most people would agree that the world will still need oil for many years to come. There are differing opinions on whether Norwegian oil is 'greener' than other oil and whether we need to extract the last remnants of this non-renewable resource. However, most could be convinced that we need more energy in the future, but that this energy must be 'green'. Both the Norwegian Water Resources and Energy Directorate, Statnett, and the Norwegian Environment Agency have peered into their respective crystal balls and come to nearly identical conclusions: the need for energy will increase significantly. For example, the Norwegian Environment Agency has calculated that to cut fossil emissions from all transport in the future, the need for power could increase by 60 TWh by 2050. That's a considerable increase, considering that we currently produce around 150 TWh.

The Energy Commission's report points in the same direction: more energy, quickly. The development of a green industry suggests increased electrification, increased power consumption, and new renewable power generation. 'We are entering a new era that requires a comprehensive overhaul of the energy system, and we are running out of time,' says the Energy

Commission. 'We are no longer talking about increasing the pace. We need to go at a pace we haven't seen before.'

Both the government and the Energy Commission have categorically rejected low-impact and emission-free energy production in the form of nuclear power. The reason? We have too little expertise here at home. If that's a valid argument, we should have thrown up our hands when the Ekofisk field in the North Sea was declared commercially viable on Christmas Eve 1969. Norwegian expertise in oil extraction was not impressive at the time.

Together, this paints a frightening backdrop for what will happen to Norwegian nature in the coming years. Here in the north, we will experience temperature increases consistently higher than further south on the planet, there will be more precipitation where it's already moist enough, and in the mountains periods of winter rain will become annual occurrences. Areas of untouched nature will diminish. New wind power projects will be established, while politicians have realised that there isn't much energy to be gained from renewing already installed hydroelectric turbines, meaning the need to re-examine our protected waterways will increase. If we add an increased interest in building cabins in snow-sure areas, the picture is complete.

For the approximately 280,000 reindeer that spend their lives on Norwegian plains and mountains, this is bad news. Whether the reindeer are perceived as wild or domesticated plays a subordinate role. There are significant challenges ahead for those who want to preserve the wide range of traditions and cultures associated with this animal. The alarm bells should now be ringing for more than just the UN Secretary-General, who has long asserted that we are on the 'highway to climate hell' and that we still have our foot on the gas pedal. Perhaps the various cultures associated with wild and domesticated reindeer can together solve the challenges we face. Hopefully, knowledge of the long relationship between humans and reindeer will give us some of the momentum we need to address the challenges. The reindeer has helped the *Homo* genus survive four ice ages, but now it needs our help to survive the new geological epoch – the Anthropocene – the age of humans. It's time for a role reversal in the mountains.

COULD THE
UNTHINKABLE HAPPEN?

Seven minutes.

Then it was definitively over. For seven minutes, there was hope on this warm July day in Aragón in 2003. The sweat beads on the forehead of Professor José Folch Pera and his colleagues reflected both the heat and excitement. They believed they had succeeded in bringing back an extinct species. Four years earlier, Spain's last Pyrenean ibex had been captured, sedated, placed in captivity, and given the name Celia. Everyone in Spain was on a first-name basis with her. Therefore, it was almost a national mourning when she was found dead under a large windblown pine on January 6, 2000. But her genetic material had already been preserved in liquid nitrogen, and it was this material that was now injected into 208 eggs from domestic goats. These eggs had previously been emptied of their original genetic material and then placed into hybrids between domestic and wild goats. The hope was that these would become surrogate mothers. Seven goats became pregnant, but only one managed to give birth to a live kid.

For seven minutes, a Pyrenean ibex breathed again on Spanish soil in a laboratory, 200 kilometres from the mountains where Celia originally lived. For seven minutes, its heart beat and pumped blood around its body. For seven minutes, science fiction became reality. For seven minutes, there was hope that perhaps the extinction of species was not irreversible. And then, after as long as it takes a good cook to make a 'soft-boiled egg', *Capra pyrenaica pyrenaica* was extinct for the second time when the kid died from defective lungs.

Genetic studies afterwards have shown that the Pyrenean ibex, which likely inhabited the mountain range during the last warm period before the last ice age about 120,000 years ago, was widely distributed during the last ice age maximum. Analyses of leftovers from ice age people's meals show that the mountain goat often appeared on the menu, and in many of the previously inhabited caves in the Pyrenees, cave walls are richly decorated with ochre-painted Pyrenean ibexes. Now, a species that had been closely associated with the people of these mountainous areas for tens of thousands of years was gone for good.

The sad story from Spain is now repeating itself more and more frequently, and most people have now realised it: our planet is not doing well. The effects of climate change are presented to us daily through the media. And as we were told a couple of decades ago – it's getting wetter, hotter and wilder. Somewhat hidden behind the big headlines related to climate change, the planet is also undergoing another change – the reduction of biodiversity. Globally, 1 million species are at risk of extinction.

'Each species is a masterpiece, assembled by a hand called natural selection,' said the world-renowned biologist Edward O. Wilson. Each species has a name, a million years of history, and a place on this earth. Yet, perhaps the sleep of many Europeans was not disturbed when the last bright red poison dart frog from Panama died in 2020, or when the mosaic-tailed rat from the northernmost part of Australia left us in 2019. But what if the unthinkable were to happen? What if the reindeer, which has been our and our ancestors' lifeline in tough climatic periods for more than half a million years, disappears from the face of the earth? In that case, we should consider ourselves fortunate that a crystal ball has not yet been invented to show us how our descendants judge us. It would hardly be a legacy we would be proud of. Squandering the cultural values associated with domestic and wild reindeer will haunt us for all time.

EPILOGUE

The Circumpolar North Year 2100

The sound of hooves striking icy ground did not carry far that morning. The reindeer's strength was dwindling, and the few mouthfuls of crusty lichen they had found on some windswept rocks earlier in the night had done little to ease their hunger. In recent years, winters had brought mild periods where precipitation did not fall as feather-light snowflakes but as rain, which froze to ice upon hitting the ground. The vital lichen – that peculiar blend of fungi and algae – had become difficult to reach for the herd. This winter, the ice cover lay thick over the lichen mats, after many long periods of freezing rain.

Previously, the reindeer herd could venture down to the forested areas where access to tree lichens and beard lichens kept the worst hunger at bay, but these areas were now inaccessible. The herd's attempts to find pasture in these areas in recent years had rather drained them of their strength. There weren't many of them left now. The last buck in the once-large herd was barely discernible through the morning mist that enveloped them like a gray blanket. Two foxes were already tearing holes in the fur to access the meaty parts behind the animal. They knew that as soon as the morning light took hold, they would be relegated to mere spectators at a feast where only golden eagles were invited. The buck's death heralded the end of an era. The few pregnant, but already emaciated, cows in the herd were unlikely to raise viable calves. It costs to produce the fat-rich milk, and in the choice between expending energy on producing new offspring or ensuring their own survival, the calves will lose. In a few years, the world will therefore be a slightly different place. Yet another species will have disappeared from the face of the earth. Initially, not a historic event. As far back as we have knowledge of the earth, species have died out. Often, new species with other adaptations to the environment have taken their place, nature has made some adjustments here and there, and our planet has continued its journey seemingly in fine form. Today, for the first time, we can actually register that species are disappearing. Whereas previous mass extinctions occurred over periods of a thousand years, we are now in what many call the sixth mass extinction, where species disappear within a single human life. The genetic material of each species is unique, representing parts of the very Library of Life. We who live today can only observe that every year books disappear from the library. Perhaps it is we who must explain to our children and grandchildren that the reindeer represented a species that for more than half a million years had a close relationship with the human race across the entire northern hemisphere of this planet. Perhaps it is we who must explain why the 36,000-year-old charcoal drawing of a reindeer in the Chauvet Cave is our ancestors' tribute to the species that was inseparably linked to them through the harshest climatic periods. Perhaps it is we who must explain why in the Norwegian mountain areas, we can come across tens of thousands of trap pits and small stone walls that provided shelter to hunters armed with spears, bows and arrows. Perhaps it is we who must explain why the culture of the Sami people in Scandinavia, the Nenets, Komi, Eveny people on the tundra in Russia, and the Inuit and other indigenous peoples in Canada and Alaska, is now in ruins. Perhaps it is we who must explain to our children and grandchildren that they are now entering what the world-renowned biologist Edward O. Wilson calls the Eremozoic – the Age of Loneliness. And – it is we who must realise that shedding tears over lost species accomplishes little. They will fall like freezing rain on ungrazed lichen mats.

Or... Could knowledge of the long history we share with the reindeer motivate us to find solutions that preserve not only the reindeer but also the identity and cultures still rooted in the animal that is Europe's most important living cultural monument?

REFERENCES

PART I

Antón, S. C., & Kuzawa, C. W. (2017).
Antón, S. C. *et al.* (2014).
Ashton, N. *et al.* (2014).
Athreya, S., & Hopkins, A. (2021).
Bermúdez-de-Castro, J. M. *et al.* (2017).
Blain, H. A. *et al.* (2018).
Blake, C. C. (1862).
Blix, A. S. (2016).
Bocherens, H. *et al.* (1995).
Byrne, L. (2004).
Campaña, I. *et al.* (2016).
De Asúa, M. J. (1991).
de Castro, J. M. B. *et al.* (2021).
Dean, D. *et al.* (1998).
DiMaggio, E. N. *et al.* (2015).
Esmark, J. (1824).
Falguères, C. (2015).
García, N. G. *et al.* (2009).
García, N., & Arsuaga, J. L. (2011).
Hestmark, G. (2017).
Hestmark, G. (2024).
Irvine, R. D. (2014).
Kurtén, B. (2017).
Lande, R. (2009).
Lister, A. M., & Brandon, A. (1991).
Lombao, D., *et al.* (2022).
López-García, J. M. *et al.* (2010).
Manzi, G. (2016).
Martinez, I. *et al.* (2004).
Mosquera, M. *et al.* (2013).
Mounier, A. *et al.* (2009).
Nash, D. J. *et al.* (2021).
Parfitt, S. A. (2005).
Profico, A. *et al.* (2016).
Rightmire, G.P. (1998).
Rivals, F, *et al.* (2008).
Rivals, F. *et al.* (2009).
Rivals, F. *et al.* (2004).
Roberts, A. P., & Grün, R. (2010).
Roksandic, M. *et al.* (2018).
Sandgathe, D. M., & Berna, F. (2017).
Schoch, W. H. *Et al.* (2015).
Schaafhausen, H. (1880).
Schoch, *et al.* (2015).
Schoetensack, O. (1908).
Schreiber, D. *et al.* (2007).
Stringer, C.B. *et al.* (1989).
Van Kolfschoten, T. *et al.* (2015).
Von Linné, C. (1788).
Wagner, G. A. *et al.* (2011).
Welker, F. *et al.* (2020).

PART II

Allen, J. R. *et al.* (1999).
Anderson, S. *et al.* (1981).
Ayala, F. J. & Cela-Conde C. J. (2018).
Balzeau, A. *et al.* (2020).
Banks, F. J. *et al.* (2008).
Barsky, D. (2013).
Blake, C. C. (1862).
Bojs, K. (2015).
Brown, P. *et al.* (2004).
Brown, S. *et al.* (2022).
Browning, S. R. *et al.* (2018).
Burroughs W. J. (2005).
Cann, *et al.* (1987).
Churchill, S. E. (2006).
Costamagno, S. *et al.* (2006).
Costamagno, S. *et al.* (2019).
Daujeard, C. *et al.* (2012).
Daujeard, C. *et al.* (2019).
Dean, D. *et al.* (2017).
Devièse, T. *et al.* (2021).
Dinnis, R. and Stringer, C. (2017).
Discamps, E. *et al.* (2011).
Discamps, E. and Royer, A. (2017).
Djacovic, I. *et al.* (2022).
Finlayson, C. *et al.* (2006).
Finlayson, C. (2009).
Gaudzinski, S., & Roebroeks, W. (2000).
Greenfield, L.O. (2015).
Hardy, B. L. *et al.* (2020).
Jaubert, J. *et al.* (2016).
Kahlke, R. D. (2014).
Kedar, Y. *et al.* (2022).
Krause, J. *et al.* (2010).
Lahr, M. M., & Foley, R. (1994).
Lalueza-Fox, C. *et al.* (2007).
Li, Q. *et al.* (2023).
Lin, Z. *et al.* (2019).
Mithen, S. (2003).
Moncel, M. H. *et al.* (2012).
Moncel, M. H. *et al.* (2021).
Morin, E. *et al.* (2014).
Päbo, S. (2022).
Papagianni, D. & Morse, M. A. (2015).
Petit, P. (2000).
Pomeroy, E. et al. (2020).
Potts, R. (2013).
Prüfer, K. *et al.* (2014).
Raynal, J. P. *et al.* (2013).
Rodriguez, J. (2011).
Rougier, H. *et al.* (2016).
Schaafhausen, H. (1880).

Skrzypek, G. *et al.* (2011).
Slimak, L. *et al.* (2022).
Slon, V. *et al.* (2018).
Solecki, R. S. (1975).
Steegmann Jr, A. T. *et al.* (2002).
Stringer, C. & Andrews, P. (2005).
Taylor *et al.* (2021).
Van Andel, T. H. & Davies W. Eds. (2003).
Villa, P., & Roebroeks, W. (2014).
Wales, N. (2012).
Woodward, J. (2014).
Wroe, S. *et al.* (2018).

PART III
Benazzi, S. *et al.* (2015).
Black, B. *et al.* (2015).
Cooper, A., *et al.* (2021).
Devièse, T. *et al.* (2021).
Fu, Q. *et al.* (2015).
Giaccio, B. *et al.* (2017).
Grayson, D. K., & Delpech, F. (2002).
Grayson, D. K., & Delpech, F. (2006).
Harvati, K. *et al.* (2019).
Higham, T. *et al.* (2014).
Hoffecker, J. F. (2009).
Houldcroft, C. J. & Underdown, S. J. (2016).
Mellars, P. A. (2004).
Metz, L. *et al.* (2023).
Skov, L. *et al.* (2022).
Slimak, L. *et al.* (2022).
Slimak, L. *et al.* (2023).
Slon, V. *et al.* (2018).
Stringer, C. (2016).
Zhang, P. *et al.* (2022).

PART IV
Baker, J. *et al.* (2024).
Bocquet-Appel, J. P. & Demars, P. Y. (2000).
Bocquet-Appel, J. P. *et al.* (2005).
Fontana, L. (2017).
Fontana, L. (2022).
Hansen, F.K. (2023).
Hayden, B. (2020).
Holliday, T. W. (1997).
Maier, A. (2017).
Pétillon, J. M. *et al.* (2019).
Posth, C. *et al.* (2023).
Rendu, W. *et al.* (2019).
Skinner, M. & Newell, E. (2000).
Slimak, L. *et al.* (2022).
Smith, C. M. (2014).
Soffer, O. (2000).
Soffer, O. & Adovasio, J. M. (2004).
Stringer, C., & Crété, L. (2022).
Vanhaeren, M., & d'Errico, F. (2001).
Willerslev, E. *et al.* (2014).

PART V
Allentoft, M. E. *et al.* (2022).
Amundsen, B. (2020).
Bang-Andersen, S. (1996).
Bang-Andersen, S. (2003).
Berger, J. *et al.* (2001).
Bjerck, H. B. (2012).
Bjerck, H. B. (2017).
Bjerck, H. B. (2021).
Bondevik, S. (2019).
Brøgger, A. W. (1925).
Ellingvåg, S. (2023).
Fu, Q. *Et al.* (2016).
Fuglestvedt, I. (2005).
Gjerde, H.S. (2008).
Günther, T. *et al.* (2018).
Ilkjær, J. (2000).
Lucquin, A. *et al.* (2023).
Lundström, V. *et al.* (2021).
Macintosh, A. A. *et al.* (2016).
Manninen, M. A. *et al.* (2023).
Recht, J. *et al.* (2020).
Skoglund, P. *et al.* (2012).
Skre, D. (2020).
Solberg, B. (2003).
Sørensen, M. *et al.* (2013).
Waddington, C., & Wicks, K. (2017).
Walker, J. *et al.* (2020).
Wee, W. & Ellingvåg, S. (2023).

PART VI
Amundsen, H. R., & Os, K. (2015).
Berge, E. & Stenseth, N. Chr. (eds.) (1998).
Berge, E. (2001).
Bergman, I., & Edlund, L. E. (2016).
Bergstøl. J. (2008).
Bevanger, K., & Jordhøy, P. (2004).
Bitustøyl, K. (2017).
Braseth, L. (2014).
Dybdal, A. (2005).
Fjellheim, S. (2012).
Hansen, L. I og. & Olsen, B. (2004).
Hardin, G. (1968).
Indrelid, S. (2014).
Jordhøy, P. *et al.* (2006).
Krzewińska, M. *et al.* (2015).
Lorenz, E. (1981).
Manker, E. (1960).
Mikkelsen, E. (1994).
Mulk, I.M. (1995).
Myrvoll, E. R. *et al.* (2011).
NOU 2001:34
Olsen, L. (2010).
Ostrom, E. (1999).
Røed, K. H. *et al.* (2021).
Salmi, A. K. (2023).
Sanden, G. D. (2016).
Schanche, A. (2000).

Stene, K. *et al.* (2015).
Vorren, Ø. (1998).
Zachrisson, I. (1984).

PART VII
Baskin, L. M. (2000).
CAFF 2006.
Descola, P. (2013).
Flegontov, P. *et al.* (2019).
Fait Fjeld. The Alaska Sámi: A Reindeer Story.
Gordon, B. C. (2005).
Gordon, B. C. (2003).
Gunn, A & Russell, D. 2023.
Jackson, L. J., & Thacker, P. T. (Eds.). (1997).
Nies, J. (1996).
Raghavan, M. *et al.* (2014).
Reich, D. *et al.* (2012).
The International Sami Journal.
Willerslev, R. *et al.* (2015).

PART VIII
Baskin, L. M. (2000).
Borish, D. *et al.* (2022).
Crate, S. A. (2010).
Crate, S. A. (2013).
Dean, J. (2008).
Duhamel, K., & Bernauer, W. (2018).
Harding, Luke. (2009).
Hebblewhite, M. & Fortin, D. (2017). Hebert,
L. C. (2015).
Hellesvik, J. 2021.
Howard-Hassmann, R.E. (2018).
Statnett 2023

Huyghe, J. R. *et al.* (2011).
Krankina, O.I. *et al.* (1997).
Lamnidis, T. C. *et al.* (2018).
Mathiesen, S. D. *et al.* (2023).
Mattingsdal, M. *et al.* (2021).
Müller-Wille, L. *Et al.* (2006).
Ravna, Z.J.V. (2019).
Rodríguez-Varela, R. *et al.* (2023).
Saag, L. *et al.* (2019).
Skoglund, P. *et al.* (2014).
Snook, J. *et al.* (2020).
Snook, J. *et al.* (2022).
Sannhet og forsoningskommisjonen Dokument
19 (2022–2023
Tansem, K. (2022).
Tonkopeeva, M. *et al.* (2024).

PART IX
Bowles, S. (2009).
Burke, K. D. *et al.* (2018).
Dirzo, R. *et al.* (2014).
Ellis, R., & Palmer, M. (2016).
Intergovernmental Panel on Climate Change.
Marean, C. W. (2015).
Marean, C. W. (2016).
Miljødirektoratet 2022.
NOU Norges offentlige utredninger 2023: 3
Prado, J. L. *et al.* (2015).
Rightmire, G. P. (2013).
Scott, M., & Lindsey, R. (2020).
Sherwood, S. C., & Huber, M. (2010).
Spilde, D. *et al.* (2018).

Allen, J. R. *et al* (1999). Rapid environmental changes in southern Europe during the last glacial period. *Nature*, 400(6746), 740–743.

Allentoft, M. E. *et al* (2022). Population genomics of stone age eurasia. *BioRxiv*, 2022–05.

Amundsen, B. (2020.) Var det en vikingtid i Norge – 2000 år før vikingene? Forskning.no. https://www.forskning.no/arkeologi-skipsfart/var-det-en-vikingtid-i-norge-2000-ar-for-vikingene/1690787

Amundsen, H. R. and Os, K. (2015). Ruseformete massefangstanlegg for villrein i nordre Hedmark-samiske eller norrøne tradisjoner? *Heimen*, 52(1), 41–53.

Anderson, S. *et al* (1981). Sequence and organization of the human mitochondrial genome. *Nature*, 290(5806), 457–465.

Antón, S. C. and Kuzawa, C. W. (2017). Early Homo, plasticity and the extended evolutionary synthesis. *Interface Focus*, 7(5), 20170004.

Antón, S. C., Potts, R. and Aiello, L. C. (2014). Evolution of early Homo: an integrated biological perspective. *Science*, 345(6192), 1236828.

Ashton, N *et al.* (2014). Hominin footprints from early Pleistocene deposits at Happisburgh, UK. *PLoS One*, 9(2), e88329.

Athreya, S. and Hopkins, A. (2021). Conceptual issues in hominin taxonomy: Homo heidelbergensis and an ethnobiological reframing of species. *American Journal of Physical Anthropology*, 175, 4–26.

Ayala, F. J. and Cela-Conde C. J. (2018). *Processes in human evolution: The journey from early hominins to Neanderthals and modern humans.* Oxford University Press, Oxford.

Baker, J. *et al.* (2024). Evidence from personal ornaments suggest nine distinct cultural groups between 34,000 and 24,000 years ago in Europe. *Nature Human Behaviour*, 1–14.

Balzeau, A. *et al.* (2020). Pluridisciplinary evidence for burial for the La Ferrassie 8 Neandertal child. *Scientific Reports*, 10(1), 1–10.

Bang-Andersen, S. (1996). Coast/inland relations in the Mesolithic of southern Norway. *World Archaeology*, 27(3), 427–443.

Bang-Andersen, S. (2003). Southwest Norway at the Pleistocene/Holocene transition: landscape development, colonization, site types, settlement patterns. *Norwegian Archaeological Review*, 36(1), 5–25.

Banks, W. E. *et al.* (2008). Reconstructing ecological niches and geographic distributions of caribou (Rangifer tarandus) and red deer (Cervus elaphus) during the Last Glacial Maximum. *Quaternary Science Reviews*, 27(27–28), 2568–2575.

Barsky, D. (2013). The Caune de l'Arago stone industries in their stratigraphical context. *Comptes Rendus Palevol*, 12(5), 305–325.

Baskin, L. M. (2000). Reindeer husbandry/hunting in Russia in the past, present and future. *Polar Research*, 19(1), 23–29.

Benazzi, S. *et al.* (2015). The makers of the Protoaurignacian and implications for Neandertal extinction. *Science*, 348(6236), 793–796.

Berge, E. (2001). Allmenningens tragedie' – frå metafor til teori. Ein litteraturoversikt. Institutt for sosiologi og statsvitenskap, NTNU.

Berge, E. and Stenseth, N. Chr. (eds.) (1998). *Law and the Governance of Renewable Resources*. Oakland, ICS Press.

Berger, J., Swenson, J. E. and Persson, I. L. (2001). Recolonizing carnivores and naive prey: conservation lessons from Pleistocene extinctions. *Science*, 291(5506), 1036–1039.

Bergman, I. and Edlund, L. E. (2016). Birkarlar and Sámi–inter-cultural contacts beyond state control: reconsidering the standing of external tradesmen (birkarlar) in medieval Sámi societies. *Acta Borealia*, 33(1), 52–80.

Bergstøl. J. (2008). Samer i Østerdalen? En studie av etnisitet i jernalderen og middelalderen i det nordøstre Hedmark. Universitetet i Oslo.396s.

Bermúdez-de-Castro, J. M. *et al.* (2017). Homo antecessor: The state of the art eighteen years later. *Quaternary International*, 433, 22–31.

Bevanger, K. and Jordhøy, P. (2004). Reindeer – the mountain nomad. Naturforlaget.

Bitustøyl, K. (2017). Tamreindrifta i Setesdalsheiane. Bokbyn Forlag. 283s.

Bjerck, H. B. (2017). Settlements and seafaring: Reflections on the integration of boats and settlements among marine foragers in Early Mesolithic Norway and the Yámana of Tierra del Fuego. *The Journal of Island and Coastal Archaeology*, 12(2), 276–299.

Bjerck, H. B. (2012). On the outer fringe of the human world: phenomenological perspectives on anthropomorphic cave paintings in Norway. *Caves in Context: The Cultural Significance of Caves and Rockshelters in Europe*, 48–64.

Bjerck, H. B. (2021). What could the 'sea ice machine' do to its people? On Lateglacial Doggerland, marine foraging, and the colonisation of Scandinavian seascapes. *Environmental Archaeology*, 26(1), 51-63.

Black, B., Neely, R. and Manga, M. (2015). Campanian Ignimbrite volcanism, climate, and the final decline of the Neanderthals. *Geology* 43 5), 411–414.

Blain, H. A. *et al.* (2018). Towards a Middle Pleistocene terrestrial climate reconstruction based on herpetofaunal assemblages from the Iberian Peninsula: State of the art and perspectives. *Quaternary Science Reviews*, 191, 167–188.

Blake C. C. (1862). On the cranium of the most ancient races of man. *Geologist*, June, 206.

Blix, A. S. (2016). Adaptations to polar life in mammals and birds. *Journal of Experimental Biology*, 219(8), 1093–1105.

Bocherens, H. *et al.* (1995). Preservation of Trophic Structure and Climatic Information Through Signatures in Fossil Mammals from a Pleistocene Cave in Southern England. *Journal of Archaeological Science*.

Bocquet-Appel, J. P. and Demars, P. Y. (2000). Population kinetics in the Upper Palaeolithic in western Europe. *Journal of Archaeological Science*, 27(7), 551–570.

Bocquet-Appel, J. P. *et al.* (2005). Estimates of Upper Palaeolithic meta-population size in Europe from archaeological data. *Journal of Archaeological Science*, 32(11), 1656–1668.

Bojs, K. (2015). Min Europeiske familie de siste 54 000 årene. Spartakus forlag, Oslo. 410s.

Bondevik, S. (2019). 'Tsunami from the Storegga Landslide', in R. A. Meyers (Ed.) *Encyclopedia of Complexity and Systems Science*. Springer, pp. 1–33. 10.1007/978-3-642-27737-5_644-1

Borish, D. *et al.* (2022). Relationships between Rangifer and Indigenous Well-being in the North American Arctic and Subarctic: A Review Based on the Academic Published Literature. *Arctic*, 75(1), 86–104.

Bowles, S. (2009). Did warfare among ancestral hunter-gatherers affect the evolution of human social behaviors? *Science*, 324(5932), 1293–1298.

Braseth, L. (2014). Samer sør for midnattsola. Fagbokforlaget Vigmostad & Børke. Bergen. 523s.

Brøgger, A. W. (1925). Det norske folk i oldtiden. A Forelesninger, Bind VIa. H. Aschehoug & CO (W. Nygaard), OSLO.

Brown, P. *et al.* (2004). A new small-bodied hominin from the Late Pleistocene of Flores, Indonesia. Nature, 431(7012), 1055–1061.

Brown, S. *et al.* (2022). The earliest Denisovans and their cultural adaptation. *Nature ecology & evolution*, 6(1), 28–35.

Browning, S. R. *et al.* (2018). Analysis of human sequence data reveals two pulses of archaic Denisovan admixture. *Cell*, 173(1), 53–61.

Burke, K. D. *et al.* (2018). Pliocene and Eocene provide best analogs for near-future climates. *Proceedings of the National Academy of Sciences*, 115(52), 13288–13293.

Burroughs W. J. (2005). *Climate change in prehistory: The end of the reign of chaos.* Cambridge University Press, Cambridge. 356pp.

Byrne, L. (2004). Lithic tools from Arago cave, Tautavel (Pyrénées-Orientales, France): behavioural continuity or raw material determinism during the Middle Pleistocene. *Journal of Archaeological Science*, 31(4), 351–364.

CAFF (2006). World Reindeer Husbandry: CBMP EALÁT-Monitoring. Expert Network Monitoring Plan. Supporting publication to the CAFF *Circumpolar Biodiversity Monitoring Program – Framework Document.* By WRH and ICRH in cooperation with CAFF. CAFF CBMP Report No. 10, CAFF International Secretariat, Akureyri, Iceland.

Campaña, I. *et al.* (2016). New interpretation of the Gran Dolina-TD6 bearing Homo antecessor deposits through sedimentological analysis. *Scientific Reports*, 6(1), 34799.

Cann, R. L., Stoneking, M. and Wilson, A. C. (1987). Mitochondrial DNA and human evolution. *Nature*, 325(6099), 31–36.

Churchill, S.E. (2006). 'Bioenergetic perspectives on Neanderthal thermoregulatory activity budgets', in Havarti, K, Harrison, T. eds. *Neanderthals revisited: New approaches and perspectives.* Springer.

Cooper, A. *et al.* (2021). A global environmental crisis 42,000 years ago. *Science*, 371(6531), 811–818.

Costamagno, S. *et al.* (2019). Approaches to the acquisition and use of animal materials. *PALETHNOLOGIE*, 10, 373–412.

Costamagno, S., Meignen, L. and Mauteille, B. (2006). Les Pradelles (Marillac-le-Franc, France): A Mousterian reindeer hunting camp? *Journal of Anthropology and Archeology* 255 (2006) 466–484.

Crate, S. A. (2010). The Legacy of the Viliui Reindeer-Herding Complex. *Cultural Survival – 27-1. The Troubled Taiga.*

Crate, S. A. (2013). Climate change and human mobility in indigenous communities of the Russian North. *Brookings-LSE Project on Internal Displacement, The Brookings Institution, Washington, DC, USA.*

Daujeard, C. *et al.* (2012). Neanderthal subsistence strategies in Southeastern France between the plains of the Rhone Valley and the mid-mountains of the Massif Central (MIS 7 to MIS 3). *Quaternary International*, 252, 32–47.

Daujeard, C. *et al.* (2019). Neanderthal selective hunting of reindeer? The case study of Abri du Maras (south-eastern France). *Archaeological and Anthropological Sciences*, 11, 985–1011.

Dean, D. *et al.* (1998). On the phylogenetic position of the pre-Neandertal specimen from Reilingen, Germany. *Journal of Human Evolution*, 34(5), 485–508.

Dean, J. (2008). Big Game and the State: The History of the Hunt in Canada. *Left History: An Interdisciplinary Journal of Historical Inquiry and Debate*, 13(1).

de Asúa, M. J. (1991). *The organization of discourse on animals in the thirteenth century. Peter of Spain, Albert the Great, and the commentaries on' De Animalibus'.* University of Notre Dame.

de Castro, J. M. *et al.* (2021). Comparative dental study between Homo antecessor and Chinese Homo erectus: Nonmetric features and geometric morphometrics. *Journal of Human Evolution*, 161, 103087.

Descola, P. (2013). *Beyond nature and culture.* The University of Chicago Press.

Devièse, T. *et al.* (2021). Reevaluating the timing of Neanderthal disappearance in Northwest Europe. *Proceedings of the National Academy of Sciences*, 118(12), e2022466118.

Di Maggio, E. N. *et al* (2015). Late Pliocene fossiliferous sedimentary record and the environmental context of early Homo from Afar, Ethiopia. *Science*, 347(6228), 1355–1359.

Dinnis, R. and C. Stringer (2017) *Britain: One million years of the human story.* Natural History Museum. London. 150 s.

Dirzo, R. *et al.* (2014). Defaunation in the Anthropocene. *Science*, 345(6195), 401–406.

Discamps, E. and Royer, A. (2017). Reconstructing palaeoenvironmental conditions faced by Mousterian hunters during MIS 5 to 3 in southwestern France: A multi-scale approach using data from large and small mammal communities. *Quaternary International*, 433, 64–87.

Discamps, E. Jaubert, J. and Bachellerie, F. (2011). Human choices and environmental constraints: deciphering the variability of large game procurement from Musterian to Aurignacian times (MIS 5-3) in southwestern France.

Quaternary Science Reviews, 30(2011) 2755-2775.

Djakovic, I., Key, A. and Soressi, M. (2022). Optimal linear estimation models predict 1400–2900 years of overlap between Homo sapiens and Neandertals prior to their disappearance from France and northern Spain. *Scientific Reports*, 12(1), 1–12.

Duhamel, K. and Bernauer, W. (2018). Ahiarmiut relocations and the search for justice: The life and work of David Serkoak. *Northern Public Affairs*, 62–65.

Dybdal, A. (2005). Folketap og kirkemakt 1350-1537. I Trøndelags historie bind 2. Tapir forlag, Trondheim. S13–38.

Ellingvåg, S. (2023). Dette er ikke en pensumbok. Debattinnlegg Aftenposten 20.12.2023. https://www.aftenposten.no/meninger/debatt/i/P4Va3p/dette-er-ikke-en-pensumbok

Ellis, R. and Palmer, M. (2016). Modulation of ice ages via precession and dust-albedo feedbacks. *Geoscience Frontiers*, 7(6), 891–909.

Esmark, J. (1824). Bidrag til vor jordklodes historie. *Magazin for Naturvidenskaberne*, 2(1), 28–49.

Fait Fjeld. The Alaska Sámi: A Reindeer Story. https://saamibaiki.org/contentConnections/Vesterheim-A%20reindeer%20story.pdf

Falguères, C. et al. (2015). New ESR and U-series dating at Caune de l'Arago, France: A key-site for European Middle Pleistocene. *Quaternary Geochronology*, 30, 547–553.

Finlayson, C. et al. (2006). Late survival of Neanderthals at the southernmost extreme of Europe. *Nature*, 443(7113), 850–853.

Finlayson, C. (2009). *The humans who went extinct: why Neanderthals died out and we survived*. Oxford University Press, p273.

Fjellheim, S. (2012). Gåebrien sitje- en sameby i Rørostraktene. Eget forlag. Røros. 275s.

Flegontov, P. et al. (2019). Palaeo-Eskimo genetic ancestry and the peopling of Chukotka and North America. *Nature*, 570(7760), 236–240.

Fontana, L. (2017). The four seasons of reindeer: Non-migrating reindeer in the Dordogne region (France) between 30 and 18 k? Data from the Middle and Upper Magdalenian at La Madeleine and methods of seasonality determination. *Journal of Archaeological Science: Reports*, 12, 346–362.

Fontana, L. (2022). *Reindeer hunters of the ice age in Europe. Economy, ecology, and the annual nomadic cycle*. Springer, 248s.

Fu, Q. et al. (2015). An early modern human from Romania with a recent Neanderthal ancestor. *Nature*, 524(7564), 216–219.

Fu, Q. et al. (2016). The genetic history of ice age Europe. *Nature*, 534(7606), 200–205.

Fuglestvedt, I. (2005). Pionerbosetningens fenomenologi. *Sørvest-Norge og Nord-Europa*, 10(200), 10. https://www.beredskapsradet.no/sites/default/files/2020-10/improfil-6.pdf

García, N. G. et al. (2009). Isotopic analysis of the ecology of herbivores and carnivores from the Middle Pleistocene deposits of the Sierra De Atapuerca, northern Spain. *Journal of Archaeological Science*, 36(5), 1142–1151.

García, N. and Arsuaga, J. L (2011). The Sima de los Huesos (Burgos, northern Spain): palaeoenvironment and habitats of Homo heidelbergensis during the Middle Pleistocene. *Quaternary Science Reviews*, 30(11-12), 1413–1419.

Gaudzinski, S. and Roebroeks, W. (2000). Adults only. Reindeer hunting at the middle palaeolithic site salzgitter lebenstedt, northern Germany. Journal of human evolution, 33(4), 497–521.

Giaccio, B. et al. (2017). High-precision 14C and 40Ar/39Ar dating of the Campanian Ignimbrite (Y-5) reconciles the time-scales of climatic-cultural processes at 40 ka. *Scientific reports*, 7(1), 45940.

Gjerde, H.S. (2008). Runde tufter i Hallingdal – en indikasjon på samisk bosetning? Masteroppgave i arkeologi. Institutt for arkeologi, konservering og historie. Det humanistiske fakultet, UiO.

Gordon, B. (2003). Rangifer and man: an ancient relationship. *Rangifer*, 15–28.

Gordon, B. C. (2005). 8000 years of caribou and human seasonal migration in the Canadian Barrenlands. *Rangifer*, 155–162.

Grayson, D. K. and Delpech, F. (2002). Specialized early Upper Palaeolithic hunters in southwestern France? *Journal of archaeological science*, 29(12), 1439–1449.

Grayson, D. K. and Delpech F. (2006). *Was there increasing dietary specialization across the Middle-to-Upper Paleolithic transition in France?* When Neanderthals and Modern Humans met. Tübingen Publication in Prehistory. Kerns forlag. Tübingen, s. 377–417.

Greenfield, L.O. (2015). *Vitamin D Deficiency In Modern Humans and Neanderthals*. Outskirts Press. ISBN-10 1478751975.

Gunn, A. and Russell, D. 2023. Rangifer status and trends. North American Caribou Workshop, Anchorage, Alaska, May 2023

Günther, T. et al. (2018). Population genomics of Mesolithic Scandinavia: Investigating early postglacial migration routes and high-latitude adaptation. *PLoS Biology*, 16(1), e2003703.

Hansen, F.K. (2023). Uvanlig spennende steinalderfunn i Trøndelag. https://www.forskning.no/arkeologi-ntnu-partner/uvanlig-spennende-steinalderfunn-i-trondelag/2232607

Hansen, L. I. and Olsen, B. (2004). Samenes historie fram til 1750. Cappelen akademisk forl., Oslo.

Hardin, G. (1968). The tragedy of the commons: the population problem has no technical solution; it requires a fundamental extension in morality. *Science*, 162(3859), 1243–1248.

Harding, L. (2009). Climate change in Russia's Arctic tundra: 'Our reindeer go hungry. There isn't enough pasture'. *Guardian*, 10/20/2009. http://www.guardian.co.uk/environment/2009/oct/20/arctic-tundra.

Hardy, B. L., *et al.* (2020). Direct evidence of Neanderthal fibre technology and its cognitive and behavioral implications. *Scientific Reports*, 10(1), 4889.

Harvati, K. *et al.* (2019). Apidima Cave fossils provide earliest evidence of Homo sapiens in Eurasia. *Nature*, 571(7766), 500–504.

Hayden, B. (2020). Archaeological pitfalls of storage. *Current Anthropology*, 61(6), 763-793.

Hebblewhite, M. and Fortin, D. (2017). Canada fails to protect its caribou. *Science*, 358(6364), 730-731.

Hebert, L. C. (2015). *'In Search of Deer': A historical ecological perspective on caribou in northern Manitoba in the context of Cree use* (Master's thesis).

Hellesvik, J. (2021). 'Vi kom først» – kom samene først? Nettside Etnisk og demokratisk likeverd. https://edl.no/2021/03/27/vi-kom-forst-kom-samene-forst/

Hestmark, G. (2017). *Istidens oppdager: Jens Estmark, pioneren i Norges fjellverden*. Kagge forlag.

Hestmark, G. (2024). A tale of two moraines and the discovery of Ice Ages. *Geological Society, London, Special Publications*, 543(1), SP543-2022.

Higham, T. *et al.* (2014). The timing and spatiotemporal patterning of Neanderthal disappearance. *Nature*, 512(7514), 306–309.

Hoffecker, J. F. (2009). The spread of modern humans in Europe. *Proceedings of the National Academy of Sciences*, 106(38), 16040–16045.

Holliday, T. W. (1997). Body proportions in Late Pleistocene Europe and modern human origins. *Journal of Human Evolution*, 32(5), 423–448.

Houldcroft, C. J. and Underdown, S. J. (2016). Neanderthal genomics suggests a pleistocene time frame for the first epidemiologic transition. *American Journal of Physical Anthropology*, 160(3), 379–388.

Howard-Hassmann, R.E. (2018). Canada's genocide: The case of the Ahiarmiut. *The Conversation*, 9. December.

Huyghe, J. R. *et al.* (2011). A genome-wide analysis of population structure in the Finnish Saami with implications for genetic association studies. *European Journal of Human Genetics*, 19(3), 347–352.

Ilkjær, J. (2000). Den første Norgeshistorien-Illerupfunnet: Ny innsikt i skandinavisk romertid. Kulturhistorisk Forlag. Tønsberg. (p 174).

Indrelid, S. (2014). Oppdagelser på Hardangervidda. Svein Nord. 222s.

Intergovernmental Panel on Climate Change. Climate change (2021). Summary for Policymakers. ISBN 978-92-9169-158-6

Irvine, R. D. (2014). The Happisburgh footprints in time: Environmental change and human adaptation on the East Anglian coast (Respond to this article at http://www. therai. org. uk/at/debate). *Anthropology Today*, 30(2), 3–6.

Jackson, L. J. and Thacker, P. T. (Eds.). (1997). *Caribou and reindeer hunters of the northern hemisphere*. Aldershot: Avebury.

Jaubert, J. *et al.* (2016). Early Neanderthal constructions deep in Bruniquel Cave in southwestern France. *Nature*, 534(7605), 111–114.

Jordhøy, P., Binns Støren, K. and Hoem, S.A. (2006). Gammel jakt- og fangstkultur som indikasjoner på eldre tiders jaktorganisering, ressurspolitikk og trekkmønster for rein i Dovretraktene. NINA Rapport 19.

Kahlke, R. D. (2014). The origin of Eurasian mammoth faunas (Mammuthus–Coelodonta faunal complex). *Quaternary Science Reviews*, 96, 32–49.

Kedar, Y., Kedar, G. and Barkai, R. (2022). The influence of smoke density on hearth location and activity areas at Lower Paleolithic Lazaret Cave, France. *Science Report* 12, 1469 https://doi.org/10.1038/s41598-022-05517-z

Krankina, O.I. *et al.* (1997). Global Climate change adaptations: Examples from Russian Boreal forests. *Climatic Change* 36: 197–216.

Krause, J. *et al.* (2010). The complete mitochondrial DNA genome of an unknown hominin from southern Siberia. *Nature*, 464(7290), 894–897.

Krzewińska, M. *et al.* (2015). Mitochondrial DNA variation in the Viking age population of Norway. *Philosophical Transactions of the Royal Society B: Biological Sciences*, 370(1660), 20130384.

Kurtén, B. (2017). *Pleistocene mammals of Europe*. Routledge.

Lahr, M. M. and Foley, R. (1994). Multiple dispersals and modern human origins. *Evolutionary Anthropology: Issues, News, and Reviews*, 3(2), 48–60.

Lalueza-Fox, C. *et al.* (2007). A melanocortin 1 receptor allele suggests varying pigmentation among Neanderthals. *Science*, 318(5855), 1453–1455.

Lamnidis, T. C. *et al.* (2018). Ancient Fennoscandian genomes reveal origin and spread of Siberian ancestry in Europe. *Nature Communications*, 9(1), 5018.

Lande, R. (2009). Adaptation to an extraordinary environment by evolution of phenotypic plasticity and genetic assimilation. *Journal of Evolutionary Biology*, 22(7), 1435–1446.

Li, Q. *et al.* (2023). Automatic landmarking identifies new loci associated with face morphology and implicates Neanderthal introgression in human nasal shape. *Communications Biology*, 6(1), 481.

Lin, Z. *et al.* (2019). Biological adaptations in the Arctic cervid, the reindeer (Rangifer tarandus). *Science*, 364(6446), eaav6312.

Lister, A. M. and Brandon, A. (1991). A pre-Ipswichian cold stage mammalian fauna from the Balderton Sand and Gravel, Lincolnshire, England. *Journal of Quaternary Science*, 6(2), 139–157.

Lombao, D. *et al.* (2022). The technological behaviours of Homo antecessor: core management and reduction intensity at Gran Dolina-TD6. 2 (Atapuerca, Spain). *Journal of Archaeological Method and Theory*, 1–38.

López-García, J. M. *et al.* (2010). Palaeoenvironmental and palaeoclimatic reconstruction of the latest Pleistocene of El Portalón site, Sierra de Atapuerca, northwestern Spain. *Palaeogeography, Palaeoclimatology, Palaeoecology*, 292(3–4), 453–464.

Lorenz, E. (1981). Samefolket i historien. Pax Forlag. Oslo. 120s.

Lucquin, A. *et al.* (2023). The impact of farming on prehistoric culinary practices throughout Northern Europe. *Proceedings of the National Academy of Sciences*, 120(43), e2310138120.

Lundström, V., Peters, R. and Riede, F. (2021). Demographic estimates from the Palaeolithic–Mesolithic boundary in Scandinavia: comparative benchmarks and novel insights. *Philosophical Transactions of the Royal Society B*, 376(1816), 20200037.

Macintosh, A. A., Pinhasi, R. and Stock, J. T. (2016). Early life conditions and physiological stress following the transition to farming in central/southeast Europe: Skeletal growth impairment and 6000 years of gradual recovery. *PLoS One*, 11(2), e0148468.

Maier, A. (2017). Population and settlement dynamics from the Gravettian to the Magdalenian. *Mitteilungen der Gesellschaft für Urgeschichte*, 26, 83–101.

Manker, E. (1960). Fångstgropar och stalotomter: kulturlämningar från lapsk forntid. *Acta Lapponica*, 15.

Manninen, M. A., Fossum, G., Ekholm, T. and Persson, P. (2023). Early postglacial hunter-gatherers show environmentally driven 'false logistic' growth in a low productivity environment. *Journal of Anthropological Archaeology*, 70, 101497.

Manzi, G. (2016). Humans of the Middle Pleistocene: The controversial calvarium from Ceprano (Italy) and its significance for the origin and variability of Homo heidelbergensis. *Quaternary International*, 411, 254–261.

Marean, C. W. (2016). The transition to foraging for dense and predictable resources and its impact on the evolution of modern humans. *Philosophical Transactions of the Royal Society B: Biological Sciences*, 371(1698), 20150239.

Marean, C. W. (2015). The most invasive species of all. *Scientific American*, 313(2), 32–39.

Martinez, I., Rosa, L., Arsuaga, J.-L. Jarabo, P., Quam, R., Lorenzo, C., Gracia, A., Carretero, J.-M., Bermúdez de Castro, J.M., Carbonell, E., (2004). Auditory capacities in Middle Pleistocene humans from the Sierra de Atapuerca in Spain. *Proceedings of the National Academy of Sciences* 101, 9976–9981.

Mathiesen, S. D. *et al.* (2023). *Reindeer Husbandry: Adaptation to the Changing Arctic*, 1 (p. 278). Springer Nature.

Mattingsdal, M. *et al.* (2021). The genetic structure of Norway. *European Journal of Human Genetics*, 29(11), 1710–1713.

Mellars, P. A. (2004). Reindeer specialization in the early Upper Palaeolithic the evidence from south west France. *Journal of archaeological science*, 31(5), 613–617.

Metz, L., Lewis, J. E. and Slimak, L. (2023). Bow-and-arrow, technology of the first modern humans in Europe 54,000 years ago at Mandrin, France. *Science Advances*, 9 8), eadd4675.

Mikkelsen, E. (1994). Universitetets Oldsaksamling skrifter-ny rekke nr 18. Fangstprodukter i vikingtidens og middelalderens økonomi. *Universitetets Oldsaksamling Skrifter* http://urn. nb. no/URN: NBN: no-85518.

Miljødirektoratet (2022). Kraftbehov til transport. Nullutslippsscenarier for 2050.

Mithen, S. (2003). *After the ice: A global human history 20000-5000 BC*. Weidenfeld & Nicolson, London. p.622.

Moncel, M. H. *et al.* (2021). Late Neanderthal short-term and specialized occupations at the Abri du Maras (South-East France, level 4.1, MIS 3). *Archaeological and Anthropological Sciences*, 13, 1–28.

Moncel, M. H., Moigne, A. M. and Combier, J. (2012). Towards the Middle Palaeolithic in western Europe: the case of Orgnac 3 (southeastern France). *Journal of Human Evolution*, 63(5), 653–666.

Morin, E. *et al.* (2014). Millenia-scale change in archeofaunas and their implications for Mousterian lithic variability in southwest France. *Journal of Anthropological Archeology* 6(2014) 18–180.

Mosquera, M., Ollé, A. and Rodríguez, X. P. (2013). From Atapuerca to Europe: tracing the earliest peopling of Europe. *Quaternary International*, 295, 130–137.

Mounier, A., Marchal, F. and Condemi, S. (2009). Is Homo heidelbergensis a distinct species? New insight on the Mauer mandible. *Journal of human Evolution*, 56(3), 219–246.

Mulk, I.M. (1995). Sirkas – ett samisk fångstsamhälle i förändring Kr.f. – 1600 e.Kr. Studia Archaeologica Universitatis Umensis 6, Umeå.

Müller-Wille, L. *et al.* (2006). Dynamics in human-reindeer relations: reflections on prehistoric, historic and contemporary practices in northernmost Europe. *Reindeer Management in Northernmost Europe: Linking Practical and Scientific Knowledge in Social-Ecological Systems*, 27–45.

Myrvoll, E. R., Thuestad, A. and Holm-Olsen, I. M. (2011). Wild reindeer hunting in Arctic Norway: Landscape, reindeer migration patterns and the distribution of hunting pits in Finnmark. *Fennoscandia Archaeologica*, (XXVIII).

Nash, D. J. *et al.* (2021). Climate indices in historical climate reconstructions: a global state of the art. *Climate of the Past*, 17(3), 1273–1314.

Nies, J. (1996). *Native American History: A Chronology of a Culture's Vast Achievements and Their Links to World Events*. New York City, NY: Penguin Random House, Inc.

NOU 2023: 3. Mer av alt – raskere. Energikommisjonens rapport.

NOU 2001:34. Samiske sedvaner og rettsoppfatninger – bakgrunnsmateriale for Samerettsutvalget. Del 2.Samiske sedvaner og rettsoppfatninger – med utgangspunkt i studier av tingbøkene fra Finnmark for perioden 1620–1770

Olsen, L. (2010). Sørsamisk historie i nytt lys. Senter for samiske studier, skriftserie nr. 17. Universitetet i Tromsø. 262s.

Ostrom, E. (1999). Coping with tragedies of the commons. *Annual review of political science*, 2(1), 493–535.

Päbo, S. (2022). Nobel Prize lecture: Svante Pääbo, Nobel Prize in physiology or medicine 2022 – YouTube

Papagianni, D. and Morse, M. A. (2015). The Neanderthals rediscovered: how modern science is rewriting their history. Thames and Hudson, London. p.208.

Parfitt, S. A. *et al.* (2005). The earliest record of human activity in northern Europe. *Nature*, 438(7070), 1008–1012.

Pétillon, J. M. *et al.* (2019). A Gray Whale in Magdalenian Perigord. Species identification of a bone projectile point from La Madeleine (Dordogne, France) using collagen fingerprinting. *PALEO. Revue d'archéologie préhistorique*, (30-1), 230–242.

Petit, P. (2000). Odd man out: Neanderthals and modern humans. *British. Archaeology*, 51, 1–5.

Pomeroy, E. *et al.* (2020). Issues of theory and method in the analysis of Paleolithic mortuary behavior: A view from Shanidar Cave. *Evolutionary Anthropology: Issues, News, and Reviews*, 29(5), 263–279.

Posth, C. *et al.* (2023). Palaeogenomics of Upper Palaeolithic to Neolithic European hunter-gatherers. *Nature*, 615(7950), 117–126.

Potts, R. (2013). Hominin evolution in settings of strong environmental variability. *Quaternary Science Reviews*, 73, 1–13.

Prado, J. L., Martinez-Maza, C. and Alberdi, M. T. (2015). Megafauna extinction in South America: A new chronology for the Argentine Pampas. *Palaeogeography, Palaeoclimatology, Palaeoecology*, 425, 41–49.

Profico, A. *et al.* (2016). Filling the gap. Human cranial remains from Gombore II (Melka Kunture, Ethiopia; ca. 850 ka) and the origin of Homo heidelbergensis. *Journal of Anthropological Sciences*, 94, 1–24.

Prüfer, K. *et al.* (2014). The complete genome sequence of a Neanderthal from the Altai Mountains. *Nature*, 505(7481), 43–49.

Raghavan, M. *et al.* (2014). The genetic prehistory of the New World Arctic. *Science*, 345(6200), 1255832.

Ravna, Z.J.V. (2019). The Inter-Generational Transmission of Indigenous Knowledge By Nenets Women: Viewed in the context of the state educational system of Russia. Ph.D dissertation. UiT Norges Arktiske Universitet.

Raynal, J. P. *et al.* (2013). Land-Use Strategies, Related Tool-Kits and Social Organization of Lower and Middle Palaeolithic Groups in the South-East of the Massif Central, France: Strategien der Landschaftsnutzung, Geräteinventare und soziale Organisation von alt-und mittelpaläolithischen Gruppen im südwestfranzösischen Zentralmassif. *Quartär-Internationales Jahrbuch zur Erforschung des Eiszeitalters und der Steinzeit*, 60, 29–59.

Recht, J., Schuenemann, V. J. and Sánchez-Villagra,

M. R. (2020). Host diversity and origin of zoonoses: The ancient and the new. *Animals*, 10(9), 1672.

Reich, D. *et al.* (2012). Reconstructing native American population history. *Nature*, 488(7411), 370–374.

Rendu, W. *et al.* (2019). Subsistence strategy changes during the Middle to Upper Paleolithic transition reveals specific adaptations of human populations to their environment. *Scientific Reports*, 9(1), 1–11.

Rightmire, G.P. (1998). Human evolution in the Middle Pleistocene: the role of *Homo heidelbergensis*. *Evolutionary Anthropology* 6, 218–227.

Rightmire, G. P. (2013). Homo erectus and Middle Pleistocene hominins: brain size, skull form, and species recognition. *Journal of Human Evolution*, 65(3), 223–252.

Rivals, F., Kacimi, S. and Moutoussamy, J. (2004). Artiodactyls, favourite game of prehistoric hunters at the Caune de l'Arago Cave (Tautavel, France). Opportunistic or selective hunting strategies? *European Journal of Wildlife Research*, 50, 25–32.

Rivals, F., Schulz, E. and Kaiser, T. M. (2008). Climate-related dietary diversity of the ungulate faunas from the middle Pleistocene succession (OIS 14-12) at the Caune de l'Arago (France). *Paleobiology*, 34(1), 117–127.

Rivals, F., Schulz, E. and Kaiser, T. M. (2009). A new application of dental wear analyses: estimation of duration of hominid occupations in archaeological localities. *Journal of Human Evolution*, 56(4), 329–339.

Roberts, A. P. and Grün, R. (2010). Early human northerners. *Nature*, 466(7303), 189-190.

Rodríguez, J. *et al.* (2011). One million years of cultural evolution in a stable environment at Atapuerca (Burgos, Spain). *Quaternary Science Reviews*, 30(11-12), 1396-1412.

Rodríguez-Varela, R. *et al.* (2023). The genetic history of Scandinavia from the Roman Iron Age to the present. *Cell*, 186(1), 32–46.

Røed, K. H. *et al.* (2021). Historical and social–cultural processes as drivers for genetic structure in Nordic domestic reindeer. *Ecology and Evolution*, 11(13), 8910–8922.

Roksandic, M., Radović, P. and Lindal, J. (2018). Revising the hypodigm of Homo heidelbergensis: A view from the Eastern Mediterranean. *Quaternary International*, 466, 66–81.

Rougier, H. *et al.* (2016). Neandertal cannibalism and Neandertal bones used as tools in Northern Europe. *Scientific Reports*, 6(1), 1–11.

Saag, L. *et al.* (2019). The arrival of Siberian ancestry connecting the Eastern Baltic to Uralic speakers further East. *Current Biology*, 29(10), 1701–1711.

Salmi, A. K. (2023). The archaeology of reindeer domestication and herding practices in Northern Fennoscandia. *Journal of Archaeological Research*, 31(4), 617–660.

Sanden, G. D. (2016). Villreinfangst i den sørlege delen av Midt-Noreg–ein studie i fordelinga av bågastø, jordgravne og steinmura fangstgroper. *Viking*, 79, 53–74.

Sandgathe, D. M. and Berna, F. (2017). Fire and the genus Homo: An introduction to supplement 16. *Current Anthropology*, 58(S16), S165–S174.

Sannhet og forsoningskommisjonen Dokument 19 (2022–2023). Sannhet og forsoning – grunnlag for et oppgjør med fornorskingspolitikk og urett mot samer, kvener/norskfinner og skogfinner. *Rapport til Stortinget fra Sannhets- og Forsoningskommisjonen*, Avgitt til Stortingets presidentskap 01.06.2023

Schaafhausen, H. 1880. Fur de in der Sipkahöhle in Mahren. Sonderbericht der niederrheinischen Gesellschaft für Natur – und Heilkunde, 260–264.

Schanche, A. (2000). *Graver i ur og berg: samisk gravskikk og religion fra forhistorisk til nyere tid*. Davvi Girji OS.

Schoch, W. H. *et al.* (2015). New insights on the wooden weapons from the Paleolithic site of Schöningen. *Journal of Human Evolution*, 89, 214–225.

Schoetensack, O., (1908). *Der Unterkiefer des Homo heidelbergensis aus den Sanden von Mauer bei Heidelberg*. Leipzig: Wilhelm Engelmann.

Schreiber, D. *et al.* In *Homo heidelbergensis-Schlüsselfund der Menscheitsgeschichte* (pp. 127–159). Konrad Theiss Verlag.

Scott, M. and Lindsey, R. (2020). What's the Hottest Earth's Ever Been? NOAA Climate.gov.

Sherwood, S. C. and Huber, M. (2010). An adaptability limit to climate change due to heat stress. *Proceedings of the National Academy of Sciences*, 107(21), 9552-9555.

Skinner, M. and Newell, E. (2000). A re-evaluation of localized hypoplasia of the primary canine as a marker of craniofacial osteopenia in European Upper Paleolithic infants. *Acta Universitatis Carolinae. Medica*, 41(1–4), 41-58.

Skoglund, P. *et al.* (2014). Genomic diversity and admixture differs for Stone-Age Scandinavian foragers and farmers. *Science*, 344(6185), 747–750.

Skoglund, P. *et al.* (2012). Origins and genetic legacy of Neolithic farmers and hunter-gatherers in Europe. *Science*, 336(6080), 466–469.

Skov, L. *et al.* (2022). Genetic insights into the social organization of Neanderthals. *Nature* 610,

519–525 https://doi.org/10.1038/s41586-022-05283-y

Skre, D. (2020). Rulership in 1st to 14th century Scandinavia (p. 545). De Gruyter.

Skrzypek, G., Wiśniewski, A. and Grierson, P. F. (2011). How cold was it for Neanderthals moving to Central Europe during warm phases of the last glaciation? *Quaternary Science Reviews*, 30(5-6), 481–487.

Slimak, L. *et al.* (2023). A late Neanderthal reveals genetic isolation in their populations before extinction. *bioRxiv*, 2023-04.

Slimak, L. *et al.* (2022). Modern human incursion into Neanderthal territories 54,000 years ago at Mandrin, France. *Science Advances*, 8(6), eabj9496.

Slon, V. *et al.* (2018). The genome of the offspring of a Neanderthal mother and a Denisovan father. *Nature*, 561(7721), 113–116.

Smith, C. M. (2014). Estimation of a genetically viable population for multigenerational interstellar voyaging: Review and data for project Hyperion. *Acta Astronautica*, 97, 16–29.

Snook, J. *et al.* (2020). 'We're made criminals just to eat off the land': colonial wildlife management and repercussions on Inuit well-being. *Sustainability*, 12(19), 8177.

Snook, J. *et al.* (2022). The connection between wildlife co-management and indigenous well-being: What cows the academic literature reveal? *Wellbeing, Space and Society*, 3, 100116.

Soffer, O. (2000). 'Gravettian technologies in social contexts', in: W. Roebroeks, M. Mussi, J. Svoboda, and K.Fennema (eds.) *Hunters of the Golden Age: the Mid Upper Palaeolithic of Eurasia 30,000–20,000*. BP. Leiden: University of Leiden, 59–75.

Soffer, O. and Adovasio, J. M. (2004). 'Textiles and Upper Paleolithic Lives. A Focus on the Perishable and the Invisible', in J. Svoboda and L. Sedláčková (eds.) *The Gravettian along the Danube*. Dolní VěstoniceStudies 11. Brno: Academy of Sciences of the Czech Republic, 270–282.

Solberg, B. (2003) Jernalderen i Norge, 500 før Kristus til 1030 etter Kristus. Cappelen Akademisk forlag. Oslo (p 371).

Solecki, R. S. (1975). Shanidar IV, a Neanderthal flower burial in northern Iraq. *Science*, 190(4217), 880–881.

Sørensen, M. *et al.* (2013). The first eastern migrations of people and knowledge into Scandinavia: evidence from studies of Mesolithic Technology, 9th-8th Millennium BC. *Norwegian Archaeological Review*, 46(1), 19–56.

Spilde, D. *et al.* (2018). Strømforbruk i Norge mot 2035. *Norges vassdrags-og energidirektorat.*

Statnett (2023). Forbruksutvikling i Norge 2022-2050 – delrapport til Langsiktig Markedsanalyse 2022–2050.

Steegmann Jr, A. T., Cerny, F. J. and Holliday, T. W. (2002). Neandertal cold adaptation: physiological and energetic factors. *American Journal of Human Biology*, 14(5), 566-583.

Stene, K. *et al.* (2015). Grimsdalen- et skattet landskap for villreinfangst og seterbruk. I: Fjellets kulturlandskap: Arealbruk og landskap gjennom flere tusen år. Eds. G. Austrheim, K. Hjelle, Sjögren, K. Stene og A. M. Tretvik. DKNVS Skrifter 2015.no 3.Museumsforlaget.207 s.

Stringer, C. (2016). The origin and evolution of Homo sapiens. *Philosophical Transactions of the Royal Society B: Biological Sciences*, 371(1698), 20150237.

Stringer, C. and Andrews, P. (2005). *The complete world of human evolution*. Thames & Hudson, London. p240.

Stringer, C. and Crété, L. (2022). Mapping Interactions of H. neanderthalensis and Homo sapiens from the Fossil and Genetic records. *PaleoAnthropology*, 2022(2).

Stringer, C.B. *et al.* (1998). The Middle Pleistocene human tibia from Boxgrove. *Journal of Human Evolution,* 34, 509–547.

Tansem, K. (2022). Helleristningene i Alta: Estetikken, geologien og figurene. Ph. D thesis. Institutt for arkeologi, historie, religionsvitenskap og teologi, UiT – Norges Arktiske Universitet.

Taylor, R. S. *et al.* (2021). Population dynamics of caribou shaped by glacial cycles before the last glacial maximum. *Molecular Ecology*, 30(23), 6121–6143.

The International Sami Journal. Baiki.org/content/alaskachron/1920.htm

Tonkopeeva, M. *et al.* (2024). Resilience Thinking in Reindeer Husbandry. *Reindeer Husbandry*, 189.

Van Andel, T. H. and Davies W. Eds. (2003). *Neanderthals and modern humans in the European landscape during the last glaciation*. McDonald institute for Archeological research. Cambridge. p265.

Vanhaeren, M. and d'Errico, F. (2001). Personal Ornaments from the La Madeleine child (Peyrony excavations): an insight into upper palaeolithic childhood. *Revd'Archeol Préhist*, 13, 201–240.

Van Kolfschoten, T., Buhrs, E. and Verheijen, I. (2015). The larger mammal fauna from the Lower Paleolithic Schöningen Spear site and its contribution to hominin subsistence. *Journal of Human Evolution*, 89, 138–153.

Villa, P. and Roebroeks, W. (2014). Neandertal demise: an archaeological analysis of the modern human superiority complex. *PLoS One*, 9(4), e96424.

Von Linné, C. (1788). *Systema naturae per regna tria naturae secundum classes ordines, genera, species,* (Vol. 1). GE Beer.

Vorren, Ø. (1998). Villreinfangst i Varanger fram til 1600-1700 årene. Tromsø museums skrifter; 28. Nordkalott-forlag, Stonglandseidet.

Waddington, C. and Wicks, K. (2017). Resilience or wipe out? Evaluating the convergent impacts of the 8.2 ka event and Storegga tsunami on the Mesolithic of north-east Britain. *Journal of Archaeological Science: Reports*, 14, 692–714.

Wagner, G. A. *et al.* (2011). Mauer–the type site of Homo heidelbergensis: palaeoenvironment and age. *Quaternary Science Reviews*, 30(11–12), 1464–1473.

Wales, N. (2012). Modeling Neanderthal clothing using ethnographic analogues. *Journal of Human Evolution*, 63(6), 781–795.

Walker, J. *et al.* (2020) A great wave: the Storegga tsunami and the end of Doggerland?. *Antiquity*, 94(378), 1409–1425.

Wee, W. and Ellingvåg, S. (2023). 12 000 år med norsk historie. Arven fra jegere, krigere og vikinger. Kagge Forlag.

Welker, F. *et al.* (2020). The dental proteome of Homo antecessor. *Nature*, 580(7802), 235–238.

Willerslev, E. *et al.* (2014). Fifty thousand years of Arctic vegetation and megafaunal diet. *Nature*, 506(7486), 47–51.

Willerslev, R., Vitebsky, P. and Alekseyev, A. (2015). Sacrifice as the ideal hunt: a cosmological explanation for the origin of reindeer domestication. *Journal of the Royal Anthropological Institute*, 21(1), 1–23.

Woodward, J. (2014). *The ice age: A very short introduction.* Oxford University Press, Oxford, p.163.

Wroe, S. *et al.* (2018). Computer simulations show that Neanderthal facial morphology represents adaptation to cold and high energy demands, but not heavy biting. *Proceedings of the Royal Society B: Biological Sciences*, 285(1876), 20180085.

Zachrisson, I. (1984). De samiska metalldepåerna år 1000-1350: i ljuset av fyndet från Mörtträsket, Lappland = The saami metal deposits A.D. 1000-1350 in the light of the find from Mörtträsket, Lapland. Archaeology and environment; 3. University of Umeå Department of Archaeology, Umeå.

Zhang, P. *et al.* (2022). Denisovans and Homo sapiens on the Tibetan Plateau: dispersals and adaptations. *Trends in Ecology & Evolution*, 37(3), 257–267.

THANKS FROM REIDAR AND OLAV

We would like to thank the publisher Porto Press and the language cleaner and proofreader, Helen Jones. Many thanks also to archaeologist Jostein Bergstøl and biologist Bernt-Erik Sæther who read and commented on parts of the manuscript. A special thanks to the esteemed Canadian biologist Anne Gunn for comments on the North American content. Financial support from the Norwegian Environment Agency has made it possible to visit key places related to the story in the book.

Despite the contributions of everyone involved, any errors and omissions in the book are our own responsibility.